Pink Boots
AND A
MACHETE

Pink Boots
AND A
MACHETE

My Journey From NFL Cheerleader to National Geographic Explorer

Mireya Mayor

Foreword by Jane Goodall

 NATIONAL GEOGRAPHIC

WASHINGTON, D.C.

Published by the National Geographic Society
Copyright © 2011 Mireya Mayor. All rights reserved.
Reproduction of the whole or any part of the contents without
written permission from the publisher is strictly prohibited.

All photos courtesy of the author.

Library of Congress Cataloging-in-Publication Data
Pink boots and a machete : my journey from NFL cheerleader to National Geographic explorer / Mireya
Mayor ; [foreword by] Jane Goodall.
    p. cm.
ISBN 978-1-4262-0721-1 (hardback)
1. Mayor, Mireya. 2. Explorers--United States--Biography. I. National Geographic Society (U.S.)
G226.M39P56 2011
910.4092--dc22
[B]

                            2010050083

The National Geographic Society is one of the world's largest nonprofit scientific and educational organizations. Founded in 1888 to "increase and diffuse geographic knowledge,"
the Society works to inspire people to care about the planet. National Geographic reflects
the world through its magazines, television programs, films, music and radio, books, DVDs,
maps, exhibitions, live events, school publishing programs, interactive media and merchan-
dise. *National Geographic* magazine, the Society's official journal, published in English
and 32 local-language editions, is read by more than 35 million people each month. The
National Geographic Channel reaches 320 million households in 34 languages in 166 countries. National Geographic Digital Media receives more than 13 million visitors a month.
National Geographic has funded more than 9,200 scientific research, conservation and
exploration projects and supports an education program promoting geography literacy.
For more information, visit nationalgeographic.com.

For more information, please call 1-800-NGS LINE (647-5463)
or write to the following address:

National Geographic Society
1145 17th Street N.W.
Washington, DC 20036-4688 U.S.A.
www.nationalgeographic.com

For information about special discounts for bulk purchases,
please contact National Geographic Books Special Sales:
ngspecsales@ngs.org.

For rights or permissions inquiries, please contact
National Geographic Books Subsidiary Rights:
ngbookrights@ngs.org

Interior design by Lindsey Smith

Printed in the United States of America

11/QGF-CML/1

human dedication

To my mother and grandmother, for always encouraging me to dream. To my loving husband and soul mate, Roland, for being an endless source of love and support. And to my daughters, Emma and Ava, for inspiring me to leave a better world behind. Your love made it possible.

nonhuman dedication

To all the furry, slithery, slimy, scaly, and feathered creatures I have had the honor of encountering in the wild. You have filled my untamed life with purpose and adventure.

contents

Dr. Mireya Mayor reminds me a little of myself. Like me, she loved being with animals when she was a child. Like me she imagined herself trekking into far off jungles. And like me she followed her dream until it became reality.

As a small girl growing up in England I spent hours alone up my most special beech tree in our garden, getting close to the birds; reading about Tarzan of the Apes; and daydreaming how I would grow up, go to Africa, live with animals, and write books about them. In those days girls did not have such adventurous opportunities—everyone laughed at me. Anyway, we had little money, Africa was far away, no tourists flew back and forth, and World War II was raging. So I studied the insects and birds in our garden and walked with my beloved dog, Rusty, on the cliffs rising up from the beach.

Mireya also began her career in her backyard, in Little Havana. She too spent hours in her special tree—hers was a mango. She watched lizards, she kept a variety of insects and other creatures in her house, she cared for stray dogs. She and I both made observations on chickens. We both had strong mothers and grandmothers. And we both owe a great deal to the National Geographic Society, which helped us to achieve our goals.

My dream led me to Africa to observe wild chimpanzees; Mireya's led her to the rain forests of Latin America, Central Africa, Madagascar, and various other exotic locations, including into the depths of the ocean. We both ended up as primatologists with Ph.D.s. I discovered that among other unexpected skills, chimpanzees have the ability to use and make tools. Mireya discovered a species of mouse lemur new to science—and persuaded the prime minister in Madagascar to create a national park to ensure its protection. Indeed, we are both passionate about conservation of the wild places where we love to be.

But whereas I stayed in the same place with my chimpanzees for years, Mireya is a true adventurer whose concern for a number of critically endangered animals has led her to explore some of the most remote places left on the planet. These journeys exposed her, time and again, to very real dangers, from charging gorillas and great white sharks to sinister bacteria that invaded her body in a place far from any hospital.

Pink Boots and a Machete is a wonderful read, spiced with descriptions of the lighter, more humorous aspects of a life spent in wild, unconventional places. But it also details the very serious side of Mireya's research. Indeed, throughout the book, Mireya the scientist is very much present. I have had the opportunity to meet many researchers and conservationists, and some of them stand out. Mireya Mayor is one of them.

Not only does this extraordinary woman have the courage and fortitude for the explorations she undertakes but she has the intellectual curiosity to answer questions previously unanswered. And she has the kind of imagination and sense of wonder that leads her to ask the right kind of questions.

Mireya understands the importance of spreading her conservation message, and she frequently speaks at colleges and universities, inspiring young people, especially women, to follow their dreams no matter how impossible it may seem to do so. She is the living embodiment of someone who did just that and who is still, vividly and enthusiastically, living and loving her childhood dream.

Jane Goodall Ph.D., DBE
Founder, Jane Goodall Institute
and UN Messenger of Peace
www.janegoodall.org

Thanks to all who devote their lives to nature, inspiring others to *marvel at its beauty, revel in its wonder, and protect its existence.*

There are many critically endangered animals that need your help. If you have any questions or would like to sponsor an animal or make a donation that will help protect some of these endangered animals and places, please email me at mireya@mireyamayor.com.

You can follow updates for my upcoming shows and track my adventures at *www.mireyamayor.com.*

To help orphan chimpanzees, please visit the Jane Goodall Institute at *www.janegoodall.org.*

There are many people whose love, talent, and support made this book possible—far more than I have space to include here. Thank you all of you—you know who you are.

My beautiful daughters, Emma and Ava, whose mere presence could make me smile during the most frustrating of times, inspired me and motivated me to want to make the world a better place, even before they were born.

Thanks to the three most influential women and people in my life, my mother—my grandmother, and my aunt—whose patience, support, and unconditional love carried me through the best and most trying times:

- Mami, thank you for always encouraging me to follow my dreams and for enabling my animal habit. I could never thank you enough for believing in me and for encouraging me to pursue the unimaginable with or without fear.
- Mima, your strength and resolve gave me my own strength to attempt the seemingly unimaginable.

- Tia Ica, thank you for paying for my braces when I was a kid, so that monkeys wouldn't now laugh at my teeth, and giving critics less ammunition.

Special thanks to Emilio, my cousin, who is like a brother, for being the man of the house, and for all the beautiful letters he wrote while we were oceans apart.

I wish to thank my family for their patience and support during all the years and holidays I spent away from them so that I could pursue my dream. Many thanks also for accepting late-night phone calls due to time zone differences.

A special thank-you to my graduate adviser, Dr. Patricia Wright, for always encouraging me and filling me with hope. Whether sharing a tent, partying with the villagers, or meeting with government officials, it was always an honor to explore Madagascar with her.

I am also grateful to Dr. Linda Taylor for awakening my curiosity and love of primates, and for inspiring me to pursue this field. Her unceasing support and guidance, and glowing letters of recommendation, have opened many doors.

I am grateful to Dr. Edward Louis for tremendous help in collecting samples, and for teaching me lab techniques at Henry Doorly Zoo in Omaha. His academic guidance and friendship were without equal.

I am indebted to the National Geographic Society Committee for Research and Exploration for its long-term financial support. Conservation International and Primate Conservation Incorporated have also provided key finances for my expeditions.

A special thanks to Tim Kelly, David Royle, Geoff Daniels, Maryanne Culpepper, and Keenan Smart for taking a chance on me and enabling me to share and speak my wonder to a large audience.

Also, thanks to all the field producers, assistant producers, researchers, and countless others (too many to name) at the National Geographic Society for their shared enthusiasm and insatiable thirst for uncovering nature and wildlife.

I am very grateful to Ashley Hoppin for her friendship and for presenting me and my research to National Geographic.

Collective thanks are expressed to my friends, professors, Stony Brook University staff, and colleagues who helped me at various stages of my research.

To the governing agencies that have granted me permission to research their national treasures and landscapes, thank you. Also, to all of the amazing people in the villages I've traveled through in far and remote places, thank you for your kindness, generosity, and hospitality.

Thank you, Elizabeth "Symmie" Newhouse, for your excellent editing, making my crazy adventures take a readable form.

Thank you, Jes Alexander, for going beyond the call of friendship and reading every single draft of this book.

Thank you to my agent, Eric Lupfer, for translating all the legal stuff I don't understand and for being awesome.

Thank you, National Geographic Book Division's Editor in Chief Barbara Brownell and the editor of this book, Susan Straight, for believing in my work and making it possible for me to share my story.

And finally, my husband, Roland Wolff, who is last on this list but first in my heart. Without his love and undying support I could not have written this book or continued to pursue my research and explorations. Thanks LOML, I couldn't have done any of this without you. For always supporting me, even when you deserved more than I could give, *thank you.*

Dripping in sweat under the Congo sun, surgically removing worms from our feet, and fighting off tsetse flies, the film crew and I were gathering the last of our gear and embarking on a grueling three-day journey home after a month of tracking gorillas. I was already beginning to suffer post-expedition blues, knowing I would miss waking up to the sounds of chimps overhead and the morning mist lingering over the forested hills. But as we hiked out of the jungle, nearly waist deep in swamp, I couldn't wait for a hot shower and clean clothes. After a few hours of paddling down the Sangha River, we saw the Cameroon border and knew we were nearing civilization. Civilization in this case was relative, but a bed, shower, and lukewarm beer were all the amenities I needed.

As the sun set, we hit the shore at Ouésso, a town in the northern Republic of the Congo, lying on the river and surrounded by rain forest. Linked by ferry with Brazzaville, it is known for its nearby Pygmy people. We would be flying out, but the journey had taken us into nightfall, so we'd overnight in a hotel and continue to the airport in the morning. One cold shower later (they lied about the hot water) and a bad night's sleep in a mosquito-infested room, I prayed our flight to Brazzaville would take off; in this part of Africa, canceled flights were the norm. After four weeks in the Congo wilderness, Brazzaville would seem like New York.

A wooden shed, a picnic shelter as a VIP lounge, and three umbrellas made the Ouésso airport seem positively bustling. Entering the shed, we stood in line, anxious that our gear would be too heavy. It was. But as the customs agent rifled through our belongings, he fixed on a copy of *Us Weekly* I had stowed in a pocket. It wasn't the actual magazine he was interested in but one of its photos.

So after some rapid-fire multilingual negotiating, it was agreed: Our gear made the flight, and the agent had my copy of *Us Weekly*, with the full-page photo of Kim Kardashian in a bikini.

We stood under the tree that marked the departure area with a small brigade of people, dogs, and chickens. When they called our flight (six hours after its scheduled departure), we dashed for the plane, finally collapsing into our seats, relieved that we were headed home.

Almost.

Before we even made our run down the bumpy runway at Ouésso, and the dust, the vivid greens, and that airport washed from memory, I had pulled out my journal and begun writing down everything I could remember of the expedition. The jet had already left the ground, ascended to about 10,000 feet, and been cruising along for some time before I looked up from my notebook and out the window. The last things I expected to see at that altitude were trees, but there we were, dancing above the treetops like we were about to land in the jungle. This wasn't good.

I shook Andy, my cameraman, who had dozed off, and said, "Why are we flying so low? I think something's wrong." That thick blanket of trees looked nothing like tarmac, much less a clearing. Andy's eyes went from sleepy slivers to oversize saucers as if he'd been awakened by a stun gun. A small panic erupted in the seats around us, as the plane bucked and shimmied along the top of the tree line. Then suddenly and without warning the plane ascended again, and we all breathed a sigh of relief.

It was short-lived.

My eyes remained fixed on the window, and I heard that sound a car makes just after the Check Engine light comes on. Except this wasn't a car—it was a commercial jet struggling to stay in the air, and I was in it. Soon the plane was descending, as if we were making an approach to the airport, but there was no airport, just a thick blanket of trees. I looked back for a crew member, only to see the flight attendants in their jump seats, heads below their knees. Then my life began to flash before my eyes. Was this it? Were these the last minutes of my life? After all the expeditions, all the dangers, all the times I had sidestepped death from disease, hunger, infestations, angry gorillas, stampedes, and so much more, I was going to die in a plane crash?

Was this someone's idea of a joke?

one

Girl Scout Reject

MAY 27, 1987: I just found a newspaper clipping with a picture of my mom making her great escape. Her face shows both fear and courage as armed men assist her onto the boat. I've heard the story endless times, but it never gets old. She said she looked at all the men carrying guns and stepped onto the boat knowing she would never go home again. It was a forced adventure. She made herself look only to the open waters, making sure she didn't catch a last glimpse of the island she was leaving with nothing but fear, anger, and the clothes on her back.

Crashing on a Congolese flight, waking up in a brothel, fighting off venomous snakes, and averting having my head ripped off by a silverback gorilla might read like a Harrison Ford movie script. But these were just a small part of my last expedition. I've come close to death more times than Elizabeth Taylor has said "I do." In fact, were I a cat, I'd have one more go at it. Maybe.

It could be argued that my job is somewhat suicidal. I've dangled on the end of a fraying rope 14,000 feet above rocky ground. And I've nearly starved to death more than once, though that was soon remedied by my mother's Cuban cooking. But still, I have looked death squarely in the eye, and that is my point.

I've come to understand that the problem isn't the close calls you are aware of, but rather the unseen ones that silently rear up, a lesson deeply embedded in me at the not-yet-ripe age of 22. Carrying a teddy bear backpack and sporting the perfect ponytail, I happily traipsed through the jungle abyss of Guyana's interior, hacking my way through impenetrable forest and thinking the main dangers to be fer-de-lance snakes and drunken miners. Little did I know that by the time I left the jungle, I would have less than one day to live. That's right. Less than one day to live.

Sitting in my dugout canoe one day, I noticed my hands were an unusual shade of pink as I lifted my binoculars to watch the squirrel monkeys wreaking havoc in the trees. Squirrel monkeys, known for being extremely hyperactive, jump from branch to branch squealing with delight and make for wonderful entertainment. I immediately forgot about my pink hands.

The next morning I woke up to hands a much brighter shade of red, with purplish, eggplant-infused accents. I attributed the odd rosy-magenta hue to the South American sun on my fair skin. I go from ghostly white to rosy pink and inevitably to lobster red. Never a golden tan. After applying sun lotion with an SPF level so high it neared triple digits, I continued on in the canoe that for the past several weeks had been my home. By dusk my hands were the size of basketballs. Had anyone decided to cut them off, they could have had themselves a good game on me. I should have been worried by then, but I continued to blame my mother for passing on her freakishly ashen skin tone.

The following morning, I could not bring my fingers close enough together to button my pants, tie my shoes, or hold a toothbrush. With much embarrassment, I asked one of the male researchers to button me up. I also made a mental note to pack more T-shirts next time instead of shirts with infernal buttons.

The fact that my wrists and forearms were oddly disfigured was concerning, but it was the wounds now covering my thighs that screamed, "Something is freaking wrong!" I was so upset about the open sores and inability to dress myself that I didn't even notice the long red streaks leading up to my heart. Yes, folks, as I would soon learn, I was on a fast track toward death.

Making my way out of the jungle meant days of hacking through dense forest, something I couldn't do without holding a machete, so I hired a villager to clear the way. The people in the village looked at my blistered hands with repugnance; my attempt to cover them in silvery white lotion and bandages had only made them look more ghastly. I would spend the next 48 hours with my hands suspended in front of my chest as I made my way back to Georgetown, Guyana's capital.

Once there I went immediately to the local hospital, where dogs and chickens outnumbered patients in the waiting room. The doctor brought me into a private room with busted-out windows and asked how I had burned my hands. The dog staring up at me looked puzzled, too. I explained that the swelling and blistering all began from tiny cuts I had acquired during the expedition. He proceeded to apply a silver cream used to treat burn patients. Severe burn patients. I could have stopped him, but at that point I didn't think it could hurt. Its only effect was to make my hands look like they belonged to a deformed tin man.

He then walked over to a little table where several open (and quite obviously used) syringes lay on a dirty tray. When he picked one up and announced, "This shot of calcium will do the trick," I knew it was time to get out. Fast. The flights back to the States were all booked; however, as this was a true medical emergency, the airline found me a spot on the plane (I actually think the clerks could no longer bear to look at me). Once back in the States, I was not allowed off the plane until a wheelchair escort arrived. Apparently, I looked incapable of making it on my own.

Odd, I thought, as the problem was my hands and not my feet, but rolling out of the plane would mark the first time during the entire ordeal that I was scared. Not scared that I might die; I was still blissfully unaware of that danger. I was scared of what my mom would say.

You see, my mom wasn't exactly thrilled with my decision to go explore one of the most remote and unknown regions of South America. My overprotective mother, who had cried and begged me not to go, stood there crying once again as she looked down at my balloon hands. Seeing me wheeled off the plane had just fueled the drama. The very thing she had repeatedly harped on was that if anything went wrong, there'd be no hospitals around. I still hate it when my mom is right. More than that, I hate to admit it. So as I was wheeled up to her, her pale, tearful face watching me in horror, I wished I was back in the jungle figuring out how to brush my teeth. As we headed into the emergency room, I assured her that I would be fine. I could see she didn't believe me and waited for the words "I told you so" to come flying out of her mouth. But staying true to her Cuban woman's persona (that of a martyr), she did something worse. She said nothing.

After several physicians inspected my bloated hands and scratched their heads, medics from the U.S. Army Special Forces were brought in. The SF medics seemed just as puzzled, however, and, before leaving, photographed my hands for reference on the off chance they'd confront such a condition again. I continued to reassure my horrified mom, until we heard the doctor telling the nurse, all too loudly, that this was the worst case of systemic blood infection he had ever seen. To Mom he added the words that may have cost her ten years of life: "If she had been delayed by just one more day, your daughter would have died." I apologized to my mom and then (in my head) strangled the doctor with my giant basketball hands.

Fact is, it's not uncommon to find me surrounded by a wild troop of chimpanzees, or waist deep in a swamp with thousands of hovering sweat bees buzzing inside my ears, or with worms living in my feet, or carrying a parasite load so heavy a doctor was once prompted to ask if I lick the insides of toilets. That is how the media labels "the female Indiana Jones" and "the real-life Lara Croft" were born. But while it might be an easy thing to give me a catchy label, "simple" would not describe my journey here.

As the sheltered daughter of Cuban immigrants, I was expected to become a nurse or a schoolteacher, something respectable and conducive to marriage and children, like my "normal" cousins. For years, on school career day, I flaunted a little white nurse's uniform that my grandmother made until one year I rebelled and announced that I wanted to be a ninja. This, you need to understand, was a very bold move on my part. All the women in my family were nurses or homemakers, and I was already showing signs of becoming a black sheep.

A tight-knit family with little means, we never ventured very far. Miami was my universe, and New Jersey, where most of my cousins lived, was as foreign and exotic as it got. A trip to New Jersey might as well have required a passport, as far as I was concerned. The world, to me, seemed small and uniform except for some differences in weather conditions. Summer vacations consisted of a four-hour car ride to Disney World, with landfills along the way the only mountains I'd see for many years to come. Truth be told, the only time I visited a foreign country as a nonadult was at Epcot. To this day, I have to remind myself that China isn't really next to Norway.

In my mom's efforts to show me the world beyond my driveway, we took frequent trips to the zoo, where I was mesmerized by the variety of creatures and the re-creations of their jungle environments. I pictured myself living in mocked-up rain forests, and that, I truly believe, is where my love affair with nature began.

At four years old, I frequently rearranged my dining room into a "jungle," lining up the chairs into a makeshift canoe

and warning my mother to watch out for the swarming crocodiles. I was also freakishly good at climbing trees and may
have even then felt a strong affinity with monkeys. My backyard—particularly the enormous mango tree, which provided
excellent climbing and the opportunity to see some wildlife—became a place of refuge. Birds loved it, insects were
bountiful, and the occasional Cuban anole lizard made for
hours-long entertainment.

Little Havana was that homogenous—even the reptiles
were Cuban. The long, slender tail of the tiny anole (which
makes up about half its length) breaks off at the slightest pressure and continues to wiggle on the ground, distracting would-
be predators. At six, that predator was me. I spent countless
hours observing and collecting lizards. Mostly, I observed them
from afar, but if I needed a closer look, I took a long stem
and tied the end into a loop, creating a noose, a skill I would
have perfected, I'm sure, if I had been allowed to join the Girl
Scouts. I would sneak up behind an unsuspecting lizard and
slip the noose around its neck, pulling ever so gently, so that I
wouldn't choke it, but I did accidentally break the tail off one
of my hostage lizards. I became entranced by that left-behind
tail, unattached but still moving. After that, you would have
been hard pressed to find a lizard with a tail within a five-
block radius of my house.

Don't get me wrong: I never killed a lizard. But I admit
to mutilating the tails of five or six. Not to worry, however;
the lizard's tail grows back over several weeks to once again
serve as a quick getaway aid.

Another striking feature of the anole is its dewlap, or throat fan. It is attached to the throat and displayed by means of a flexible rod of cartilage that the lizard can swing downward and forward, revealing a brightly colored patch of skin. Males display their dewlap during courtship and when defending territory. This display is often accompanied by a series of head bobs and push-ups. Years later I would observe similar behavior in overly muscular males at the gym.

Though I thought of myself as a tomboy and was hardly squeamish about worms and lizards, I was also very much a girlie-girl who loved pink and shopping. To this day I am a walking contradiction, setting off for remote jungles carrying pink boots, a little black dress (should an unforeseen occasion arise), and a machete. A budding fashionista even at four, I would capture the little lizards and latch them, still living, onto my earlobes as earrings. Most girls wouldn't touch them; me, I thought they completed the outfit.

Despite my adventurous spirit and the imagination that would transport me to distant places, my mom dismissed my desire to experience the natural world. I'll never forget at age seven asking if I could join the Girl Scouts. I could already see myself rubbing sticks together, learning to identify bear tracks, and watching the stars outside my tent. But Mom said no. Joining the Girl Scouts would no doubt lead to camping, and that, my mom said, was far too dangerous. Before I could earn my first badge, I was officially a failed Girl Scout. Instead, I was to go back to the piano and practice for an upcoming recital—a most grueling weekly task for an outdoorsy child. And when finally released from my sentence on the piano bench, I would need to get into my tights and leotard for ballet class. My mom, the parole officer overseeing my after-school activities, couldn't possibly have dreamed that I would one day lead expeditions to the most distant, remote, and unexplored jungles in the world. God forbid if I had dirtied my leotard.

It should have come as no surprise to her that I followed my Girl Scout dreams right into the River of Darkness. As much as my mom might hate to admit it, the apple doesn't fall far from the tree. Though in our case, the fruit was a mango.

Seeking political asylum, my mom left Cuba at the age of 20 with literally nothing more than the clothes she wore. She was a refugee venturing to a strange land in which a different language was spoken, with no idea of what she'd do once she got here. I often ask my mom to tell me the story, despite having heard it a thousand times. Each time, she vividly describes stepping onto the boat, holding her gaze toward the water, swearing never to look back at the island she loved. She was, in my eyes, an explorer, one I greatly admired. However sheltered she'd been as a girl, she would now have to provide for herself, her younger sister, and her parents. She had grit, the kind I like to think made its way to me.

Despite raising me to become a traditional woman, my mom had earlier tried breaking that mold herself. Hardworking and resilient, she had been accepted to medical school in Cuba in 1965, the very year Cuba's sole political party was renamed the Cuban Communist Party, but she was expelled before she could hold her first scalpel when she refused to sign papers professing loyalty to Fidel Castro's regime. Under that regime, her father and brother had been jailed without explanation, her opinions had been suppressed, and her sense of security had been destroyed. Even at the expense of her dream, my mom refused to sign away her freedom. I think she always hoped I would follow in her never taken footsteps and become a doctor myself. In the end, I did become a doctor but, as I am reminded by my cousins, "not the normal kind."

My upbringing itself was not traditional with a mom-and-pop scenario. I was raised in Miami by not one but three very opinionated and headstrong women: my mother, whom I call Mami; my aunt Ica; and my grandmother, forever remembered as Mima. My father, as my mother would later explain, was in medical school when she became pregnant. They'd met while taking an English class at the University of Miami. He was an exchange student from Madrid—tall, handsome, and witty. My mom fell hard. When Mom announced she was pregnant, my father replied that he didn't want kids. To him, having children at that time would interfere with his career plans and mean giving up on the very dream my mom had relinquished years before. My mother never married, and I would never have any brothers or sisters. I would also never meet my father. I suppose that technically I did meet him once, but from what I'm told it was only for a few seconds when I was nine months old. A few seconds was all it took for him to slam the door once he saw it was us. My mom thought if he met me, he would change his mind. I sometimes felt a void because of this, but my mom was both mother and father to me, and I observed the strength and integrity with which she handled both those roles. I may have lacked the physical presence of a father, but I never lacked a strong role model in my life.

The majority of the more than two million Cuban exiles in the United States live in or around Miami. So, though I was born and raised in Miami, I might as well have called Cuba my motherland. Only Spanish was spoken at the house, as neither my mother nor Mima spoke a word of English. I didn't learn to speak English until I was five years old and had entered the American school system. To this day, when I'm asked my nationality, my immediate response is "Cuban." That response nearly got me arrested in Mexico, when officials thought I must be presenting them with a fake passport. But that's how strong my Cuban roots grow.

It wasn't always the case. Like most kids, I disliked anything that made me different. Not knowing a word of English at the age of five was a nightmare. As a little girl, I thought my Cuban roots were a hindrance. I'd have given anything to be named Jennifer or Beth, something other than the very Spanish and weird-sounding name bestowed on me (which no one could pronounce). I would shudder when my mom started speaking her foreign tongue in front of my friends.

My upbringing was fit for a princess, a Cuban princess, complete with homemade frilly dresses that my grandmother sewed and more dolls than I could have ever hoped for. But to my mom's dismay, I would get home from school and instantly rip the dresses off, opting for shorts and tees. I often thought I would have made the perfect son. My interests all involved the outdoors—climbing trees, catching lizards, and going fishing. To feed my girlie side, Mami, Ica, and Mima countered with pink dresses, ballet, and piano.

Fortunately for them, growing up in a big city, I didn't have too many opportunities to experience wildlife in the backwoods. But we did spend lots of time on the beach, and while most kids were playing in the surf, I would wander off with a net, collecting anything unlucky enough to swim into it. Occasionally, I was swift enough to catch a hermit crab scurrying into a sandy hole. I spent hours observing the birds hunting for meals, and many times supplied the bread from my ham and cheese sandwich.

Despite not supporting my desire for merit badges and sleeping in the great outdoors, my mom did tolerate and even encourage my love of animals. I had a lot of pets as a kid. The family room was lined with birdcages; tanks of fish quickly took over the rest of the house.

Our house was basically a zoo, and I considered charging admission to support my animal habit. The menagerie included several dogs of various colors, shapes, and sizes; cats abandoned by neighbors; rabbits; hamsters; fish (both saltwater and fresh); birds; and even a chicken named Maggie, an Easter present. She came to me as a chick small enough to fit in a teacup and quickly grew to be my favorite pet. Despite county zoning laws against chickens, my otherwise law-abiding grandfather, Pipo, built her a huge, wire-mesh cage. I pretended, or perhaps really believed, I was a farmer. I still have memories of throwing on overalls and getting ready to feed my chicken. In the mornings I would collect the eggs that Maggie had left for us and then go in for breakfast. It would be years before I realized those eggs had been planted by Mima. Such was the life of a Miami farmer.

My menagerie grew exponentially when I became old enough to walk home from school. Growing up, I thought myself a dog whisperer. If there was a stray dog within a two-block radius, it found me and followed me home. Once there, it became part of the extended family. But as much as I loved my pets and capturing bugs and lizards, it was mostly the freedom of animals I reveled in. Butterflies were of huge interest simply because they seemed to embody more freedom than any other creature, with their aimless, carefree fluttering. My interest led to a butterfly garden that enraptured my mom and me each morning over our cafés con leche. To this day, I am mesmerized by the beauty of butterflies, and my garden is full of the kinds of flowers that attract them.

Unbeknownst to my mom (Mima knew), I kept snails, worms, and an array of creepy-crawlies under my bed. Technically, it was our bed: mine, the snails', the worms', and my mom's. It was a small house, so I had to share a room with my mom, and my secret was safe until she accidentally freed them while cleaning under the bed. The memory of her shriek still sends chills down my spine. She unequivocally put her foot down when I wanted to leave the bedroom windows open with lights on to attract moths.

In the end, it was a turtle that got me into the worst trouble. My fascination with turtles began not by the water but on my front porch. One day, there sat a turtle no bigger than a softball. My mom agreed that I could keep it after much whining and wheedling from me, skills I mastered to talk her into every animal I wanted. My plastic pool became the perfect island home for the turtle. I loved watching it swim, its little legs pedaling like crazy. So I named it Bicicleta. It quickly grew, and in hurricane season we would transfer it to our bathtub for protection. During one of those bathtub transfers it refused to let go of my grandmother's finger. I had made my first personal scientific discovery: a snapping turtle!

After that, my mom and Mima insisted Bicicleta be returned to a nearby canal, its likely original home. With tears in my eyes, I let it go. It was my first heartbreak. Mom had suggested I paint a little pink dot on its shell so I could spot it in the future, but I never expected to see it again. Fast-forward several years, and you can imagine the shock when I once again found Bicicleta, with its perfect pink dot, sitting on my front porch. I don't know how it found its way back home from the canal. Or how it had gotten across a very busy street that even I wasn't allowed to cross. I returned Bicicleta to the canal once again, satisfied that it knew the way if ever it wanted to visit.

Eventually, I got over the turtle. In fact, the turtle was the least of my future heartbreaks. But it taught me two life lessons: "What is meant to be will be," and "If you set something you love free, if it's yours, it will come back to you."

Having three mothers with Cuban tempers wasn't easy. The fiery temper of a Cuban woman may be a stereotype, but it is also a reality. However, my collective mothers instilled in me a boundless resilience, confidence, and strength. Little did I know that the strength these women possessed, that allowed them to leave their own country, would be essential for me in my future calling. Then there was the daily diet they fed me of Cuban rice and beans: For months at a time in the field, it would be the food I'd eat every day.

My mom is a very sharp woman. She graduated at the top of her class in Havana and had been on her way to medical school, but the only job she could get on arriving in Miami was at Burger King, sweeping floors. Adding insult to injury, BK, a fast-food giant in the country of freedom, justice, and workers' rights, paid her 90 cents an hour under the table, even less than minimum wage at the time. Talk about a whopper.

After she was granted political asylum in the U.S., my mom still hoped one day to go to medical school. But with a language deficit and a family to support, that dream would have to wait. Instead, she worked so that her only sister, who was five years younger, could go to nursing school. My mom saved whatever pennies remained after food and rent to replace the piano her sister had left in Cuba. Ironically, the piano my mom worked so hard to buy would become the bane of my existence, the one I was compelled to practice on. Though it has long been deemed untunable, that piano still sits in Aunt Ica's house like a piece of furniture.

Self-sacrifice is a very Cuban trait. Everyone pitches in for
their loved ones. In 1961, when Castro proclaimed Cuba a
communist state, my Uncle Pedro, who had just been selected
to play professional baseball, fought against the revolution,
making himself a target. But it was not his fight alone. My
grandfather's younger brother, Gonzalo, risked his life to
hide Pedro in his produce truck and drive him to the Colombian embassy in Havana to seek political asylum. The Colombian ambassador personally told Pedro that the regime would
tolerate his taking refuge in the embassy but under no circumstances would allow him to leave the island. Still, the
ambassador offered to help him escape by allowing my great
uncle Gonzalo's produce truck onto embassy grounds. With
Pedro hiding inside a crate in the back, my great uncle headed
for Varadero Beach, where a boat would whisk Pedro to Florida. Armed militia stopped them on the way but luckily never
checked the contents of the fruit and vegetable crates. The pen-
alty would have been death for both.

My grandmother, who was a schoolteacher in Cuba,
also endured her share of heartache. Among the fear tactics
employed by Castro's regime, she was made to "volunteer" to
cut sugarcane, not much different than forced labor. Her oldest child, my tio Nene, was jailed for spending three months
vacationing in the U.S., which to the regime made him a suspected CIA agent. He was 17.

When they arrived to arrest him, my mother asked one of
the soldiers, who had been a longtime family friend, how he
could do that. The soldier responded, "If my own father had

to be executed for the purposes of the regime, I would put the bullet in him." Those words would haunt her for many years.

Regular incarcerations ensued, completely at random. In 1961 there was an unsuccessful attempt to overthrow the Castro government by a U.S.-trained force of Cuban exiles supported by the U.S. military, famously known as the Bay of Pigs invasion. During the invasion, Castro ordered that all suspected dissenters, my grandfather and Tio Nene among them, be picked up and jailed to keep them from joining.

The prisons were so crowded that my grandfather described having to sleep in turns, sometimes standing up. Executions were brutal and not uncommon. It was at that time that my grandmother made the wrenching decision to help her son flee the island.

Cuba's borders had yet to be closed, so with breaking heart Mima arranged to have Tio Nene sent away as soon as he was released. She signed the necessary papers for him, a minor, to travel by plane to the U.S., ostensibly to visit a friend. But this was no vacation. Shortly after, Cuba's borders closed. Mima did not know if she would ever see her only son again.

In 1965, four years after both my uncles had made their escapes, Fidel Castro stood in the Plaza of the Revolution and announced that anyone who wanted to leave Cuba could go. My grandfather didn't want to abandon his mother, but my grandmother wouldn't take no for an answer. She begged him to think of their children. Less than 24 hours later, police arrived at their home to inventory their belongings, making sure that nothing but the clothes they were wearing left the island with them.

I often try to imagine how difficult it must be to leave your country, your relatives and friends, your home and all its contents—all the people and possessions that make up your life—fully knowing that there is no turning back. My grandmother made that life-altering decision overnight.

It was a fortunate decision. By the end of the 1960s an estimated 15,000 to 17,000 people had been executed.

But my grandmother didn't leave everything behind. Living up to the adage "Well-behaved women seldom make history," she hid her most valued possessions under her clothes. She boldly left the island with photographs of her children, to this day their only tangible memories of their cherished childhood.

Although she eventually became a nurse, my mom's dreams of becoming a doctor were first reduced to working for one. She became secretary to one of the top oncologists in Miami and put in extremely long hours. As a result, I spent most of my time with Mima. My grandmother's job was to take care of me, which was, I admit, no easy task. Mima never learned to drive, so most of our time was spent on long bus rides, one of the most exciting parts of my childhood. Something about the treks to the bus stop and the ensuing trips seemed adventurous. There were journeys in the making, my first expeditions, even if the destination was only the park or the shopping mall.

At the park I would disappear into the trees and come back with handfuls of tamarind, which I would proudly watch Mima eat on the park bench. I showed early that I had skill as a hunter-gatherer, like the BaAka, the Pygmy people of Africa I would come to know and love years later.

My grandmother, who in the mother-chain was second in command, was a bit more permissive of my exploratory tendencies. In my mother's absence, I would get permission from Mima to ride my bike in areas I knew very well Mom wouldn't allow. As soon as I got home from school, I wasted no time in ripping off my skirt and jumping into what my grandmother called "street clothes," so that I could join in a neighborhood ball game. Baseball glove in hand, I'd take off on my bike and race down the street, crossing the railroad tracks and hollering at the prostitutes who plied their wares there, racing on as they hollered back. I'm not sure why we did this, but I do remember loving the adrenalin rush. It also seems to have been good training for fleeing elephants.

After some pedaling, I would find myself in a much more affluent area, where banyan trees lined the avenues. These trees are majestic, with limbs that grow thick and wide from their trunks. In order to support the tree's great weight, the limbs grow shoots at stress points that stretch downward and take root when they reach ground.

The banyan always makes me think of my family; in many ways they are alike. Both are resilient, surviving even the harshest of storms. And like the shoots that help support that great tree, my family was always there with the support I needed to get where I wanted to go.

two

Antithesis of a Scientist

JANUARY 7, 1995: It's a little like leading a double life. I rehearse the dance routines for hours on end and save just enough energy to pore through the science text and memorize Latin names of species. It makes me wonder if Darwin had some surprising hobby. Sure, he spent all his time on voyages to far and remote lands, coming up with scientific theories on evolution. But perhaps he was a good dancer, too. Yes, in my mind, Charles Darwin was a closet cheerleader.

I admit I didn't take the typical scientist route. Though my love of animals continued as I got older, in fear of being labeled the creepy critter girl, I stopped harvesting eight-legged creatures under my bed. I was a very good student, but in school I wasn't very good at science or math. Even today I think the teaching of those subjects is geared toward boys. Rather than fight the system, I focused on what ballet had trained me for: I joined my first cheerleading dance squad, the West Kendall Wildcats.

Mami and Mima were happy I was back in skirts.

In high school I cultivated my artistic side and let the nerdy boys have science. I excelled in writing courses, largely because of my vivid imagination, and became editor of the school paper. This gave me the opportunity to get some life experience outside of the classroom. To pursue a story, I embedded myself in a homeless camp in downtown Miami. My mom thought I was staying at a friend's house. When she realized I'd been living in a tent amid vagabonds, she encouraged me to pursue other extracurricular activities. To this day I feel a strong affinity with the homeless as fellow wanderers and survivalists. It was with them that I first learned to camp.

But in life there are detours, and for a brief time I headed not toward the wilds but in the opposite direction.

My grandfather Pipo passed away when I was six. We'd always lived in the same house and been very close. I would often go to work with him at the cinema, where he was a handyman. He could usually sneak me into screenings of films before they were released. It was very exciting to go to the back room, where all the films were stored and previewed. I fell in love with movies.

Most of all, I fell in love with stardom.

My grandmother looked like a blonde, green-eyed starlet. She loved to watch television and often said that I was destined for fame. Apparently I was, though not in the Hollywood way she surely had in mind. But knowing I would have my grandmother's support and approval, I began auditioning for school plays and quickly landed a lead role. After glowing reviews, I received an internship at the Actor's Playhouse, a local professional theater, where I continued performing in musicals. I'm Cuban. Drama queen runs in my blood.

When I graduated from high school, I got a two-bit agent and appeared as an extra in feature films. Yes, I am that

unrecognizable girl walking past the camera in *that* movie. I
didn't even consider applying for college. I honestly believed
that school would get in the way of an acting career. Oddly
enough, my mom and Mima were OK with this decision. In
fact, they were proud. My grandmother, in particular, loved
watching me in the limelight. Though I had yet to get a speaking part, I considered myself a professional actress.

In reality I was a professional secretary and waitress who
got fired a lot.

My big break finally came when I began appearing regularly as a bikini-clad model on Mima's favorite Latin TV program, *Sabado Gigante*. Sadly, Mima did not live to see me on
it. But I always had the feeling she was somehow responsible,
smiling from heaven.

(Years later, in a funny twist of fate, I appeared on that show
again, not in a swimsuit but as a wildlife expert with lemurs in
tow. "The snakes," I was told, would have to "wait outside."
Turns out my grandmother's crush, Don Francisco, the effer-
vescent host who is a household name in Latino circles, was
terrified of snakes and highly superstitious.)

Much to my mother's delight, I had become a full-fledged
girlie-girl and performer, putting to good use all those years
of ballet classes. But the truth is I was spending more time
behind a desk than in front of an audience. I didn't mind the
work, though it was often tedious, and the long hours didn't
scare me, but I quickly realized I wasn't cut out for a nine-
to-five job. The woman who sat next to me, though not my
supervisor, got her kicks from bossing me around. She was so

miserable and frustrated with her dead-end job that I vowed never to become her. You know when people ask you what that moment was when you *knew*? Fran was my moment. It was watching her belittle an assistant at the fax machine that made me realize the only thing that could save me was to sign up for college. It seemed my only ticket out.

It turns out that campus life suited me, and I surprised myself by how much I loved academia. I particularly enjoyed creative writing and philosophy. I even fell madly in love with my philosophy professor, an older, free-spirited vegetarian whose lectures on animal cruelty, ethics, and religion mesmerized me. Plus, he was really cute and even dedicated one of his books to me.

Philosophy and logic classes were a natural fit for me. Given my Cuban background, I was very good at arguing and excelled at coming up with a rationale where none existed, a talent I had no doubt learned from my three mothers. Repeatedly, I was told by professors that I'd make a great lawyer, a statement I had often heard from my moms. When I graduated from my two-year college, I received a full scholarship to the University of Miami, where I went on to finish my bachelor's degree.

Much as I was loving college life, something was missing. I was no longer performing in plays, and I'd stopped going to commercial castings. Throughout junior high and high school, I'd been good at basketball, even receiving a full basketball scholarship to the University of Mississippi, but I had by now stopped playing sports competitively.

Then in a simple twist of fate on the beach one afternoon I met Vivian.

She was a gorgeous blonde with a Colgate smile, and I couldn't help but notice that she was flaunting the tan I had always yearned for. We hit it off, and I asked her what she did. "I'm a cheerleader," she responded. My puzzled look may have prompted her to add "For the NFL," as if to say "a professional one."

A professional cheerleader?

I loved watching football, but somehow I had never given a thought to the bouncing beauties on the sidelines. Vivian said, "You should try out next week." Me? I thought. I hadn't even made the high school squad. How could I possibly be selected among hundreds to be a cheerleader for the Miami Dolphins?

"OK, I will."

My mom had always encouraged me to go for the seemingly impossible (as long as camping was not involved), so I convinced myself to give it a try. The mere thought that there might be something I couldn't do ignited my competitive instincts and gave me the push to audition. I really wanted to believe I could do it and figured I had nothing to lose but my pride and dignity. Plus, I thought the uniforms were cute.

But let there be no mistake. I auditioned not because I really wanted to be a cheerleader, but rather as a way to get into the games. As an avid football fan, I knew standing on the sidelines would give me a far better view than any ticket I could buy. And did I mention the cute uniforms?

On arriving at the stadium for the auditions, I could see just past the parking lot hundreds of beautiful, scantily dressed girls stretching and practicing their best yoga moves. I walked back to my car and called Mom to tell her I had changed my mind. In her usual way, she boosted my confidence and urged me not to take myself out of the race. As I paced back and forth, never straying more than 20 feet from my little red convertible, the blond goddess Vivian walked by. In her bubbly, professional cheerleader way she said, "So glad you decided to come!"

Not wanting to admit defeat, I walked into the sea of beauties.

I signed in and was assigned a choreographer and given a number. For the next several weeks I would answer to #325. Later that afternoon, I was one of 75 selected from the initial hundreds to go on to compete for the highly coveted pom-poms. The audition process was grueling, both physically and emotionally. I gave up several days a week to rehearse and was regularly humiliated by the coach for missing a step or standing slightly out of line. Luckily, I was used to being yelled at. You can't live with three Cuban moms and not be.

After hundreds of hours, badly bruised hamstrings, and more high kicks than a 50-year run of the New York City Rockettes, I was deemed flexible and coordinated enough to hold the title of professional cheerleader. One of only 32 spots. Vivian was not so lucky. She was the last to be cut.

I had reached stardom, I thought, even if I got paid only $25 a game. Regardless of the pay, I still smile when I think back to being on the football field in a stadium filled with 70,000 screaming fans and the emotion that would come over me every time I stood listening to the national anthem.

Though if I'm honest, the height of gratification came the following year when some of the cheerleaders from my high school who had snubbed me from their squad came to audition and got cut. Very like a cheerleader, I realize.

I continued going to university, slightly more popular now, and was breezing through a double major in English and philosophy. I excelled, in fact, never failing to make the dean's list. There came a point when I was just a few credits shy of graduating and needed to fulfill one last science requirement. The women's biology course I wanted to take was full, and all my pleading did not convince the professor to let me in. Even batting my lashes failed to do the trick, a tactic that up to that point had been foolproof.

I had no choice but to scroll through the list of available courses to find something else, and I settled on an anthropology course that seemed vaguely interesting. More important, it was scheduled at the perfect time—it didn't interfere with prime poolside hours for tanning. OK, burning.

The anthropology professor was tough, and I considered dropping the class more than once. But it was during that class that my passion for animals was rekindled. When she began talking about primates, our closest living nonhuman relatives, I was transported to places exotic and faraway. I came to learn of the plight of these animals, so many of which were on the verge of extinction. As I researched my newfound obsession, I saw that there were no photographs, only line drawings, of some of these animals. I started to ask more and more questions in class and discovered that even at a time when we had set foot on the moon, many places here on Earth had yet to be explored.

After class one day, I nervously approached my professor—who looked me up and down, stopping at what I'm sure she thought was an all-too-revealing top and too-short skirt, along with platform shoes—and began to ask her a question. But before the words came out of my mouth, she said, "I saw you on TV. You're a cheerleader." I thought I would die. She'd seen me wearing the little uniform and shaking my pom-poms. All this before handing me back the assignment I'd turned in late as a result of that Monday night game.

I gathered my courage and said, "Dr. Taylor, I think I would like to become a primatologist. How do I do that?" I immediately realized how silly I must have sounded, but without missing a beat, she replied, "You need to develop a research question, formulate a hypothesis, and apply for a grant. There's actually a university grant for women in the sciences, and the deadline is in a couple of weeks." Noticing that she had answered my question without so much as cracking a smile, I felt like a scholar for the first time.

Dr. Taylor then asked me about my "other" life as a cheerleader, which had obviously intrigued or puzzled her for some time. As it turned out, Doc, as she soon let me call her, was a huge Dolphins fan. Despite her stern exterior, we shared another couple of interests: shopping and shoes.

And so began our lifelong friendship. I soon found myself hanging out less with friends, opting instead to spend hours in her office.

I remember watching *Gorillas in the Mist* one day and thinking, Oh, my God, that's it! That's exactly what I want to do! I want to go live with mountain gorillas in Africa! I was picturing myself wearing camouflage gear in the Rwandan forest, befriending a 400-pound silverback, and waving a machete at poachers when I glanced up at my pink Hello Kitty clock.

Realizing I was late for practice, I jumped off the couch, wrestled my way into a small black leotard and tights, grabbed my pom-poms, and ran through the door. I figured I could fix hair and makeup in the car. But what I *really* wanted to do was pick up the phone and call this Leakey guy, who obviously had the financial means and seemingly peculiar bad sense to send Dian Fossey, Biruté Galdikas, and Jane Goodall to live in the wilds, all of whom had little to no background in primate research.

I wanted to become one of Leakey's Angels.

I wondered if Prada would design me a functional yet stylish backpack. I mean, even if the gorillas didn't know labels, I saw no reason to go out there looking like, well, a bush woman. Designer khakis and fashionable field boots would become all the rage if I had anything to do with it. But even in my dreamlike state, I realized that my newly found ambition to go live in the forest among apes would not excuse my being late to rehearse next week's halftime routine, which, curiously, had been choreographed to Robert Palmer's "Simply Irresistible."

I arrived at our rehearsal site, Don Shula's Gym, where I was greeted by my 31 cheerleading colleagues. Funny how the words "colleague" and "cheerleading" don't exactly roll off the tongue together. I dabbed on some lip gloss and eavesdropped on the week's latest gossip, which I have to say almost without exception involved a blonde. "Did you hear that Christine is getting kicked off the squad? She was caught out on a date with one of the running backs!" First or second string? I thought. This was a real no-no in the world of professional cheerleading. We all signed contracts clearly stating that fraternizing with the players would be cause for immediate dismissal. Maybe she didn't know what "fraternizing" meant, I chuckled to myself. Christine was the best cheerleader on the squad, certainly the prettiest. I was sure she'd be given a stern warning, get benched for a game or two, and then all would go back to normal. But just then Christine came out of the locker room with red, swollen eyes, grabbed her belongings without so much as a word or looking at anyone, and exited the gymnasium. Our coach, without wasting a second, clapped her hands to get our attention back into the room and yelled at us to start stretching. The music came on, fear and curiosity filled the room, and everyone just focused on not becoming the target of our coach's wrath that day. A wrath that had earned her the secret nickname Hitler.

After practice, a few of the girls and I decided to get something to eat. We had just spent nine hours burning thousands of calories and had passed our weigh-in for the game with flying colors. We had earned a salad with nonfat dressing on the side.

After we discussed Christine's fate and the difficulties of the routines, I asked the girls what they saw themselves doing in the future. It seemed a silly question, even to me. I mean, what better way to spend your weekends than cheering on one of the best teams in the NFL? We did have Dan Marino and Don Shula at the time, and two years in a row we had almost gone to the Super Bowl. Besides, in addition to the $25 we were paid for each game, we were entitled to two free tickets for family and friends.

OK, life was good. But I meant the FUTURE. I told them I had watched *Gorillas in the Mist* and was thinking about quitting after the season so that I could venture to a remote country, live in the rain forest, make friends with the natives, and track primates.

"You mean, like monkeys?!" After they stopped laughing, they asked me if I was serious. "I mean, you'd what, like live in a tent? There's no electricity—how would you dry your hair?" asked one of the girls.

I had not thought of this.

I made the point that cheerleading was not something any of us could do forever and that I was thinking of giving it up for the experience of exploring uncharted territory and contributing to science. They thought I was nuts. A few took me seriously, but most laughed, and the conversation devolved to comparing football players and apes. Offended, I grabbed my unsweetened tea and excused myself so that I could give further thought to this "no electricity" business.

[three]

Cheerleader in the Mist

JULY 21, 1996: We spent an entire day on the river rowing a dugout canoe, trying to elude the rains. As dusk settled, we spotted monkeys high in the canopy along the water's edge foraging for fruit. It was my first wild primate observation and I am feeling invincible. Last night—my first night in the jungle—seemed romantic, too. I cooked on a fire, read by candlelight, and went to sleep to the sounds of frogs and a cascading waterfall. But my love affair with nature is over after having spent the entire night in bed with a mosquito.

That year, with the help of Doc's glowing letter of recommendation, I received my first grant to study a rare species of monkey in South America, the white-faced saki. I thus started my travels to distant and remote places, in pursuit of some of the most critically endangered animals in the world.

I had never traveled outside the country before, but how hard could it be to chase monkeys? I approached my coach and let her know that I would not be returning to cheer the following season. She warned me that if I missed summer rehearsals, there was no coming back. That thought had occurred to me, but I was determined to trade in my pompoms for a pair of hiking boots. Pink ones.

The cheerleaders thought I was crazy. But it was my mom who took my news the hardest. She cried, but she still felt compelled to iron my field clothes, a clear sign that on some level I had her support. She probably convinced herself that it was a phase and that her dreams of me becoming a good housewife would not in the end be shattered. I'm pretty sure she was also convinced that I'd been brainwashed by this "Doc" character. But nothing would stop me. I was heading to the Amazon with a few key supplies—a teddy-bear backpack and stylish, black Ralph Lauren vest. Those oversize fishing vests just wouldn't do.

Doc introduced me to the director of the Smithsonian Institution's Guyana project, Dr. Shawn Lehman. He was six four and at one time had played college football, so at least we had football in common. At some point during that meeting, Shawn, whom I secretly nicknamed Dr. Handsome, said, "You don't look like a scientist." I was deeply offended, but he was a really good-looking guy, so I smiled. Had it ever occurred to him that maybe *he* didn't look like a scientist? What does a scientist look like? I've asked myself that many times since. As a former NFL cheerleader, I would not feel welcomed into the scientific community for years. In graduate school I know I was graded more harshly. Later, producers remarked on my looks and said things like "You're a Sexy Jane running around in the jungle." "You don't look like a scientist" was a statement I would come to hear and loathe for years.

Regardless, Dr. Handsome took me under his wing, offered me a place to stay, and introduced me to other Smithsonian researchers and botanists working in Guyana who could tell me in which trees to look for the sakis and which plants I should avoid. Later, he would poke fun at the high heels and dresses displayed in my room at the research house.

Feeling confident about my plans, I purchased my plane tickets, the impractical teddy-bear backpack, and a pair of trendy hiking boots. I even had a little room left for a Calvin Klein field shirt and the black Ralph Lauren field vest. Neither of those was officially field clothing, but the CK shirt was military green and the vest looked like real field vests only it had a more flattering fit. The coolest part was that Dr. Taylor took me on the shopping trip. Turns out she's a bit of a label addict too.

I dutifully checked off all of the necessary gear on my list: tent, sleeping bag, backpack, water bottles, tweezers, water filter, hair dryer, survival manuals, first-aid kit, hiking boots, flashlights, binoculars, field notebooks, little black dress, and waterproof pens and paper. Who knew there was such a thing as waterproof pens and paper? I certainly didn't. I also didn't know that because of deadly snakes and other creatures roaming the forest floor, I would never use that tent or sleeping bag, opting instead for a locally made hammock.

I weighed my bags, which I knew to be too many, and noted the overweight. I tried to choose which heels and platforms to leave behind but thought it best to pay the extra charge, as I didn't know which dresses I'd need to match. I justified packing the little black dress, as it weighed nothing and didn't take up much space. Mine was not at all a bag Charles Darwin would have carried on an expedition, but I explained that thought away by telling myself that men are simply not as fashionable, and, anyway, in the 19th century shoe styles were limited.

As for cheerleading, I would not return to audition the next season, or any season after that. The cheerleaders took the news of my departure well, though most of them never believed I would go through with my crazy idea. The ones who did believe never thought I would survive to write about it, and the rest never thought about it at all.

It was finally time to leave. As my mother finished ironing the last of my field pants, I hugged her and assured her that everything would be all right. She reluctantly drove me to the airport, yet she seemed excited that her little girl was flying off to see places she had only read about. My promise to bring her a nice doily seemed to help. I checked myself and my overweight bags in and set off for an adventure that would change not just the course of my life, but also my entire perspective of the world.

I arrived in Georgetown, the capital of Guyana, to the unfamiliar smells and sights of a developing country. The first thing I noticed was the inordinate number of dogs and chickens on the runway, not exactly what you'd see at Miami International Airport. The city looked like the setting for a fairy tale, with tree-lined streets and quaint Dutch colonial and Victorian houses dating from its days as a Dutch and then British colony. I marveled at everything I saw like someone who'd just been sprung from prison. Off U.S. soil for the first time in my life, my heart beat with anticipation for the adventures that were sure to follow.

After two weeks of uncertain electricity (it came and went randomly) and no television, no hot water, no telephone, and no air conditioning in that hot and humid country, I started having my doubts. And that was before I even stepped one foot into the forest. In that big, overcrowded city I found myself missing the amenities of "civilization." Where was a Taco Bell when I needed one? I eventually discovered that Georgetown's first-ever fast-food chain, a Kentucky Fried Chicken, had just opened within walking distance of my guesthouse—the line to get in went out KFC's door and past the guesthouse. Suddenly, I began to think of how I could tell my coach that this was all a big mistake and beg her to take me back. But I knew it was too late. Tryouts had passed, and a new blonde had surely filled my place and was now the sole proprietor of my pom-poms. I also missed my mom terribly. But I decided to make the best of a dreadful situation.

One day I wandered into the market to stock up on supplies. It teemed with the sort of energy you feel in Times Square on a Friday night. I browsed the colorful stalls and purchased nonperishables like peanut butter and sardines. I even bought some reeking dry fish, though I refrained from putting them in my backpack. Fortunately, because Guyana is a former British colony, everyone speaks English. The produce seemed brighter and bigger than I had ever seen in American supermarkets. But it was the reaction to one purchase that really threw me. At a stall I asked, "How much for the Kool-Aid?" and got a very startled look. I found the reaction odd and only later learned that Kool-Aid was synonymous with group suicide in Guyana after the infamous Jim Jones had poisoned more than 900 people with cyanide mixed with it in 1978—this would be the first of many faux pas during the expedition. I picked up a few fruits and vegetables, even though they'd been sitting out in the sun with hundreds of hovering flies. More than ever, I longed for Miami and take-out sushi.

It was time to sort out the permits, and I was glad to have packed a nice pantsuit and pumps to wear at my meeting with the forest ministry officials. When they invited me to join them for dinner later that week, I knew the little black dress would also come in handy. In all it took—or rather wasted, given my dwindling funds—two full weeks of meetings with government officials and University of Guyana authorities to finally get approval to conduct research in the jungle. It was frustrating how many people's hands each paper had to pass through and with what precision each and every stamp was applied. But in the end, we were legit. We had successfully convinced the authorities that we weren't there to steal their saki monkeys.

Now we could head to the jungle. Dr. Handsome and I and our team would leave early the next morning. As I helped load things into the car, I noted that my backpack weighed more than the others and that my never-broken-in hiking boots were already giving me blisters. Other than that, I was feeling pretty good. Shortly after, one of the scientists, a well-seasoned botanist, succumbed to malaria and had to stay back at the house. A harsh reality, I thought, of life in the wild.

We spent one day driving dusty, potholed roads, two days on a small riverboat, and three days hiking. It was a grueling trek, as I'd been warned; at night we'd sleep in hammocks attached to trees. We were in pure wilderness, with few amenities to ease the way. This area was called the Land of Many Rivers, and to cross them we had to throw ourselves in waist deep. The worst was that the rivers were infested with piranhas, which are known to bite their victims once, ripping out a chunk of flesh and leaving a round, crater-shaped wound. Stories of people being attacked and eaten by ferocious schools of piranhas quickly came to mind, despite reports that there is little scientific evidence for such behavior. The same reports said that at least three of the people supposedly killed that way actually died from heart failure or drowning and were feasted on only later. Suddenly, my enthusiasm for venturing farther into the wild was replaced by fears of the unknown, of not being able to keep up, and of being attacked and eaten by fish, whether before or after drowning. We were almost at our destination, and I was wishing I were dead. Just not because of piranhas.

We arrived at an Amerindian village on the jungle outskirts, and I showed the villagers our hard-earned permission papers. Not a building in sight, just a sea of green, a jumble of trees, and rivers that had yet to be explored. But here in the middle of nowhere I was far from alone. In fact, within minutes of arriving I was at the center of a circle of villagers who had somehow heard of our arrival. They had rarely if ever seen foreigners. Finally, a group of brave little girls approached. I thought for sure they could smell the last of the Jolly Ranchers hiding in my bag. But it wasn't the candies they were after. One little girl reached out and touched my arm with a finger, then yanked it away as if burned. The other girls followed suit. They then proceeded to touch my hair, giggling uncontrollably. I didn't think it would be all right for me to do the same, so I just stood there. Proclaiming that the show was over, a village elder came to my rescue and took me into his thatched hut like you would a lost puppy.

I knew then I would be OK.

Living in that village was an incredible experience. Though I felt hugely out of my element, at the same time I couldn't have felt more at home. The villagers were very friendly and hospitable. Here was a place where food was scarce and people went shoeless and wore clothes with more holes than my scientific theories, yet they were feeding and sheltering me, treating me as their own. Subsequent travels to other impoverished countries showed me that that generosity was not the exception but the norm. I felt immensely humbled.

I had settled into my new life rather well, I thought, especially not speaking the local dialect. It always amazes me how far hand signals and pointing can take you. In the mornings I helped the women prepare the meals. Truth be told, unlike the other women in my family, I am not a good cook. Luckily, a lot of the cooking involved spitting, lots of spitting, and I can spit with the best of them. You see, the Amerindian staple diet is cassava. Cassava is used to make alcohol, known as *chicha*. And Guyana's national dish, pepperpot, is typically stewed meat strongly flavored with cinnamon, hot pepper, and cassareep—a special sauce made from the cassava root. Cassava, also called yucca or manioc, has a high level of toxic cyanogenic glycosides, a pure 40-milligram dose of which can kill a cow. Improper preparation of cassava can cause a condition in humans called konzo, a neurological disease that results in paralysis, impaired vision, goiter, and cretinism. To release the toxins, cassava is soaked in water for several days. The enzymes in saliva help further the process—thus the spitting. I tried very hard not to think about the preparation while eating or drinking.

A Guyanese wildlife trader and his family lived nearby, and, hearing the village had visitors, came over to welcome us. He invited me to come along on his hunts, so on most days (with a very dry mouth after cooking) I joined the men in the forest. I didn't enjoy this part of the day, but I wanted to learn about the hunting practices. Granted I was naive, but it was a shocker.

Monkeys, mostly squirrel and capuchin, were rounded up and crammed into small cages to be sold as food or for illegal export. The hunters would chase monkeys into trees and isolate them by pulling down surrounding trees. They often killed the females, ripping babies from their backs. Strikingly beautiful birds such as macaws and toucans were trapped, and sometimes I had to hold them on my lap in the boat for transfer to market. The trader's wife didn't understand why I wanted to go into the forest, saying, "It's dangerous, you know.

There are jaguars." I knew that. But it was not the jaguars that made me want to cry. I was witnessing atrocities committed toward some of the world's rarest and most magnificent creatures, and I could do nothing but document it.

Not only did my colleagues not know I'd been an NFL cheerleader, they didn't know I'd never left the country before—or even gone camping. But it was now irrelevant. Yes, I had grown up a sheltered girl with a love for animals and ballet, but now I was chasing wild animals and spitting on my food.

After a few days of village life, it was time to go on in search of the sakis. The team now included an elderly Amerindian villager whose knowledge of the forest would prove invaluable; his daughter, who seemed to be in her early 20s; and her teenage brother, who was partly deaf from quinine, the malarial cure he'd taken since birth. The kids would paddle and assist us in hacking through the nearly impenetrable wall of trees. Then, of course, there was me and Dr. Handsome, who weighed in at more than 200 pounds. We would all climb into an unstable dugout canoe together. Buckets were essential to bail water whenever one of us shifted position.

We left with not much more than a bag of food, a few camping supplies, and hearts filled with hope. We planned to be away three months. After paddling for a while, we set up camp. Sleep did not come easily. Though during the day the forest seemed like a tranquil place, at night the sounds were deafening. Frogs, bats, even monkeys made up the chorus. I wouldn't say I was scared exactly. But I was. Between that and the malarial dreams that had me covered in blood, I wasn't overly eager for shut-eye.

The next morning we loaded our belongings into the canoe and pushed off again. I took notes on the wildlife and mused at just how small humans figure in nature. I noted the quiet surroundings. Suddenly, our guide motioned me to duck down as a boat of "port knockers" was coming around the river's bend. What are port knockers, I thought, and why does everyone look so scared?

As it turned out, port knockers are small-scale miners who pan for gold along rivers and streams. They are the prospectors of Guyana, intrepid individuals who, like the cowboys of the Wild West, are part of the national identity and the subject of many tales. And judging by the guide's reaction, they can be your worst nightmare. That is, if your worst nightmare is to get robbed, beaten, and possibly raped and killed if you put up too much of a fight, or if they're simply drunk enough. We hid the boat and ourselves under some fallen trees and sat in frightened silence as the loud, drunken sailors cruised by.

Unfortunately, we wouldn't see any monkeys that day, and as the sun was setting, we tied up our canoe, set up camp, and rested our bodies on damp hammocks. I was starting to think we would never find them and that, anyway, I wasn't cut out for this. That night I learned how the rain forest got its name. It rained longer and harder than any storm I had ever endured in Miami during the hurricane season. On the upside, the pots and pans we left out overnight sparkled in the morning. Nature's Maytag, I thought. But then I noticed that in the mad rush to get the tarps up I had forgotten to bring in my designer field vest. I glanced at the label and swore it was mocking me: Dry Clean Only.

The rain never really let up, and over the next several weeks I was awakened daily by howler monkeys. Howler monkeys are like rats in South America. Anyone who has spent the night in a South American rain forest has at the very least heard them from a distance. I think they actually take great pleasure in waking people they have identified as "not a morning person." Howlers will find the tree you are under and perch there while making their incredibly loud cry. At first, I thought it was exciting and added to the experience of living in the wild. Soon I just found it annoying. But since there was no chance it would stop, I'd get out of my hammock, bathe in the river, filter some water, take my antimalarial pills, throw on my boots, and wonder what the cheerleaders were doing that day.

Tarantulas soon became an even greater nemesis. They would climb to the top of my backpack and nestle in my long, tangled, wet hair. It was not easy digging them out. Leafcutter ants cut highways through the backs and tongues of my boots left on the ground overnight. A vampire bat took a chomp at my foot hanging off the hammock during sleep, and mosquitoes had a field day on wrists and ankles that rubbed too close to the mosquito net. Somehow they made it under the net, too, and most of the night I was killing them and checking for spiders. I quickly learned that mosquitoes actually love deet. Though I can't prove it, I think deet makes them stronger.

We were starting to run out of food, and morale was sinking, so we decided to seek a village to restock our dwindling supplies. We found a lovely elderly Guyanese couple living on the river's edge who seemed more than happy, eager even, to have us stop. Given how remote the area was, I suspected they didn't get many visitors. As a city girl, I could see the appeal of living far from the masses under the tall forest canopy, with only the sounds of birds, frogs, and monkeys. This had to be one of Earth's last remaining paradises, recalling places written about by 19th-century explorers. No roads at all. At night nothing but stars and the pale light cast by the moon. It was surreal. The couple had created a beautiful floating garden that I hoped to emulate someday when I got back to civilization—whatever that meant. They stuffed us with papaya and delicious pink juice made from a local fruit I had never heard of, and told us stories about saki monkeys. I would have gotten more excited had our first sighting not been in their pot.

We spent two days there, resting and taking refuge from the rains, and then it was time to push on. We traded some of my batteries and a lighter for papaya, the mystery fruit, and condiments. As I looked back, the couple stood waving, and I was sure there was a tear in the woman's eye. I knew exactly how she felt. For two days the place was magical, but I don't think I could have lasted there very long. The only buzz in these parts came from bees.

Another day passed, and we continued on our journey to find the rare monkeys. At that point I wanted to proclaim all monkeys in Guyana, except howlers, extinct. And then for the first time . . . SAKI MONKEYS! I screamed, "Look, sakis!" Dr. Handsome asked where. "There! In that tall tree!"

I took a GPS reading, jotted our sighting in my waterproof notebook with my waterproof pen, and followed the creatures until the sun went down.

I was officially a scientist.

As we were drifting to sleep that night, we heard loud splashing in the direction of our boat. I stumbled to turn on my headlamp and prayed it was not a port knocker who had found us. I saw not one but two intruders. Inside our canoe, a couple of very large, curious river otters were playing with our gear. They jumped out at the sight of my light. It made an already good day perfect.

Feeling optimistic and reenergized, we continued our search. Along the river's edge, we spotted sakis again. But what were they doing in a group? These were supposed to be monogamous creatures, their units consisting of only male, female, and offspring. Monogamy had disappointed me once again. I came to realize later that this was a very interesting finding, indeed, and that it had recently been written up in a scientific journal.

We spent a few weeks hacking through thick forest, following the animals as best we could. I was no longer as terrified of tarantulas as the first time one perched on my backpack, though I still scoured the forest floor with my light at night. My eyebrow tweezers, which had been ridiculed by my colleagues, got new respect as the favorite tool for removing ticks and leeches from hard-to-reach areas. I learned that, in addition to the havoc wreaked by leafcutter ants, leaving boots out overnight was a very bad idea because of all the things that could crawl inside, which you only discover after you've given them your foot for breakfast.

I had also found various clever ways of avoiding our assistant's request to help trap the very large and deadly fer-de-lance snakes. Her brother, in particular, had a fascination with these animals and wanted us to help stuff them into a box for closer observation. Luckily, they were only able to find one on their own. I never let on that I seemed to trip on these fearsome snakes at every bend.

The snakes and tarantulas were a small price to pay for the beauty of Guyana's interior. Nothing describes a wonder like Kaieteur Falls. This waterfall is about five times higher than the more well-known and relatively wimpy Niagara Falls and about twice the height of Zimbabwe's Victoria Falls. Its distinction lies in the unique combination of height and volume, making it one of the most powerful waterfalls in the world. It is no less than a four-hour vertical climb from the base at around 280 feet to the summit at just under 1,900 feet. One point on the hike is now officially called the Oh My God, as that's what people say when they realize what they have to climb. I was grateful to be as fit as a professional cheerleader.

Perhaps more impressive than its size is the fact that the waterfall sits in a nearly pristine rain forest atop an ancient plateau known as the Guyana Shield. This geological phenomenon is said to be the oldest layer of rock on Earth, at 2.99 billion years. On the edge of the plateau I got to see some rare wildlife, such as the golden frog and the harpy eagle, and tracks of the elusive jaguar. Every winded step was made worthwhile.

Kaieteur Falls is said to be named after an Amerindian chief by the name of Kai, who canoed over the falls to his death. Apparently, he did this in order to protect his tribe from a rival Carib tribe and the disease that had affected them. The word *teur* is native Amerindian for "falls." Whether Kai's sacrifice worked is unrecorded, but I have to wonder how plunging to your death over a waterfall would act as a vaccination, however good the intention. There are still no safety rails at Kaieteur Falls, and approaching its edge is risky. But looking over its rim, I could feel the power. Before I knew it, my arms lifted, and I felt I could take to the air and soar. Perhaps the great Amerindian chief had felt a similar compulsion.

The Guyana expedition was soon over, and I returned safely to the joys of hot showers, electricity, and a comfy bed, but I was a different person. Comfort could not keep me around for long. I had been bitten by the bug, quite literally. I switched majors and applied to the top-rated anthropology graduate department in the country, at Stony Brook University, where I would go on to pursue a Ph.D.

I would return to Guyana the next year, just long enough to almost die. As earlier recounted, that return trip ended a few weeks short, with my hands becoming increasingly more swollen and red. By the end, they looked as if I had dipped them in a pot of scalding water they were so blistered and distorted. They got so bad I had to cover them with a blanket in town to avoid the stares.

I never did find out what caused my hands to reach the size of basketballs. Apparently, the red streaks on my legs signaled that I had a blood infection traveling toward the heart, spelling doom. To this day, I do not discuss the details with my mom. But I can't help wondering if I should have stayed away from the Kool-Aid.

During the course of two expeditions, I had evolved from naive cheerleader to daring explorer. Or perhaps I was a daring cheerleader and naive explorer. Either way, as I lay in a hospital bed for almost two weeks, hooked up to antibiotics and steroids, I never stopped dreaming of my next adventure. After a full recovery I applied for another grant. I had found my calling. Guyana would not be the last place where I contributed my spit to a village meal.

[four]

Seduced by Sifakas

JUNE 2, 1997: I walked for hours today with blistered feet, and the only thing that kept me going was thinking about the possibility of seeing one of the rarest and most endangered primates on earth. It amazes me that there are animals we still know nothing about. It has been weeks, and we have only caught glimpses of these forest ghosts. I fear that this expedition will fail. I fear for their future. These strange creatures leap from tree to tree unaware that they and these forests are on the verge of extinction.

I had come to Madagascar to do what no other man or woman had done before, to look for and study an almost extinct form of lemur called Perrier's sifaka. There were no photographs of these animals, only line drawings. A sobering article entitled "Death Row" in a 2000 *Time* magazine declared the animal nearly vanished. I was going in search of one of the most critically endangered primates in the world.

I learned later that, although nothing was known about the Perrier's sifaka, a beautiful, all-black, elusive creature that lives in a forest in Madagascar's northeast, I was not the first to attempt to study it. A number of highly respected primatologists had tried. After a fleeting glimpse, or at most a momentary observation, these researchers, one by one, had returned empty handed. Seems like these ancestral primates sometimes dubbed "dumb monkeys" were capable of outrunning, if not outsmarting, world-renowned scientists. Desperate to learn about this mysterious tree dweller and to make a small dent in the science, I became passionate about studying them.

It may not surprise you to learn that most donors were hesitant to hand a former cheerleader a wad of money and send her off to one of the most isolated regions of Madagascar in search of a needle in a haystack. But one grantor did. His name is Russell Mittermeier, president of Conservation International, a primatologist and herpetologist with a Harvard Ph.D., a successful activist, and a kid at heart. With an enviable head of thick gray and white hair, Russ continues to collect Tarzan novels and memorabilia, and his sense of wonder and amusement is intact after more than 30 years of fieldwork. For fun he still likes to go out and catch frogs. Perfectly at home in the forest, he himself is not unlike Tarzan.

Thanks to Russ, I found myself in Madagascar, and one day I ran into him on the streets of Antananarivo, the capital, recognizing him instantly from his picture in *Time* magazine, in which in 1998 he'd been named one of the "EcoHeroes for the Planet," and in the many books he had written. We agreed to meet for lunch that day. I not only wanted to thank him for his financial support, I also wanted to pick his brain about the black ghosts I was going after. Russ had been one of the lucky few to briefly see these sifakas while researching a feature he was writing for *Outside* magazine. Sitting in the restaurant of one of the city's ritziest hotels, the Hilton, Russ warned me of the difficulties I would encounter. The list was long. I studied his face and the charming, nonchalant way he talked about his travels and adventures. Here was an academic legend, a hero in the flesh. I found myself with a bit of a schoolgirl crush and awed that I, a poor excuse for a Jane, was having lunch with Tarzan.

As Russ spoke, I began to identify qualities in him that I like to think I possess myself. He is a go-getter. His curiosity and passion are insatiable. And best of all he likes to follow his gut, which must be what caused him to take a chance on me. It was clear that, like me, he was a bit of a paradox. While he could endure the grueling heat of the jungle and months of living out of a tent, he also had a taste for the finer things in life. A wine connoisseur, he was as comfortable talking to the A-list celebrities he entertained at fund-raisers as to village elders. As we sat and ate what would be my last good meal for quite a while, I knew he liked my enthusiasm and felt he noticed the same stubborn qualities in me that had led to his own success. With a boyish laugh, he asked me about having been an NFL cheerleader. I could tell he would soon become the one cheering me on. "You're going to go far," he said. With that, he sat back, smiled, and continued to ask about my days as a pom-pom girl. I think the fact that I had been a cheerleader had only helped seal the deal. Perhaps he saw in me some Jane and just enough Tarzan.

That I would "go far" was an understatement. To see this lemur, I had already traveled halfway around the globe. From

Miami, I'd flown across the Atlantic to Paris, then through the islands of Réunion and Mauritius to Antananarivo. Almost 48 hours after setting off, I had landed in Madagascar. The final leg, to Antsiranana, on the northernmost tip of the island, would be reached aboard an old prop plane.

Larger than California and about the size of Texas or France, Madagascar is the world's fourth largest island, isolated in the Indian Ocean off the coast of southern Africa. About 70 percent of the estimated 250,000 species of fauna found on the island exist nowhere else on the globe. They are animals that can only be described as evolutionary oddities.

Madagascar is a scientist's dream come true.

This true living laboratory has given rise to creatures reminiscent of something out of Dr. Seuss. The aye-aye is an iconic example. Although a primate, this nocturnal lemur looks like a large cat, boasts ears like a bat, a bushy squirrel-like tail, an elongated extraterrestrial-looking middle finger, and beaver teeth that never stop growing. Once thought to be extinct, the aye-aye was rediscovered in 1961. It remains an endangered species because its habitat is being destroyed and because of native superstition. Ancient Malagasy legend says that the aye-aye is a symbol of death. Some villagers believe its mere appearance predicts your death. I was both excited and terrified to see one.

Having traveled all over the world, I can attest to the claim that Madagascar is unlike any place on Earth. Entire books have been dedicated to the question of just what caused Madagascar to become so different. Why is it that almost everything that exists in Madagascar exists nowhere else in the world? Some argue that these animals were already there when the land that is now Madagascar drifted away from Africa some 160 million years ago. But animals akin to lemurs didn't arise until about 58 million years ago, so that throws a huge wrench into that theory. Did they walk, swim, or drift there? Nobody knows. Naturally absent from Madagascar are dogs, rabbits, cats, monkeys, squirrels, gorillas, elephants, pangolins, antelopes, zebras, camels, giraffes, hyenas, lions, cheetahs, monitor lizards, adders, vipers, cobras, pythons, hornbills, woodpeckers, and other animals prevalent in nearby regions of Africa. Why didn't they come, too? Nobody knows. What we do know is that of the more than 150 mammal species that live on the island, about 90 percent are endemic. To this day no one is sure how they got there. But that's only one of Madagascar's unsolved mysteries.

Madagascar is home to screaming reptiles, hissing giant cockroaches, and a curious beast, the indri, that sings a song of indescribable beauty. Many a day I wished I could have been one of the first people to arrive on the island, when it was a real-life Jurassic Park. How I would have loved to witness giant lemurs the size of gorillas sharing the forest floor with dwarf hippopotamuses and 600-pound tortoises. Flightless elephant birds, standing more than ten feet tall, raced through the island's forested savannas on legs no smaller than tree trunks carrying their half-ton bodies, laying eggs that could hold the fluid content of about 180 chicken eggs. With a single egg, an entire village could have feasted on omelets for a month. Sadly, those jumbo-size creatures, along with the rest of Madagascar's aptly named megafauna, went extinct 2,000 years ago.

But the curious creatures that remain, if more compact, are no less impressive. The giraffe-necked weevil could inspire a Steven Spielberg movie, and I dare say the aye-aye might have been the muse for *Gremlins*. In the trees, two-foot-long chameleons have tongues that can be longer than their bodies. They extrude their tongues faster than the human eye can follow, at around 26 body lengths per second. They have a bizarre way of moving, in which they slowly rock back and forth between steps, often in time to the rustling of nearby leaves.

Camouflage is a fashion staple here, and no one wears it better than the geckos. The humbly named fantastic leaf-tailed geckos have a flattened, leaflike tail complete with notches to resemble a decaying leaf. Its close cousin, the fringed leaf-tailed gecko, sports some 300 teeth, more than any other reptile or mammal on earth. And the lemur's wild nemesis, the fossa (pronounced foosa), is Madagascar's shorter and stockier version of the puma. Dubbed the pink panthers of Madagascar, fossas are killing machines, eating pretty much anything that moves with powerful jaws filled with canines as big as any guard dog's and long, retractable claws on both front and hind feet. The coolest thing about the fossa is that their feet are reversed. The biggest toe lies on the outside of the foot rather than the inside, so it can grip trees. What gets most scientists' attention is the fossa's penis. An adult fossa is about 3.5 feet long and has a penis of about 7 inches, a sixth of its body length. If a man had the same ratio, he would be 3 feet tall and very smug. These creatures only begin to scratch the surface of Madagascar's carnival of animals.

Perhaps it was my own island roots, but when I stepped off the plane in Madagascar, I was struck by a feeling of familiarity and homecoming, almost recognizing the distinctive sights and smells of this peculiar place. Perhaps as a child I had been there in my vivid imagination. I instantly loved how the dust coats every surface, leaving houses and plants and even cows looking dry and reddish, like they'd been colored by a brick-red Crayola.

Dr. Handsome, the Smithsonian director I'd worked with in Guyana, had come with me. Seems that the sight of my basketball hands there had not scared him off. We were headed to Analamera Special Reserve, a 34,700-hectare nature reserve and the only place in the world where Perrier's sifakas and most other animals on the island are found. But first we would need food and supplies. The port town of Antsiranana, also known as Diego Suarez, was the jumping-off point for Analamera. Diego Suarez was named for two Portuguese sailors: Diego Diaz, who first landed on Madagascar in August 1500, and Hernan Soarez, who arrived six years later. This slightly decaying but hauntingly picturesque town of 100,000 inhabitants has one of the world's most beautiful and widest bays. It was hard not to be captivated. The town retains the charm of its French colonial past, with balustrades and columns lending it an elegant and aristocratic air. Important strategically since 1884, the port was used as a naval base by the French until 1973. This would be our only opportunity to buy food and supplies to last us through the expedition.

The seemingly simple task of shopping in Madagascar's colorful, open-air markets is an expedition in and of itself, and an exhilarating experience. Walking through the hundreds of rickety wooden stands crowded under a sea of umbrellas, I watched as men hacked big chunks off a side of beef and women stacked fruits and vegetables into tidy pyramids. Despite trying to look like I belonged, I was swarmed by young men offering to act as guards. After repeatedly declining their services, I realized I had been pickpocketed. Luckily, a woman witnessed the crime and screamed at the perpetrator, madly waving her broom and insisting he return my money until he did. I thanked her profusely, completely in awe of her ability to rescue me while carrying a dozen live geese in a woven basket on her head.

With my money back in my possession and tucked into the very bottom of my backpack, I needed to figure out how to convert the local currency. In my pocket I carried a huge clump of cash, bills far too big to fit in an American wallet, and in denominations starting in the thousands. I had no idea how much a 5,000-unit bill was worth. To make matters more confusing, coins and banknotes were denominated in both Malagasy francs and ariary, with the subunit of the ariary, the iraimbilanja, worth one-fifth of an ariary and equal to a franc. The trouble was, besides the difficulty in telling the difference between the two types of bills, posted prices were

arbitrarily given in either ariary or francs. Yes, it was that confusing. With ariary worth five times more than the currency
marked Malagasy francs (MFG), on more than one occasion I paid 25,000 MFG when I thought I was paying 5,000.

One of the more stressful tasks in the market is bargaining—unless, of course, you've been trained by the best. And
Mima was the best. I had many years under my belt of watching my grandmother score unbeatable prices in Miami flea
markets. No salesman at any level of experience was a match
for her bargaining skills, and I felt sure I had inherited her
shopping genes. But to bargain in Madagascar you have to
know what the local price is. Is the equivalent of a dollar
too much to pay for a kilo of tomatoes? Am I being taken?
Should I try to get my tomatoes for 80 cents? Is it really worth
pretending to walk away to save 20 cents? Mima would say
yes, so that's what I did. I came to learn that paying a third of
the price you were quoted as a foreigner was fair—more than
the locals would pay but fair. When I learned that the average
Malagasy yearly income is $200 per family, I felt guilty argu-
ing for those 20 cents (or 437 ariary/2,200 MFG) and made
it a point to overpay for my tomatoes thereafter.

I thought for sure that once we were in country, getting to
the field site would be the easy part. However, I discovered that
only two trucks in the entire town of Diego Suarez could make
the off-road, muddy trek, and both those vehicles were sitting
on cement blocks. "The roads are impassable without a good
vehicle," said the hotel owner, who also rented the cars and
manned the restaurant. "I may be able to sort you out a truck,

but it won't be ready for another couple of days." It wasn't ideal, but it's not like we could just dial up the local Hertz. We agreed to wait. With that he brought us Madagascar's beer of choice, Three Horses. Seeing as how I wasn't going anywhere, I downed several, finding it curious that every bottle tasted different. Perhaps it came down to which horse.

A week later we were jumping into the back of an old four-wheel drive loaded down with camping gear and enough food to last us a month. The driver took us to the local office of the National Association for the Management of Protected Areas (ANGAP), where we picked up a guide and presented our permits. There we met a short, fit Malagasy ranger in his late 20s, who would lead me and Dr. Handsome to the lemurs and make sure we didn't make off with any. In truth, he was our babysitter. We then set off for the forest along a dirt road barely wide enough for a bike, getting stuck numerous times en route and trashing the area's last good truck.

After several hours we arrived at a spot where fallen trees prevented the vehicle from going farther, so we jumped out and unloaded our gear. We began walking. Where to exactly I had no real clue, but I was happy to be on my way there.

For days on end we trekked, set up camp, ate, slept, broke down camp, and trekked some more. The area was in large part devoid of trees, and where trees did stand, there were barely enough leaves for shade. Steep cliffs rose in the distance above two rivers. Small streams flowed toward the Irodo River in the north, fracturing the plateau. Rice grew on the Irodo plain, flooded by a reservoir. In the valleys and well-watered areas stood deciduous dry forest, with canopies 50 to 65 feet high. The area looked nothing like the dense jungle vegetation I had grown accustomed to. It was difficult to imagine that anything could survive in this dry and desolate environment.

The absence of trees made it difficult to escape the sun. That would have been tolerable if we were seeing animals along the way, but we had not set eyes on a single one. It wasn't just the lemurs we hadn't seen. I would have been content to spot a snake, or chameleon, or even one of those freaky long-necked weevils. I was beginning to think the island dubbed the "most biologically diverse place on the planet" was a sham. Was it too late? Had all the animals gone extinct already? I asked our ranger to show us where we were on the map. When pressed about where exactly he'd seen the sifakas, he admitted he'd never actually been there before. The man whose job was to protect this critically endangered animal's territory and on whom we were relying to take us to them *had never been there*.

We needed a Plan B.

Clearly, the guide was less than enthusiastic about the pilgrimage. He did not appreciate the outdoors the way you'd expect a park ranger to. Besides not liking to be there, he pointed out that the area was far too vast for one man to cover. Built like a runner, he did like to do one thing. This man could eat. As a result, we were running out of food two weeks earlier than expected. Where he might eat one bowl of rice in his town, he was eating five bowls of rice with us. The expedition was beginning to rip apart at the seams, and the only man who could help us was hungry and in no mood to do so. His hunger pangs finally prevailed, however, and he agreed we'd take a detour to a village, a three-hour detour, as it turned out.

The village was small and rudimentary without any electricity or wells, only a few thatched houses and no sign of a market. We could hear thumping like a giant's footsteps from the huge mortar and pestles villagers use to remove the chaff from the rice. Clotheslines aired tattered yet sparkling white shirts. However lacking in financial means, the Malagasy are very conscious of cleanliness and appearance. Like human washing machines, women beat clothes against rocks by the rivers, often becoming prey for crocodiles. I have yet to figure out how they get muddied clothes to look so clean. I have tried beating my clothes, too, but all I seem to do is injure myself.

Dr. Handsome and I were immediately besieged by children. Their parents followed. Then the parents' parents showed up. Soon we were surrounded by no less than a hundred people, none of whom said a word, only stared at us the way zoogoers observe the gorillas mating. I stood there feeling much like an extraterrestrial, wondering whether they were expecting us to break into a song and dance and whether I dared dig to the bottom of my backpack for my last granola bar. The fact that I could say hello in their dialect probably gave them something to talk about all week. It made them laugh for minutes.

One of the little girls finally broke out of the circle and ran up to me. I stood very still. She reached out, touched my arm, and then ran back to the circle screaming as if she'd pressed her finger to a hot stove. The little girl next to her then ran up and touched my hair. This prompted the rest of the kids to run forward and touch any exposed part of me and then run away howling with laughter. Turns out, this wasn't some strange Malagasy ritual. This would mark the first time this village had seen a white woman.

I was a hit. Or so I thought.

Malagasy in remote areas learn from their folktales that white-skinned *vazas*, or foreigners—also called *mpakafo*, meaning "heart-takers"—come to the island to kill them and eat their vital organs, especially those of women and children. I thought perhaps I should eat my granola bar and try to ease their fears.

I would learn that night that despite their poverty and fear of whites, there is no more generous people. We feasted on an authentic Malagasy meal, a *sakafo*, consisting of *ravitoto*, a pork stew with ground cassava leaves, and the ubiquitous rice and washed it all down with *ranon 'apango*, a watery drink made from burned rice. The latter is an acquired taste. Over the next weeks I would also learn that trekking was only part of the challenge of an expedition. Every visit to a village required a rum-soaked meeting with tribal elders that lasted through the night, occasionally for days. The rum, a home-brewed jungle concoction, burns the throat like jet fuel. So not only was I hiking under a scorching sun for hours on end in my lemur search, I was doing it sporting a king-size hangover.

From this village we added members to our expedition. Zaralahy was the village elder, with more than 20 grandchildren. A sweet, soft-spoken man weighing no more than 90 pounds, Zara seemed to have more energy than a Duracell bunny. He was also nimble and had a fantastic, toothless grin.

He uttered the words we so needed to hear, "I know where those sifakas are," and, with an elfish laugh, jumped up to gather a few belongings.

The villagers helped us gather food to take on our journey, and Zara offered his son Bendanalana's services as camp cook and guard, an offer we happily accepted. Trying to make up for lost time, we rented a zebu cart to help transport our gear and waved goodbye to a group of new folks who had trekked out to see the crazy white people. Seven hours into the forest and not a single animal later, I considered us crazy white people, too.

My feet were swollen, sore, and close to quitting. I jumped on the back of the zebu cart to give them a break but jumped quickly off; with no suspension, the ride was too hard on the rear end. While my body kept urging me to quit and call off this failing expedition, my stubborn Cuban genes told it to shut up. I asked Zara how far we were from our destination. He pointed to a small clearing on the map between two even smaller forest patches. "Antobiratsy," he said. I looked up the meaning in the Malagasy dictionary. My heart sank. We were headed, if literal translation was to be believed, to "bad camp."

Several hours later, Zara gestured to us to drop our packs, as we had finally arrived at the clearing. No sooner had our bags hit the ground, putting them at the same level as our morale, than little black faces peered through the branches and stared at us like the villagers a day before. Here at last were Perrier's sifakas! Immediately, I whipped out my camera, before they could disappear into the forest. But they were in no hurry to go; the photo session went on so long, I actually started to get bored.

I couldn't understand it. How was it that there were no photographs of these animals, when they were quite clearly not camera shy? Amid beaming smiles around the campfire, I asked Zara how this marvelous place could have been given the name "bad camp." He explained that villagers came here to mourn the death of a family member. It was considered a holy ground, and many local people believed their ancestors were there in the form of my beloved lemurs. This reincarnation had been the lemurs' saving grace, as locals deemed it *tavy*, or taboo, to hunt them. After experiencing generations of mourners, the lemurs in this spot had become habituated to human presence. "Bad camp" was the best camp ever. That night my spirits lifted, and I went in search of chameleons and mouse lemurs. Wouldn't you know it? They were there, too.

This wondrous, lemur-filled place, Antobiratsy in Analamera Special Reserve, is protected on paper but still encroached on by villagers, miners, and hunters. Over the next several months in Antobiratsy, passing miners would stop to show me gorgeous sapphires bunched in handkerchiefs from their pockets. Sapphire is my birthstone, and not so long ago I would have leaped to buy one. But having learned that those precious stones are the source of deforestation and the destruction of entire ecosystems, I would tell them to get lost.

Each day began at 5 a.m. with a bowl of mushy rice doused with sugar, which mimicked the texture and taste of oatmeal, and coffee sifted through Bendanalana's sock. I convinced myself it was a new, unused sock. After breakfast we would split up into teams. Zara and I would follow one group of sifakas, while Dr. Handsome and the ranger went after another. The goal was to take down as much behavioral data as we could on the various groups. Since forests in that area are sparse and trees often completely devoid of foliage, lemurs have little protection. The area is so dry that the sifakas come down to the forest floor to drink from the river, exposing themselves to predators, especially fossas and birds of prey. Observing this behavior at the river was a scientific first. Each day the lemurs would travel extensively, making our days very long. Often we would not reach camp again until dusk, when the sifakas had finally settled into a sleep tree for the night. By the campfire we would sit and talk, the only other sound our forks scraping against metal plates as we ate to a serenade of frogs and geckos.

One night I suddenly felt a sharp pain on my right foot, and off the dim light of my headlamp I saw a small, black scorpion scuttling away. I let out a yelp. The ranger calmly placed a mug over the perpetrator and continued eating. Dr. Handsome helpfully pointed out that scorpions with small claws have the strongest punch, as they rely on the potency of their venom to kill their prey. I looked: It had small claws. The pain was unreal. My foot felt like it was being attacked with a jackhammer, and it was rapidly swelling. As sweat streamed off my forehead, I worried that I was going to lose consciousness. I remembered hearing somewhere that if you're stung by a scorpion, you should crush it in a mortar and pestle and rub it into the wound. I wasn't sure if this was for medical purposes or revenge. All I could do was treat the bite with antiseptic cream from my first-aid kit, shove painkillers down my swollen throat, and pray for the best.

Despite my miraculously brief incapacitation, followed by an equally traumatic encounter with swarming wasps, the project was going well. We collected data documenting every morsel the sifakas ingested, their proximity to other group members, and the distance they traveled. We would sometimes spend hours looking up into the trees, a task that I found rather painful, given a neck injury I'd suffered as a cheerleader. I had opted not to have it surgically repaired and still had a bulging disk in my upper spine.

Other times these acrobatic monkeys put us to the test; they may have found it humorous to watch us struggle up the rocky terrain as we chased after them. The area was covered in *tsingy*, razor-sharp peaks of limestone, demanding slow and deliberate climbing or else suffer the bloody consequences. The sifakas, which made their way across the treetops, often paused to stare at us below as if to say, "What's taking you so long?"

Back at camp one day I discovered we were out of food. Not *almost* out of food . . . completely out of food. That we were *suddenly* out of food came as a shock (how could we have even run low without anyone noticing?) but it's been my experience that the Malagasy will not come to you with a problem until you have discovered it. It turns out that our park ranger had been cooking up extra portions while the rest of us were out chasing lemurs. With more than a month to go, we were in trouble. The following morning we set off bright and early to trek ten hours back to Zara's village for more food.

On the way we stopped in several other villages but came up with nothing more than six tomatoes, a few potatoes, and less than a kilo of rice. There was a drought and crops were sparse, leaving everyone worried about where the next meal was coming from.

Desperate, we asked the ranger if he would be willing to head back to Diego Suarez. Not surprisingly, he was thrilled. The rest of us would continue to starve until he returned. I gave him money, some tomatoes for the journey, and a note to be delivered to Dr. Patricia Wright, who was hours south of us. In addition to being my advisor and now lifelong friend, Pat is a housewife turned world-renowned lemur expert, creator of Madagascar's Ranomafana National Park, discoverer of two primate species, a diplomat, and a proud Jimi Hendrix fan. In fact, she had been on her way to a Hendrix concert when she ducked into a pet shop to escape rain and saw an owl monkey, a nocturnal South American primate that would become her passion. Having endured criticism for wearing miniskirts as a social worker and, after being a housewife, struggled to be accepted in the Amazon to study owl monkeys, she could not have been a more appropriate mentor for me. Pat in many ways is very much a cheerleader herself.

In my letter I explained to Pat the hardships we were encountering, as well as our successes in finding and following the lemurs. I also explained that besides food we needed men. Not just any men, but George and Loret, the two top Malagasy lemur capturers who worked with her. Our experience with Perrier's sifakas convinced us they were more than a mere subspecies of other sifakas. Their distinctive appearance, peculiar behavior, and geographic isolation led us to question the conventional wisdom that they were only a color variant of the species. With starvation setting in after weeks of an inadequate food supply and several days with no food at all, I wondered if we would ever find out.

Later that week our ranger returned with food, George, Loret, and a letter from Pat. In the note she wrote, "Congratulations on your success! Enjoy the sausages and cheese. They are a gift from Michael Apted!" I was stunned. *The* Michael Apted, director of *Gorillas in the Mist,* the movie that had inspired me to follow in the footsteps of Dian Fossey, had sent *me* sausages and cheese?! What a fateful turn of events, I thought. This would be the second time the film director had rescued me. The first time was back at home with the film that changed my life. This time, with sausages.

Apart from our food dramas and encounters with miners and scorpions, camp life could be pretty mundane. You get up, you drink sock coffee, you chase lemurs, you eat rice, and you go to sleep, so that you're rested and ready to do it all over again in the morning. But this morning was different. I had washed my clothes down by the river the day before and laid them out to dry overnight just outside my tent. In the morning I grabbed the pants and slipped in one leg at a time. I wasn't alone. I yelled so loud I swear it's the reason we didn't see any lemurs that day. Before I knew it, my pants were flying through the air and I was standing in my underwear in front of the entire camp. Cockroaches had nested in my pant legs, hundreds of them, and I could feel each one scurrying up and down my calves and thighs and hissing up a storm. It was the last time I put my pants on in the field without checking their contents first.

Now it was time to try and save the lemurs by taking samples of their blood and tissue. That was the long-term goal; the immediate goal was to not kill any during capture. I worried about misfired darts. But George and Loret were the best, and Dr. Handsome and I had had experience capturing primates in South America. We loaded the injectable darts with Telazol, a sedative that would knock out the lemurs just long enough for us to collect samples before returning them to the trees. Next we identified a target, which had to be sitting in just the right position. It was the sifaka butt we were after, not a vital organ. Gun loaded, Loret would take aim, while George and I held a hammock to catch the animal plunging from the tree. For the most part, the sifakas cooperated, but one continued to hang on to the tree fully sedated. Just as we were deciding who would climb up and risk a wasp attack, the sifaka's grip loosened and it came plummeting down. It landed on my head, uninjured.

By now we had named the lemurs. One group became the Flintstones (Fred, Wilma, Barney, and Betty), while the other group was named after beers (Corona, St. Pauli Girl, Coors, and Bud), a sign of our alcohol deprivation. Fred was the oldest and by far my favorite. He had a very sweet disposition, and the abuse he took from the females made me feel sorry for him. Sadly, it was his remains I found on the trail several weeks later. Not much more than a tail and a clump of hair were left, evidence that a fossa had gotten him. His death took a toll on all of us, even Zara, who had initially thrown logs at the sifakas if they came too close due to his tribal belief that these all-black creatures, like our black cats, could bring bad luck. Only their existence on sacred ground enabled them to survive that superstition. Zara, like all of us, had grown to love these creatures as individuals. Until his passing years later, Zara would dedicate his life to the protection of sifakas, assisting research teams and educating his grandchildren on the importance of protection. His son Bendanalana is now one of the area's most sought-after guides.

As time went on during our study, and mutual trust grew, I often found myself in the middle of a sifaka group moving cautiously from one forest patch to the next. As if crossing a treacherous highway, the creatures would pause at the edge of an open patch where aerial and ground predators might lurk, look right, then left, then right again before moving ahead. Side by side we made the journey. I began to delight in my new role as the lady who walks with lemurs.

five

Caught on Film

NOVEMBER 20, 2000: I stood underneath the tree, my eyes fixed on the target. My hands held the rifle nervously. With a film camera crew watching and recording my every sweat bead I felt the pressure mounting. I couldn't miss. I closed my eyes and concentrated on not shaking. Then eyes wide open, I took the shot. The lemur jumped, reacting to the feel of a sharp dart hitting his butt. The race began. With little effort the animal glided through the trees while we incompetent humans tried to keep up. If we didn't make it on time, he would plunge from the canopy to his death. Crap, that would be filmed, too.

Years before I appeared on television pointing out little-known facts about snakes or describing the mating behaviors of gorillas, I was putting in the legwork. Anyone who knows me knows I am not a morning person. But no matter. In the field a typical day for me began around 5:30 a.m., when the first fingers of light started to reach into the forest canopy. Home was anywhere I could pitch a tent, more often than not in some distant jungle, and chances were that I hadn't been able to communicate with my mother in months and she was worried to death.

Yet the question I am most frequently asked is "How did you get to where you are?" This question refers not to my career as a scientist and explorer, but rather to my frequent appearances as a wildlife correspondent on television. Frankly, it was a lucky break that first got me on TV. And although there has certainly been a lot of luck and good timing throughout my career, I firmly believe that the harder I work, the luckier I get. The path was slippery and arduous, like the muddy, rugged terrains I've spent years traversing.

After my first trip to the eighth continent, as Madagascar is sometimes called, I was soon a regular fixture there and could hold my own in Malagache, the local language spoken mostly in the villages. As a result of my track record with Perrier's sifaka, I was entrusted by people at various conservation agencies, not least of all Russ Mittermeier, the president of Conservation International, with the laborious task of locating and gathering data on another species of sifaka, the ghost-white silky sifaka, an even more endangered species than the Perrier's. In the January 2000 *Time* magazine article on endangered primates, the silkies were listed as the world's sixth most endangered primate, and like their cousins in the north, no photographs of these animals existed. With only a few hundred left in the wild and none in captivity, they, too, had never been studied.

I spent most of my time in Antananarivo, the capital of Madagascar, waiting at MICET, the Malagasy sister office of the Institute for the Conservation of Tropical Environments at Stony Brook University, while my permits were being sorted.

MICET provides logistical support for scientists and environ-
mentalists working in Madagascar. More than once the staff
there had bailed me out of trouble, and it was a great place to
check email and meet just about any researcher worth knowing. A swirling hub of activity, the MICET office was where
many expeditions and collaborations originated.

On this particular day, I was waiting to meet with my
advisor, Dr. Patricia Wright, who would be joining me on this
next expedition. As I sorted through some field gear, a stocky,
hairy young man dripping with brand-new North Face gear
came stumbling into the office. He introduced himself as Mike
Kraus. Mike had apparently shown up in Madagascar to
study lemurs the way someone pops over to the zoo to look at
zebras. He wasn't aware of the long and difficult permit process or the challenges of getting to field sites. "I was mugged
last night, and they took all of my money," he moaned. He had
wandered into one of the areas in Antananarivo where only
a tourist would go wearing a fancy camera and a fanny pack
full of money. Those items were no longer in his possession.

Pat emerged from a meeting with permits in hand and
announced that a car had been arranged to pick us up the
next morning for the 18-hour, bumpy, kidney-crushing
drive north. I introduced Mike and his predicament. In her
usual generous and relaxed way, Pat invited him to join us,
a move I hoped we would not regret. Also joining our expedition would be Felix, Safia, and Desire, Malagasy graduate
students and guides; Loret, who had captured innumerable
lemurs with Pat and me; Peter Tyson, a writer doing a story

on our groundbreaking expedition; and Jacinth O'Donnell, a British wildlife filmmaker.

With Land Rover fully loaded, we were squished like sardines in a can, but it was still more comfortable than my last taxi-bus experience, in which a runny-nosed toddler and a chicken were thrown onto my lap for eight hours. A Madagascar experience not to be missed. After months of preparation, we were finally on the road, and not just any road but the very artery of life here. Through the car window I watched the island's hard-working people as they went about their everyday lives: women streaming to or home from the markets; uniformed children returning from school; herders with loaded carts pulled by zebu cattle; drivers in minibuses hustling passengers aboard. It was not unusual to see beggars no older than six or seven years with infants on their backs in the middle of the busy road. Most impressive were the men and women carrying enormous bundles of charcoal, sticks, or wheat in reed baskets perfectly balanced on their heads as they dodged traffic. Small bungalows and market stands lined both sides of the road. Past the traffic and into the hills lay fields of wheat, vegetables, and rice in various stages of cultivation. The fields are farmed by hand with primitive plows pulled by cattle. Also on the side of the road stood traditional brick-making furnaces and stacks of raw red bricks left drying in the sun. Most of the houses along this central road were made from the bricks and were a far cry from the shacks on stilts I was accustomed to seeing. From a distance, the little rust-red houses sitting in the hilly landscape evoked small villages in Tuscany.

Our destination was Marojejy, a 60,150-hectare reserve in the northeast and one of the few places in the world where you can hike from a dense, vine-cloaked jungle to a treeless plain in the cloud forest just shy of 2,400 feet in altitude. Home to the silky sifaka. Our aim was to hike a single-track trail to a narrow opening on the mountain where the rare primates were known to visit. It would be a five-hour, strenuously steep climb up a slippery trail made even more miserable by the rain. But leeches between my toes were a small price to pay for being one of only a handful of researchers to see these sifakas, thought to be the most beautiful in the world. I would soon dub them the angels of Marojejy.

Less excited was Mike Kraus, gasping for air in the back of the line all the way. Even the porters carrying the generator for Peter's computer had flown past him. Several times during the trek I stopped to wait for Mike, whose bulky body struggled against the mountain's slope. I suggested he remove some of his many layers before he succumbed to heat exhaustion. But he confidently refused, saying that his pricey, state-of-the-art, "breathable" clothing was designed for just this sort of trek. Well, he was a big boy entitled to make his own mistakes. As I stood aside and let the porters pass so I could check on him, I heard the frequent mention of "crazy *vahza*." Not long after, from around the corner appeared Mike, wearing nothing but his boxers and hiking boots.

"So the clothes didn't breathe?" I said, ribbing him. Drenched in sweat, he could only gather enough breath to say, "Can I have some of your water?" Normally, on an expedition you guard your water like your life depends on it, since often it does, but I'm a bit of a camel and don't require much to drink, so I handed him my almost full, pink water bottle. Seconds later he returned it. Empty. (The next year Mike returned on another expedition but almost never left his tent and went home early. Point being, not everyone is cut out for the explorer's life.)

Once we had made it to the plain, I collapsed, journal in hand, beside a waterfall plunging over a lip of stone. One false move on this slippery edge and I was toast, but the view was incredible. Treetops literally brushed the clouds. An ocean of forest rolled off into the distance. But no tree in Madagascar is safe. Sitting on the cliff's edge, I could just make out bare slopes where the Malagasy had cleared hillsides to plant rice. Poverty and the ever increasing population have put tremendous pressure on the island's dwindling forests. Slowly, they've been slashed and burned for rice fields. It's what Malagasy ancestors did for centuries, but now less than 10 percent of the original forest remains. I have yet to find a place on the island where I could escape this harsh reality.

Setting up camp on a small ridge, Pat and I shared a tent. As I am usually the only woman on my expeditions, the thought of girlie chitchat into the night was welcome. But by the time nature's lights had gone out, we were too exhausted to talk; we listened to the nocturnal woolly lemurs just beginning their day, crawled into our sleeping bags, and passed out. Gab about boys and shoes would have to wait.

The following morning I woke to the sound of cascading water, unzipping of neighboring tents, and clanging of metal pots. Our camp cooks, Nestor and Jean, had a fire going and water boiling for coffee and tea. Breakfast was a rice pudding–like fare mixed with raisins and condensed milk. By 6:30 a.m., when small rays of light began to creep through the forest canopy, a family of five silky sifakas appeared just across the stream. We gazed wide-eyed at the two-legged creatures for a quarter of an hour before they vanished into the forest. Flushed with excitement, I looked over at Pat and said, "This is one of the best days of my life." I noticed she had a tear in her eye and knew she felt the same.

Peter arrived in camp that day, too late to see the sifakas' brief debut and with less than good news. On the long hike up, a blister on his foot had become infected. As I knew all too well, infections in the tropics can turn deadly in a matter of hours. His foot, red and swollen, would make it impossible for him to maneuver the terrain. Feverish, he had lost his appetite, and you could barely see where his foot ended and his toes began. The infection was already beginning to show signs of going systemic. I recognized the signs from my Guyana basketball hands, gave him medication, and volunteered to clean his wound.

We decided to try antibiotics for a night before deciding whether to get Peter out of the forest. Even with two good feet, the five-hour hike was treacherous; using a crutch, it was impossible. Less than two days in the field, and we already had a crisis. Fortunately, by morning Peter's foot had improved and, eager to stay, he decided to remain in camp writing dispatches. We quickly scarfed down a breakfast and divided into two teams.

The team consisting of Pat and Mike with Felix, Safia, and Desire would scour the forest in search of the silky sifaka. With Loret and me, the second team would walk the transect lines. One of our goals was to conduct a census of the number and kinds of lemurs in Marojejy. To do this, we set up transects along the existing trails and posted small, bright-orange flags every 82 feet from base camp. This would allow us to identify and reference exactly where we were when we found the animals. Once we'd established transects, we walked quietly, stopping every 50 feet to look up and around in the trees.

At first it seemed as if the forest was still asleep; the only sounds were raindrops falling and what our guides called the "barking crab," which may have been a frog. Suddenly, we heard lemurs directly over our heads. By their loud grunting noises we knew they were not silkies, but rather a group of white-faced brown lemurs. We noted what we saw and continued the search. Shortly after, we came upon a group of gentle gray bamboo lemurs, which quickly scuttled into the treetops, prompting an excited whisper from our guide, "Maybe we've found our lemurs," as this species is often seen traveling with silkies. We all looked and hoped, but we had not.

We hiked up our mile-and-a-quarter transect and then turned back because we had reached the mountaintop and the trees had become shrubs. Discouraged, I had to remind myself that the trek had not been a total waste. We had seen lemurs, even if not the ones we were looking for; observed a paradise flycatcher with its gorgeous, long tail feathers; spotted a black, squiggly fungus resembling its name, dead man's finger;

and found several miniature waterfalls spilling out of the hill-tops. A great day, indeed, by anyone else's standards. Besides, as our guide, Desire, had pointed out in the beginning, it can take more than a week to catch a glimpse of these animals. So we had already been lucky. But as we descended to camp, the morale seemed to plunge like a waterfall. We had climbed (and slipped) all day and had not seen or heard our sifakas.

At a point only about 1,000 feet from camp, I happened to look up at what resembled a soft cloud. There were our angels, the silky sifakas. They came down the trees and sat close, within five feet of us. They seemed to be just as curious about us strange, bipedal creatures as we were about them. Needless to say, we were elated. I had every piece of camera equipment out, and in the dark understory my flash went off constantly. But it didn't seem to bother them. On the contrary, they appeared to be more than happy to pose for the camera.

A half hour later we realized they were not running away as before. They continued to sit, munching on young leaves and grooming one another, seemingly ignoring us. At one point, they even hung suspended by their hind feet and twined together in play. More than three hours later, they seemed to have had enough of performing for their newfound friends and continued on to the sleeping tree. We followed and it was there we left them, all snuggled up together.

Back at camp we gathered beneath the cook's tent for a meeting. Just then the skies opened up, and everyone squeezed in tight under the overhanging cloth. Monsoon-like conditions notwithstanding, tomorrow would be a big day. This site was one of only two for the silky sifakas, and in the morning Marojejy was to be designated a national park. With an audience of politicians and bigwigs at the base of the mountain, we would attempt to capture some animals for study. "God forbid anything goes wrong," said Pat in a tense and excited tone. Silently staring into the coals of the fire while awaiting our dinner of rice and corned beef, I think we were all praying to the ancestors. Exhausted from the day's trek, Pat and I made a dash for our tent with rain pelting down, while the Malagasy sang traditional songs by the fire. Once we were in our sleeping bags like two schoolgirls at a slumber party, I opened one of the bottles of wine I had swindled from Air France. It was the first time I'd seen Pat nervous. We talked about all the things that could go wrong the next day, like accidentally wounding or even killing a lemur. With park ministry officials there as witness, such a mistake could spell death to our careers. A couple of bottles of wine later, we were asleep.

Nerves awakened me before dawn. Today was the day. Looking outside my tent door, I could see our field assistants Zoky and Randriansy fanning the fire and readying the pots. Loret, Felix, Pat, and I set out from camp before the water had even begun boiling to make sure we would find the sifakas sleeping in the tree where we'd left them. It was still dark as we crossed the stream and headed up a slick trail, making long slip marks in the mud. The rest of the team would find us easily. By 7:30 a.m. Loret's blowgun was in full swing, and we had four drugged sifakas in our hands, three males and one

female. The trails were too slippery and dangerous to make it
back to camp with the lemurs. Instead, we would improvise
a makeshift field lab in the forest and work up the animals
then and there. Pat and Safia ran back to get more supplies
and alert Peter, who was still tending to his foot but would
manage to join us.

Loret and I laid the sifakas on burlap sacks, fast asleep,
white-furred chests gently breathing in and out. We shielded
their faces from the sun with broad green leaves. I stepped
back and looked at these gorgeous animals. With black and
pink faces, ears nearly lost in the plush, and white fur covering their long, sinuous bodies, they looked more like stuffed
toys from FAO Schwarz than anything real.

We began taking the first sifaka's measurements, laying
a measuring tape along its long limbs and tail. Felix and I
weighed each animal using a handheld scale and measured
its teeth with calipers. Their fur was soft and silky, and it was
easy to get lost in their beauty, though I did notice their nails
were as badly in need of a manicure as mine. Pat, who had
returned with the supplies, instructed me to repeat the measurements aloud as I wrote them down so that there'd be no
errors, reminding us, "If we get the number wrong, it's the
wrong number for this species." She was right. Scientists and
government officials would rely on our data to help preserve
the silky sifaka and its little remaining habitat.

With a steady hand but racing heart, I began to take blood
from each animal's vein before the anesthetic wore off. The
blood samples, once processed back in the States, would tell

whether this geographically isolated species warranted eleva-
tion from subspecies to full species, thus increasing its chances
for protection. While Loret and I did most of the work on the
animals, Pat kept a watchful eye, offering direction, advice,
and—by her beaming smile—support and approval.

While the park officials looked on, Pat, Peter, and I—like
kids with a new puppy—took turns holding the sifakas, keeping them warm as they came out of the anesthetic. "Tomorrow,
June 5, is the National Day of the Environment in Madagascar," said Pat as she cuddled one of the slowly awakening
males. "It's a big celebration. The prime minister will be there,
and many other important Malagasy officials. With the new
Marojejy National Park, it's such an auspicious moment to be
helping these beautiful animals." Peter sat happily with a sifaka
on his lap, knowing he was witnessing history in the making.

Cradling the young female, I was relieved that our mission
had been successful and the future of these animals held promise. As the fleshy pad of her finger curled around mine like a
human baby's, I hoped one day my as-yet-unborn children
would be lucky enough to witness her gliding through the trees.

When they began grunting, a "moving call" sound sifakas
use, we knew it was time to return them to the trees. Loret and
I carefully placed them in breathable rice sacks, which would
keep them calm until they were fully restored to consciousness. Then, under a darkening sky, we carefully opened the
sacks and offered them branches to cling to, their opportunity
to climb back to freedom. Eagerly, one by one, they wrapped
their fingers and opposable thumbs around the branches and

scurried up into the tree, pausing halfway up and looking back at us as if to say goodbye. They would not remember that anything out of the ordinary had happened. I, on the other hand, would never forget it.

So what is the connection between this story and how I became a wildlife correspondent? Timing. I neglected to mention earlier that back at MICET I had also met my soon-to-be boyfriend, and now ex-boyfriend, Luke Dollar. A handsome and charismatic Southerner, Luke is the world's foremost expert on fossas, the pumalike creatures that eat my sweet-faced, slow-moving lemurs for lunch. Clearly, our relationship was destined to fail, but my visit to his field site would forever change my life.

Still feeling green from the previous night's soiree celebrating the new park, I made my way to Luke, flying across the island to Mahajanga, a seaport with beautiful beaches, a coconut-lined boardwalk (La Boru), and a hot climate that is virtually rain free for eight months a year. Obviously, Luke had excellent taste in field sites. He met me at the Hotel La Piscine, and we took long walks on the beach and talked about our shared love for Madagascar. He mentioned that a National Geographic film crew would be spending a few weeks at his field site, a 2.5-hour drive away, starting early the next morning. I was excited to see the film crew and fossas in action.

A far cry from the beachy scene at Mahajanga, Luke's site, Ampijoroa, was a mosaic of dense, dry forest on the country's west coast. Temperatures soared above 100 degrees, causing sluggishness and malaise in the camp. All work was done before noon, followed by a long nap; work resumed in the late afternoon when temperatures subsided. Here you would have killed for a dip in the ocean.

With the National Geographic crew at the site, the fossas lived up to their reputation for elusiveness, failing to surface or rather succeeding at remaining undetected. Fearing the crew would have to leave with no footage, the film producer asked if I at least would be willing to go on camera and talk about the lemurs found there. I agreed to do so, of course.

At 7 a.m. about two weeks after the film crew arrived, the temperature already into the high 90s, we headed to the fossa traps that so far had yielded only disappointment. At last, in a trap baited with chicken, stood the sleekest and most feral mammal I'd ever seen. The fossa's muscular head turned to watch us, its catlike eyes focusing on the blowgun Luke was preparing with an anesthetic dart. Patiently, we waited for the animal to position its body correctly to receive the drug. In minutes, we were rushing toward the cage. I helped Luke carry the fossa back to camp, where a series of measurements, not unlike the ones I made on the lemurs, would be carried out. It would have been hard not to notice the fossa's pungent odor. Musky would be the nicest way to describe it. Once again I felt lucky to be working with sweet-smelling lemurs.

Fossa now filmed, the producer asked if she could pitch my story—namely, the "bubbly ex-cheerleader primatologist studying critically endangered lemurs"—to National Geographic for a second film. Delighted, I said yes, not really believing it would happen. Several weeks later, en route from another expedition to one of my previous field sites, I received an email saying a film crew was flying in and would arrive soon. It had been weeks since I'd checked email, and when I looked at the date, I realized "soon" meant tomorrow.

The film crew arrived and completed a one-hour documentary on me and the silky and Perrier's sifakas, which would air as part of National Geographic's acclaimed *Explorer* series. Later, back in New York, a cryptic yet intriguing phone call invited me to visit Geographic headquarters in Washington, D.C.

The minute I walked through the doors of the National Geographic building in 2001, I knew I wanted to be hired. I had spent years studying primates in remote jungles of South America and Madagascar. I had gotten a taste of exploration and adventure, but I wanted more. Don't get me wrong, I'm not an adrenaline junkie. But as a correspondent for National Geographic, I would go places and work with animals I'd never seen before.

I got that dream job.

The next thing I knew I was covering stories for the *Explorer* series on great white sharks, gorillas, leopards, and giant squids, just to name a few. Luke and I broke up. Let's face it, I was rooting for the lemurs and he was rooting for the creatures that eat them. We would always be at odds. But my marriage with National Geographic grew strong. I, the Cuban ex-professional cheerleader, was now National Geographic's first female wildlife correspondent. Mima would have been so proud.

My life hasn't been the same since.

six

Don't Let the Lip Gloss Fool You

MARCH 7, 2001: After all these years, I still don't get it. If I'm on an expedition with a handsome man, he gets revered. If he's less than attractive, he is described as "rugged." Most of the time, their looks are just not addressed. But as the only woman on most expeditions my looks somehow take center stage. I'm either too pretty or not pretty enough. One found me to be "the voice of reason" but then commented on my boobs. Have to keep reminding myself not to read TV critics' reviews.

In the animal kingdom, most boys are prettier than girls. For example, among birds of paradise the males are much more colorful and pleasing to the eye than the females. While the male's spectacular plumage attracts mates, the female needs to be camouflaged and inconspicuous to avoid predators while pregnant or hiding in a nest with newborns. As in many species, the male bird of paradise has no part in child care, so he has less selective pressure against ostentatious display. Without even looking it up, I can tell you that that bird is clearly not from Cuba.

Cuban women are very proud and conscious of their looks and are not to be out-plumaged by a male. My grandmother would make sure her hair looked perfect before going to the hairdresser, and if you've ever attended a Cuban function, you may have noticed that there is no such thing as overdressed. To this day, my mom will spend hours fixing her hair and makeup before going out, even to a doctor's appointment, and dress no differently than if she were going to a wedding.

Perhaps I was overly sensitive about being judged growing up in a house full of Cuban women, but one of the things I love most about animals is that they don't judge you. An animal may avoid a human if it senses danger or act hostile if it is securing food or protecting its offspring or mate. But animals don't judge people like humans do.

Don't get me wrong. I know that my family's love is unconditional, and my mom didn't judge me, but she made it clear that everybody else would. Though she often called me the "most beautiful child on the planet," I was never the prettiest girl in the class. I didn't always click with girls, since I wasn't as interested in playing with dolls or making brownies in an Easy-Bake Oven. And all the bugs hidden under my bed kept me from being able to throw slumber parties like the cool girls did. My idea of fun was chasing lizards, climbing trees, and playing stickball. I had inherited an aptitude for fashion, or perhaps a style obsession, and was admired for my trendiness, but I was always more comfortable playing basketball than house. As a result, most of my friends were boys. My best friend, Marcelo, was a brown-haired, doe-eyed Colombian boy who was the male version of me. He nicknamed me Chicken Legs because of the long, skinny legs that stretched like strings from underneath my shorts. But those chicken legs could outrun and outclimb any of the boys, so until my teenage years I wasn't bothered.

I was in college before I began to receive male attention as a woman. It felt strange after always being "one of the guys." I think that earlier experience is the main reason I feel so comfortable as the only woman at a field site in the wilderness. While I was a slave to fashion, often parading the halls in cute summer dresses and uncomfortable platform shoes, I loved sports, especially basketball, and could swear like a sailor. Perhaps it was that dichotomy that made me attractive to men. In college I was still the girlie-girl tomboy I'd grown up as and didn't mind spending the weekend watching football and going fishing. I was a dream girlfriend, even if I'd not been pretty enough to make the high school cheerleading squad. But blossoming into an attractive young woman did not make my life easier. As a matter of fact, it was more of a hindrance than a blessing.

I know I haven't always helped my own situation and still shudder to think of the first time I left for an expedition, with an entire suitcase of sandals and heels to complement my outfits. Not only could I not give up my love for stylish clothing and makeup, but I also needed to keep close tabs on the tweezing. Most people assume that women do this for the benefit of men, but Mima always said that women dress for women. She argued that while men are easy to impress, women judge other women harshly. I wasn't doing it for either. First of all, I am usually the only woman on an expedition. Let's face it:

Most women wouldn't want to disappear for months to somewhere without phones, malls, hair salons, or electrical outlets. Frankly, I don't know very many men who would, either. And, second, more often than not I find myself the only woman amid 30 to 50 men (including film crew and porters). Field producers and videographers are overwhelmingly male. If one was looking for Mr. Right, this would not be a bad thing. But I wasn't looking for love—all I ever needed to find was a private place to pee. So the lip gloss and well-fitting field pants were just for me and for no one else's benefit. Out in the remote wilderness I was still a cheerleader, a cheerleader with a machete, hiking boots, and few opportunities to shower.

Because of my cheerleader background, which everyone seemed to know about, in graduate school I was graded more harshly and initially treated like an outcast. To me it seemed that some of my professors wouldn't give me the time of day and looked at me with amusement, as if to say, "Cute of you to ask and I love your dress, but you're in the wrong field." I quickly tried to look more like a field researcher—or, better said, their idea of what a field researcher should look like. I took out my contacts and wore glasses. I began dressing more sloppily, went without lip gloss, and even forsook manicures. By the end of my make-under, I looked like a cross between Janis Joplin and someone who'd been locked up in a lab for months. But I couldn't keep up the charade for long, and the Cuban former cheerleader soon prevailed.

At the time I was convinced that professors actually tried to fail me because passing me might suggest that their classes were too easy. Or, worse, if the professor were male, it would be assumed I had flirted if I did well in class. Never mind that I was the first to show up for class and the last to leave. I felt I had to work harder than anyone to prove myself and get past my background, in spite of having by then at least as much field experience as some of the instructors grading me. I found myself with the opposite problem I had had in high school. Now I was too pretty.

I'd be lying if I didn't say that in my first semester I thought of quitting and called my mom on more than one occasion to say I was coming home. But by the end of that semester, my hard work was paying off and I was regularly receiving the highest marks in the class. I will even go as far as saying that I had finally earned the esteem of my professors. This was a huge feat, as the anthropology program at Stony Brook University is one of the most highly respected in the country. The professors are tops in the field; the fact that they were tough on me made me stronger, and in retrospect I am nothing but grateful. At the time, though, it seemed their approach was not to select the best and help them swim, but rather to select the best and try to drown them. My entering class consisted of seven students, of which only two of us remained long enough to earn a degree. I had always been a good swimmer.

If I were a monkey, my place in the hierarchy would have been well established within the group by this point. But my battle was far from over. Though I now had the support and respect of my professors, my colleagues had yet to be convinced. I think that part of the problem stemmed from the

fact that I wasn't the smartest in the bunch, yet I was receiving more scientific grants than the average student. Once
again, my Cuban roots might have had something to do with
it. I was very good at setting up a question and then arguing
to no end its importance and what a disgrace it would be not
to fund it. Yes, the fact that funding success largely depended
on the ability to argue cogently was a definite plus for a girl
who'd been trained by the very best—Cubans. But to some
of my colleagues who felt I wasn't Ph.D. worthy, in large part
because of my fashion sense and background in pom-poms,
it simply seemed unfair. I regularly found myself feeling like
I should apologize for wearing concealer. The National Science Foundation and Fulbright both saw past the concealer,
however, the first awarding me a fellowship and the second a
research grant to study one of the most critically endangered
primates in the world in Madagascar.

Needless to say, I was most comfortable in the field, where
far from civilization and critical eyes, I could just be me. And
it was in the field that I got to know best who "me" was. Every
morning in the middle of nowhere, without electricity or anyone to impress, I'd take great care in picking out my outfit and
hover in front of a business card–size mirror to apply my lip
gloss and check my eyebrows. I also felt I had a strong case
for bringing a little black dress on expeditions. Village parties
spring up more often than you might expect, and despite never
having been a Girl Scout, I like to be prepared.

The judgments of fellow students were soon of no conse-
quence, as I was to spend more time in Madagascar than at

grad parties. And luckily for me, lemurs don't judge. Well, that's not exactly true. More accurately, lemurs don't judge humans. It probably was not a surprise to anyone who knew me that I'd end up spending most of my adult life among lemurs. Lemurs, you see, are female dominant, and I come from a long line of dominant females. Male lemurs have it rough. They are booted out of the best sleeping sites, displaced from preferred feeding trees, and as a general rule made to feel useless and inferior. It was hard not to feel sorry for those poor guys. Female lemurs sometimes take off and leave a lonely male to finish their leftovers. I have hung back with an abandoned male and listened to his cries as he beckons for the females to acknowledge him so that he can rejoin the group. As if to mock him, the females will often ignore his pathetic pleas and continue munching while he looks around helplessly. This emotional torture can last for hours. Yep, female lemurs can be witches.

Once into my bitchy-lemur jungle element, I thought I was home free, especially since before I was even out of graduate school, I was already a wildlife correspondent for National Geographic, one of the most prestigious scientific and educational organizations in the world. Think about it. Among the greats associated with National Geographic are Jane Goodall, Jacques Cousteau, Dian Fossey, and Louis Leakey, to name just a few. These were the heroes in whose company I aspired to be, and, though I by no means think I have achieved their rank, surely I have done something right. But I quickly learned that like the female lemurs, there are sometimes bitchy female scientists.

In nature, there are plenty of examples of female alliance. Scientists studying lion females have found that there isn't a "queen" to match a lion "king," and there exists a sisterhood among the females. Groups of female lions typically hunt together and forge a bond that even includes sharing the duties of raising newborn cubs. They've been compared to soccer moms, who benefit from helping each other out. It raises the question of why the term "catty" is used to describe conniving and backstabbing women. I suppose I was disappointed that this sisterhood was not as prevalent among female human researchers. It was usually the female researchers I interviewed for TV who were the most hostile. They would regularly say hello with teeth clenched, and I swear I'd read "I hate you" in their expressions. At first I thought I was paranoid; I mean surely a strong, independent woman wouldn't be so quick to judge a scientific comrade. My attitude was Girls of the field, unite! But as much as I would have liked to believe that the antimalarial drugs were making me delusional, I wasn't paranoid. I overheard one scientist turn to my producer, just five minutes after meeting me, and ask him, "Is she here because she has a pretty face?" I felt the urge to both thank her and smack her. I heard another say she would have preferred a male host to interview her, as my "look" would now force her to have to shave. Nothing like being welcomed to a field site with "Why is she here?" Let it be noted that this would mark the first time I questioned shaving my armpits, though after years of picking ticks off my body, I know that body hair only helps conceal them.

At this early point in my career, still in my mid-20s, I had led dozens of expeditions around the world, I'd published numerous articles in scientific, peer-reviewed journals, and I'd made a groundbreaking scientific discovery of the world's smallest primate. Would hairy armpits really have made me more credible? And it wasn't just the researchers. It seemed I wasn't even safe from a few of the television producers, some of whom remarked on my looks before they even said hello. Rather than focusing on my experience or noticing my firm grip as we shook hands, they'd say things like "How do we make you look more like a scientist?" Did my credentials not speak for themselves? I *was* a scientist.

But none of them beat my personal favorite, which was "Are you going to wear that? We need to make you less attractive, or you'll look like Tarzan's sexy Jane running around in the jungle." It's my favorite because inevitably that is the image that was encouraged. I can't begin to count the number of scenes of me bathing in rivers or showering under a waterfall. But that is a part of everyday life in the field that people are often curious about, so I never objected. More ridiculous and somewhat amusing, I think, were the conversations that preceded such filming, centering on whether it would be appropriate or sexist. Would producers discuss such things if I were Jack Hanna? Just curious.

And then there are the TV critics. Here's an excerpt from one: "The show can't decide whether to treat Mayor as an expert, or as the title ["Wild Nights with Mireya Mayor"] and location hint, a bit of a sex symbol." He then added, "But throughout the show she wears a wool cap and drab clothes that just beg us to take her seriously." This was in contrast to the observation of another critic, who wrote, "Explorers require rugged gear, the sort Indiana Jones girds himself in. Then there's Mireya Mayor, a sexy blond explorer. She fills out a tank top nicely." I can't win. If I wear tank tops, I'm vying for attention. If I cover up, it's only because I want to be taken seriously. Regardless, the first critic lost all credibility when he called my clothes drab. They were both hip and designer.

Don't get me wrong. I realize that this cuts both ways. I got my job in television not only because of my credentials but also because of how I looked. National Geographic liked that I didn't look like a typical scientist. I know that criticism comes with the territory if you're a scientist and a woman who likes wearing pink boots and tank tops.

But when I'm being charged by an elephant bull, I never have to wonder if he's chasing me because I'm a woman. Nope, I can rest assured that he's coming after me simply because of my stinky human scent. Elephants do not discriminate in whom they trample. This is why I love working with animals. Animals are more perceptive than humans and don't pay any attention to my gender or the color of my boots.

Being a woman in the field has advantages and disadvantages, but at the end of the day it is only experience, performance, and skill that ensure survival. It hasn't been an easy road, but it has been an amazing one. I was in my early 20s when I first took a field job, full of energy, excitement, and hope. My dream to work with animals had come true. Every day that I step out of my tent is different and unpredictable. I never know if I am going to be tracking gorillas in Congo, capturing giraffes in Namibia, scaling a mountain in Venezuela, chasing monkeys in Japan, or herding wildebeests from a helicopter. The one thing I can be sure of is that it isn't ever going to be boring. I've grown some thicker skin and learned to accept that even after getting dangerously close to spitting cobras and black mambas, I will always have to contend with some reporter commenting on how I fill out my tank top.

No, I never thought I'd one day set foot in the Explorers Club, let alone be invited to join. As a former NFL cheerleader, I would not feel welcome in the scientific community for years. Now when someone says, "You don't look like a scientist," I simply say, "Well, this is what a scientist looks like," and smile. I will never apologize for being a woman. Or for shaving my armpits and wearing lip gloss. The lemurs would argue that it is my alpha-female right.

seven

Gorilla Warfare

MAY 30, 2002: This morning the sweat bees were absolutely atrocious. They were inside my ears, nose, throat, eyes. I couldn't look up for more than a fraction of a second without inhaling them. That's all I could think about until we were charged by Mlima's group—the whole group. First the female, Matata, then the juveniles then Mlima. It was terrifying. It was not a classic textbook display charge where only the male bluff-charges—the whole group got really close. The screams were so loud and powerful. It was so intense I didn't even notice the sweat bees anymore.

Deep in the heart of darkness in the lush rain forest of the Congo, the gorillas were dozing under the rays of morning sun that pierced the dense vegetation, exuding their infectious, albeit misleading, aura of calm. I, on the other hand, was swatting at sweat bees trying to make their way into my ears and up my nose. These bees are attracted to salt in human sweat, and although their sting is almost painless, their constant presence is a total pain in the butt. Especially when one is trying to observe gorillas and share in their Zen-like state. Ironically, the more I waved my hands to get rid of the annoying creatures, the more I sweated and added to my appeal. By the dozens, they clustered on my arms and legs and dive-bombed into my eyes. What satisfaction it gave me to crush them.

While digging a bee out of my eye, I heard a noise behind me. Like most primates, gorillas are usually heard before they are seen. Not having a mirror, I was using the lens of my camera to pick sweat bees out of my pupils. Suddenly, reflected behind me was a gorgeous, 400-pound silverback. As if responding to an inaudible command, the gorillas had stopped dozing and now surrounded me. This wasn't good. The females let out a piercing shriek. There were only three of them, but it sounded like a dozen or more. Frozen, our guide whispered to me to cower and pretend to eat leaves. Why pretend? I ingested several. Evidently feeling threatened, the females prodded the silverback to charge. So like a husband, at first he pretended not to hear, but the females began running at us. Our only weapon a ballpoint pen, I quickly ate more leaves. The silverback joined in the charge. Just inches from us they all stopped and began furiously slapping the ground. Now pacified, the wives went back to foraging.

Being charged by gorillas is part of my job description. I am a primatologist first and foremost, so in spring 2002, when National Geographic asked me to do a film on gorillas, I was ecstatic. At long last, I would have the chance to live out my Dian Fossey fantasy! I would be working with a British film crew, including Dave Allen, an award-winning natural history producer and cameraman, a soundman, and a field producer. I had spent many years in Madagascar, but this would be my first time on the African mainland. I could barely contain my excitement, never giving a thought to just how difficult and dangerous this mission would be. Central African Republic, on the border of war-torn Congo, was in the midst of military upheaval. Government forces were burning entire villages to the ground and executing large numbers of suspected rebels. And the rain forest is never safe, even at the best of times.

To reach this besieged tropical outpost I flew from Washington, D.C., where National Geographic headquarters is based, to Paris, where I met up with the film crew, and then to Bangui, the capital of Central African Republic (CAR), one of the world's poorest countries. Bangui is a heartbreaking city, its inhabitants intimidated and browbeaten by decades of violent coups d'état by officers of the ruthless national army. Soldiers walk the streets carrying automatic rifles, and at checkpoints around every turn your passport is inspected and payment exacted.

Slightly smaller than Texas, CAR is a sweltering and searing remnant of French colonialism plagued by run-down buildings, eroded roads, and crumbling monuments to former dictators. In Bangui I watched fat Frenchmen solicit prostitutes as young as 12, and hotel pool areas and bars were crowded with seedy characters speaking sotto voce in French or Sangha, the local language. In the many open-air markets, flies swarmed over stacks of dried fish and smoked bush meat, including great ape and elephant. The multihued dresses of Bantu women resonated against the gray and dusty backdrop of the city.

Film crews don't travel light, so with some 30 bags piled onto the one SUV the city offered, we departed Bangui headed southwest. The heat was intense, and through our open windows a fine layer of dust settled on us and our gear. After a while the only other vehicles we saw were huge logging trucks, which came at us at such incredible speeds we'd have to swerve into a ditch to avoid collision. There goes one of my nine lives, I thought to myself each time this happened. The closer we got to our destination in the Dzanga-Sangha forest, the more BaAka Pygmy villages we saw, their domelike huts made of sticks and leaves. Nomadic hunter-gatherers standing only four to four and a half feet in height, the BaAka ("forest people") are one of CAR's more than 80 ethnic groups, each with its own language. Village children would run alongside our SUV and wave excitedly. Just as excitedly, I waved back.

Twelve hours after we started out, we arrived in Bayanga, a small logging town at the edge of the forest, which featured a landing strip of beaten red dirt used by cars, planes, pedestrians, and goats. It was only a few miles from Bai Hokou, the camp that would be our window to the gorillas. On this night, we would stay in simple bamboo huts with mosquito netting. I was exhausted and could barely wait to eat, take my antimalarial pill, and crash. But through the night, visions of black hands reaching through bars kept waking me. I'd force open my eyes, but even awake the images got closer and closer. There was no escaping those hands. Terrified, I ran to Dave's bungalow and begged to sleep in one of his bunks. I fell asleep there, and the images stopped. In the morning I realized the antimalarials had caused the hallucinations. Dave looked at me as if I were crazy when I described them, but as I handed in my key, the hotel clerk told us my bungalow sat on land once used as a prisoner burial site. Neither Dave nor I spoke, but we both looked as if we had seen a ghost. Only difference was, I actually had.

The trip from Bayanga initially followed an old logging trail and then a meandering elephant trail, taking us through open fields until gradually the forest canopy closed in. The base camp, Bai Hokou, was named after a forest clearing in which elephants had dug a large hole for its mineral-rich soil (*bai* means "clearing," and *hokou*, "hole," in Sango, the BaAka language). It was a series of basic, wooden, thatched huts for dining and office work. Sleeping took place in tents and bathing was done under a beautiful sandy-bottomed waterfall, a five-minute walk away, close to a bat-filled cave.

At Bai Hokou we met Chloe Cipolletta, an Italian wildlife biologist who knew these gorillas better than just about anyone else. She had spent the last five years following and gaining the trust of a family group she and her trackers named the Munye, meaning "good thing" in BaAka. Chloe and her team had revolutionized the strategy for saving western lowland gorillas in this remote corner and for the first time were showing success in habituating them to humans. If the program succeeded, tourists instead of loggers would be trekking in to visit the gorillas.

No more than a minute after we arrived at camp, the bees moved in. The soundman got stung in the eye, and it soon bulged grotesquely from its socket. Amid this possible medical emergency, Chloe came out to greet us.

It was easy to see why she had succeeded where many others had failed. Chloe's feistiness and determination came through before she even opened her mouth. She is the daughter of an Italian banker and could have lived a luxurious life in a Roman villa with a closet full of Dolce & Gabbana. How appealing an idea, I thought, as I stood drenched in sweat, waving off bees! Instead, she ran around in ripped tees and unshaven legs and lived in a thatched hut at Bai Hokou. I was eager to ask her questions, but there was no time for more than a quick introduction before she ordered me into a vehicle. We quickly headed out to pick up the BaAka tracking team, who'd had two weeks off in their village. A swarm of bees accompanied us.

Later that afternoon, as I pitched my tent at the edge of the Bai, I noticed cans a few feet away attached to barbed wire surrounding the camp. Chloe later explained that this was an elephant alarm system. The cans were filled with rocks, and should the elephants try to break through the fence, the cans would cause such a racket you would at least have a few seconds to escape. She warned me that elephants did frequently come into camp and that under no circumstances should I attempt to engage them. The thought had never crossed my mind. She explained that a young male elephant gored a young Italian woman here. "And," she added, "the large hole in the kitchen that looks like a window—elephant." Visions of being trampled in my sleep consumed me. I spent my entire first night at camp awake, listening for rattling cans.

Exhausted from my vigilant night, I staggered out of my tent to a thatched hut for a breakfast of fresh bread the BaAka had baked in a stone oven. I spread preserves and took a bite, then felt a sharp sting on my left shoulder, which left my arm almost paralyzed with pain. Then another and another. Bees. I instantly became aware of a growing hum and realized it was hundreds of African honeybees, also known as killer bees, hanging out in the dining area near the sugary treats. From then on, whether in camp or the forest, I could count on not only the annoying sweat bees but also multiple stings a day from the killer bees. We began documenting who got stung first, most, and least. Even in my tent, I wasn't safe; bees flew down my pants and into my shoes, making getting dressed hellish. Freaking bees! Their presence here had taken me completely by surprise. Had this been edited out of *Gorillas in the Mist*? Getting trampled by elephants somehow didn't seem nearly as bad.

Chloe and the trackers briefed us on how to find and track the gorillas, and, most important, what to do if a gorilla charged. I learned you must stay at least 20 feet away from one to prevent passing on germs. No matter how tempting, no hugging allowed! If charged, Chloe said, you must look confident but not overly, letting the gorilla know you're not scared but keenly aware of who's boss. I wondered if waving a white flag would work. For centuries our close, forest-dwelling relatives have known humans only as hunters, who have killed them by the hundreds. Not surprisingly, the relationship between man and gorilla has been based on violence and fear. Early explorers described gorillas as "half man, half beast" and slaughtered as many as they could in the name of science. Given that horrible track record, the silverback, named Mlima, was still aggressive, Chloe warned. A silverback's job is to protect his family, and it is not uncommon for them to fight to the death. Mlima had attacked, bitten, and clobbered two trackers. In one instance, he charged a tracker and ripped his shirt off in a single motion.

My fantasy of sitting among a group of gorillas having a tickle fight had quickly vanished. Because of their habitat, western lowland gorillas are much more difficult to follow than Dian Fossey's mountain gorillas. Whereas you can see mountain gorillas—and they you—from miles away, dense vegetation serves as a shield for lowland gorillas, making it easy to stumble upon and surprise them. Not until the 1960s did scientists try to study lowland gorillas in the wild. And then their fear of humans made it difficult to habituate them, so that they would go about their normal activities tolerant of human observers. After many failed attempts, it was assumed they were simply unable to accept a human presence. Because of this, lowland gorillas were the least understood of the great apes.

As Chloe was well aware, her project's stakes were very high. Habituation was not without risk. Habituated animals are easy prey for poachers. When Chloe first encountered them, the Munye group consisted of the silverback Mlima (Swahili for "mountain"), four adult females, two infants, and possibly a subadult black male. Chloe and her team had devised a nonthreatening clucking sound to alert the animals to the team's presence even in the densest forest, in the hope they'd eventually associate clucking with friendly humans. At first Mlima tried to discourage the approaches with impressive charges, but gradually over the years the team earned his trust and were allowed to get close enough to gain knowledge of the family.

The most testing stage of habituation, the aggressive period, can last for more than a year. But, as Chloe learned, that was only the beginning of the process. After that period, silverbacks may ignore human observers, but females resist far longer. The reasons are unclear. Perhaps the females are just more sensitive to us as risks to their young, or as competition for food. Funnily enough, it might also be that they think we are after their mates. Mlima was handsome, but I could assure the females that big, hairy males were not my type.

There is absolutely no glamour in gorilla tracking. Covered in sweat-bee residue, bitten by chiggers, and usually soaked by rain, we would spend up to 14 hours in the forest, half of it searching for the animals. Despite their massive size, they left only the slightest of trails, whose signs the BaAka deciphered like a CSI team. No one goes into the forest without the BaAka. These guys can spot a snapped twig at 50 paces and then recognize it as snapped by a gorilla. Female. Thirty minutes ago, give or take. Extraordinary.

One day I lay down in one of the nests the gorillas build every night and noticed how much more comfortable it was than my tent's foam mattress. Clearly, these are intelligent beings that enjoy comfort. Then I realized that my head rested on a mound of gorilla crap. We collected the dung in bags made of large leaves to later analyze for the fruit species the beasts consumed. Suddenly, Chloe and the trackers sensed something. We clucked and looked around, but there was no gorilla in sight. All of a sudden, I was hit by a very strong, musky, distinct odor. For a moment I thought it was me needing a bath. But it wasn't. It was the smell of the silverback.

Watching gorillas is not unlike watching a soap opera. The Munye family had its history of drama, jealousy, and violence. Though Mlima initially looked like a smooth operator with a four-female harem, he did not seem to have an easy time with the ladies. In November 1999, Chloe and her team found him horribly wounded. Adding insult to injury, two of his females, one with a still dependent infant, had deserted him. Based on the evidence, it was thought that a leopard, or perhaps another silverback, had attacked. Mlima slowly recovered, but two months later a third female departed, leaving Mlima with a sole female, Matata ("problem" in Swahili), and their infant, Ndimbelimbe (named for a local herb). It was while the silverback was injured and weak that Chloe was able to move closer and begin to earn his trust and the group's.

One day, as we stood watching, Mlima's now teenage son, Ndimbelimbe, like a typical teenager, was doing his best to annoy Dad. Finally losing patience, Mlima took a swing at his son. An infuriated Matata rushed to her boy's defense. Ndimbelimbe shot his Dad a smug look as his mother pulled him by the arm and dragged him away. Of course, not before giving Mlima a good scolding. Typical male, Mlima continued eating, probably thinking that this would blow over and the nagging wife would come to her senses. But the next day, his wife and son disappeared and Mlima, usually the picture of pride and strength, was a big, weeping mess.

Matata did not return that night. Or the next few nights. It is not typical for a female to sleep apart from her mate, so this was serious. Somewhere in the dense forest, divorce papers were being filed. Forlorn cries from Mlima rang through the trees for days. He had lost his only remaining female and son. This would mean a life spent alone, socially isolated from other gorilla groups. It was difficult not to feel sorry for this blubbering male, and I wanted desperately to find Matata and persuade her to take him back. A few days after Matata had left Mlima, we were standing in the forest watching him when, upset and frustrated, he charged us. I tried not to breathe, though he could surely hear my heart pounding like a drum. But it was a bluff charge, and as soon as it was over, he just sauntered past. I did a quick count of limbs, four—the correct number—and it occurred to me, not for the first time, just how soft and pink we are. Now we needed to back off. The disintegration of the Munye group meant much more than a lonely male gorilla. It could be the end of Chloe's project and her many years of hard work.

I decided to try to lighten the mood back at camp. I turned up some music and asked the trackers to teach me a dance. Then they asked me to do the same. At first I tried swing, but that was a little tricky. I had to think of a dance that didn't require partners. Then it dawned on me: La Macarena. It caught on like wildfire. In the forest behind their huts the trackers practiced constantly thereafter, much to the dismay of the film crew, who pictured coming back another year to film the BaAka's traditional dance only to have La Macarena spring up. The BaAka had taught me so much I was happy to be able to leave a little Cuban cheerleader culture behind.

But the smiles did not last long, as more bad news arrived. A call over the high-frequency radio shook us to the core. Poachers had been caught with the remains of two dead gorillas. Hoping against hope it wasn't Matata and her son who'd been found, I jumped in the truck and headed over to the poacher bust. When I arrived, I saw what looked like a barbecue pyre piled high with dismembered gorilla body parts, hands and feet severed to sell as souvenirs. Uniformed guards holding rifles stood watch. A dead gorilla can bring five dollars, a big sum here.

As I got closer, I could smell the distinct odor of burning gorilla flesh, little different from a human's. I picked up one of the hands and felt like crying. It was still warm to the touch. As I looked through the remains, I was painfully aware that they belonged to a female and a youngster. Had Matata and Ndimbelimbe been killed? Had the habituation project led them straight into the barrel of a poacher's gun? I pulled myself away from this tragic scene and let flow the tears. Back at camp I stood under the waterfall, hoping to wash off the horrible scent, though it would never remove the horrendous memory of the murdered gorillas.

The mood was somber. News of the murders had affected everyone at camp. With no gorillas to follow, I picked up a book in Sango written by missionaries and began learning useful phrases such as, "There are rocks in my rice." When I tried practicing on the trackers, they invited me and the film crew to go into the forest with them for a three-day spear hunt. Welcoming a break and curious as to how these forest dwellers survived, I accepted. The BaAka eat berries and other fruit, as well as honey and animals; their constant moving allows the natural wealth of the forest to replenish itself. The plan was for the BaAka and me to hunt in the farthest depths of a forest reserve where no guns are allowed, taking very little, including tents, with us. I thought about the bees and just how little I relished being rained on. Authentic was good, but my tent was coming along.

We retraced the route back to Bayanga, their village, and I was led through an array of igloo-shaped dwellings to meet somebody I assumed would be a local chief. You can imagine my shock when a tall white man in a military green T-shirt, ripped jean shorts, and a pencil-thin mustache greeted me in very American English, introducing himself as Louis Sarno. Twenty years before, while sitting in his living room in New Jersey, Louis had heard Pygmy music on the radio and was so spellbound he came to record it and never left. He married a local woman and learned the language. He had become an advocate for the BaAka, whose way of life, much like the gorillas', was now seriously threatened by logging. Other groups were moving in to settle and grow crops in the clearings. As BaAka are much smaller than most Africans in the area (they were traditionally called Pygmies, but some now consider that label pejorative), they have often been mistreated and forced to work as slaves for others, such as the Bantu.

Louis frequently went on hunting trips with the villagers. Despite towering over them and, by his own admission, being a lousy spear hunter, he and his New Jersey accent fit in surprisingly well. Thirteen BaAka families, Louis, the film crew, and I all piled into two pickups. I was handed a little boy no older than two with a runny nose and no diaper. For hours the women sang, their voices powerful and the rhythms complex. I could see why their music had compelled Louis to travel halfway across the world. It was extraordinary. There was amazing energy as we drove from village to slash-and-burn logging area, to marginal forest, to second-growth forest, and finally to ancient, primal rain forest. The BaAka were home.

We hiked through the undergrowth, carrying cassava, cooking items, and hunting equipment. While I struggled with a small backpack, the women carried loads as big as the men's strapped to their heads and on their backs, with babies in their arms. BaAka people are built strong. Most of them went barefoot. They have short and very wide feet, most likely an evolutionary adaptation, with soles as thick as the soles of my boots.

After a three-hour hike we stopped to set up a campsite, intending to get farther into the forest the next day. The women, who wore nothing but a wrap, began cutting branches and setting up the shelters. One woman in particular, whom we dubbed "Superwoman," stood out to me and the crew. With breasts hanging down to her belly and a baby in tow, she quickly built her shelter, got a cooking fire going, and climbed a tree to collect honey before I'd even figured out where to put my tent. To bless the hunt, the men chanted to the forest spirits and whacked their nets with plants they believed to be magical.

The next day, armed with nothing more than porcupine quills, crossbows, and nets, the BaAka men and women began moving through the forest. I was told to make noise to aid in chasing out the duikers and porcupines. The noise would also help clear out elephants and gorillas before they'd be forced to charge. I helped carry a 70-foot net made of vine bark to form a barrier, but I could sense from the looks on some of the faces that I was not moving fast enough. That annoyed look is universal. The BaAka depended on these hunts. I tried going faster.

The men were chasing a duiker, a small forest antelope, and suddenly three blue duiker were running our way. The men yelled and chanted, forcing the animal to run toward the net. We women, along with the children, stood at the periphery of the net. If the animal changed direction, we would adjust its position. Everything was perfectly organized and at the same time chaotic. A very unlucky duiker was caught, and I could sense both victory and disappointment at having caught only one.

Then came the brutal part of the hunt, which I will never be prepared for. The little antelope was hog-tied, and I made the mistake of looking into its brown eyes before its screams sent chills down my spine and blood began splattering. I determined to become a vegetarian again. But we can't judge these hunters. They have lived sustainably off the land for centuries. For most Westerners, meat comes nicely prepackaged, sparing us the gruesome reality of the kill.

I joined the women who were now fishing at the stream. They built a canal to divert the water and then used sand to create a dam and corner the fish. I attempted to catch some but soon realized it was a huge effort for a few small fish. Behind us, other women climbed the trees, collecting honey from stingless bees. This I liked. They handed me a honeycomb, and I let the honey drip into my mouth. Nothing ever tasted as sweet or delicious.

At midnight the camp erupted in celebration for the successful hunt. BaAka men drummed on pots and pans and jugs, and the women sang and yodeled, thanking the forest spirits and asking for a fruitful hunt the following day. There was a lead singer, with call and response. Under the stars in the deep forest their haunting music seemed otherworldly, and it would only get more so. As if a piece of the forest were moving, men under shaking branches danced, representing the forest spirits. From the shadows, we could see the movement, and as the "spirits" came closer, we could make out glowing shapes, men covered in phosphorescent mold or algae, illuminating the forest. It was surreal and magical, and I never wanted it to end. "This is the BaAka's place," whispered Louis. How tragic it was that their forest and way of life were so rapidly vanishing.

As we drove back to Bai Hokou, I braced myself for what news might be waiting. I hoped that the forest spirits had lent a hand in reuniting the Munye family and that the dead gorillas I had seen were not Mlima's son and mate. But a glance at Chloe's face told me that as yet there was no good news.

Mlima was still alone, and there'd been no sightings or traces of Matata and Ndimbelimbe.

Over the next few days, I joined in the search. Eventually, the trackers thought they spotted Matata in the thicket. No one dared breathe, but we clucked softly and prayed it was them. Indeed, Matata's eyes peered out through the leaves, and next to her sat Ndimbelimbe munching. Mlima had won his family back! It was the most touching and beautiful moment of the journey, tainted only by the sweat bee in my nose.

[eight]

King Kong in My Pocket

JANUARY 23, 2003: Tonight we waited until almost midnight to start making our way through the jungle. The silence was almost deafening. At night the forest seems still, and there is sometimes enough light from the moon to see the large tree trunks silhouetted against the forest floor and background. But on this night only the light from our flashlights guided our path. In the near distance we heard a sound. Something was crashing in the trees. We ran as fast as we could, tripping over the roots and foliage under our feet. We were running not from, but toward the sound. As I looked up into the canopy, what looked like glowing charcoals stared down at me from a tree. We were not alone.

The world's most famous primate, King Kong, once enthralled movie audiences by cupping a delicate Fay Wray in his hand, not harming but protecting her. Deep in the jungles of Madagascar, the roles were now reversed. Life was imitating art, but with a twist. I wasn't the beautiful damsel in distress. And no,

I didn't have a gorilla-size lemur cupped in my hand. Those prehistoric giants lost their habitat and were hunted to extinction more than 2,000 years ago. Today their descendants are still hunted, and the loss of habitat is worse than ever. The tiny primate in the palm of my hand needed the protection of a damsel—me—to survive. This little lemur could share the fate of its giant cousins if I didn't act fast. That's a lot of pressure.

Working under pressure is nothing new to me. Even when I was an NFL cheerleader, I had to perform under the gun. Dancing in front of more than 75,000 screaming fans, remembering to smile, and making sure my hair remained in place in scorching heat after twisting an ankle—that's pressure. But I was about to experience a whole new level. I was in Anjanaharibe-sud, a mountainous rain forest in northeastern Madagascar, working with geneticist and veterinarian Dr. Edward Louis, director of the Omaha Zoo's Madagascar Biodiversity Project. Eddie and I had met in the capital, Antananarivo, a year before. At times, talking to Eddie was a bit how I imagined a conversation on quantum physics with Stephen Hawking might go. Lots of technical words from him, very little comprehension by me.

Despite the language barrier, I was instantly drawn to Eddie's quick wit and sarcastic sense of humor. We became very good friends and grew quite close during our expeditions together. This puzzled some of my colleagues, who saw him as an ill-tempered "cowboy," one who'd come into an area with disregard for everything and everyone and captured every animal in sight. I attributed this view to professional jealousy and, rather, considered Eddie a determined, albeit slightly mad, scientist with a huge heart. I had seen him lose his temper, even at a tent, but it didn't faze me. On the contrary, I would laugh at him, which always seemed to put a smile on his face. I was the bubbly cheerleader, Eddie the grumpy cowboy. We were yin and yang.

Eddie and I were in Anjanaharibe to capture everything with a heartbeat, whether it had four legs, slid on its belly, or hopped for a living. In a mammoth undertaking, Eddie was investigating the genetic makeup of Madagascar's vast and endangered fauna, taking blood and tissue samples of all its creatures to create a complete genetic map. This meant walking through every parcel of forest in Madagascar and collecting multiple samples from every living life-form. Conservation planning would be greatly enhanced by this research. Identifying all species present in an area would allow the government and policymakers to know which areas were in most dire need of protection.

I was there to capture sifakas and indris, the largest of the lemur species. I was finishing up the fieldwork for my Ph.D. and needed more samples to complete my studies. This expedition would widen the range of the individuals I'd sampled so far and possibly elevate them to full species status. In conservation speak, that meant more attention, higher priority, and more money. I was hugely excited to be a part of Eddie's groundbreaking research and loved learning about the frogs, snakes, and amazing chameleons that camouflaged themselves above us in the trees. It became routine for me to jump off the trails to catch tiny mantella frogs, among the most brightly colored and spectacular of all frogs. Like the poison arrow frogs of the New World, the mantellas of Madagascar are capable of storing poisons (which they get from the ants they eat) in their glands. I was mesmerized by these lethal beauties.

Eddie and I were sitting around the campfire one night, when the small lemurs really got our attention. We had two different lemur guidebooks: One said the eastern mouse lemur occurred here, which made perfect sense since we were on the east coast; another said it was the western species. Clearly, one of them had to be wrong. Intrigued, we decided to put out small mammal traps baited with banana. The idea is that the animal smells the bait, goes in for a free lunch, and releases the little trap door. It is later let go, unharmed. We started baiting and setting traps that very night.

Mouse lemurs are the smallest primates in the world. Nocturnal and known for their frenetic chirping and activity, they feed on insects, small vertebrates, fruit, and flowers. The combination of tiny and nocturnal makes them a difficult species to study. But we weren't trying to uncover secrets of their personal lives; we just wanted to know which kind of mouse lemur lived there. Metal mammal traps should have done the trick.

Every morning we sprang from our tents and raced to the traps, hoping to get a glimpse of this mysterious little creature. Morning after morning, we would return to our tents empty-handed. The last night before we had to pack up our gear and head to another field site, it was raining hard even by rain forest standards. Like me, lemurs don't like to move around much in the rain. I just wanted to curl up in my warm sleeping bag. Experience told me our lemur traps would be empty, but I thought I'd run over and take a look.

I was wrong.

Inside the trap sat a tiny, drenched, shivering primate. The large eyes that made up most of its face looked at me from the bottom of the trap. For a moment, I froze. The lemur was so small I could put it in my shirt pocket. And in an effort to warm it up, inside my pocket is where it went.

Jagged, bumpy, and rutted like a potholed street, the surface of the forest floor is covered in roots that unexpectedly pop up out of the ground. As I was running back to camp, thoughts of tripping and crushing the endangered lemur crowded my head. I could see the headline, "Former NFL Cheerleader Squashes World's Smallest Primate With Her Left Breast." I slowed down just a bit.

In my mad dash I hadn't paid any attention to the little lemur's appearance. Afraid it was already hypothermic, Eddie and I agreed we must increase its body temperature immediately. At the campfire we warmed some water, poured it into a ziplock bag to use as a hot water bottle, and pressed the lemur close.

Now we had a chance to look at it. At first glance it resembled the eastern species (which made sense given where we were). Upon closer inspection, we could also see some characteristics of the western species. Then I noticed that the color was slightly off. We began noticing other very subtle differences that meant, in fact, it looked like neither. It appeared both guidebooks were wrong. We didn't have to say a word; Eddie and I were completely aligned in our thinking. We both realized we might have something new here and understood the implications. As soon as we took a blood sample and the animal warmed up, we released it.

Back in the States, Eddie and I began processing the DNA samples at his genetics lab in Omaha, Nebraska. I hate the lab. There, I said it. Television shows make it appear as if you pour something into a test tube, shake it around a little, and bam! Results. Don't fall for it. Every step of analyzing DNA is a long and painstaking process with endless trial and error. You spend hours working on a sample, paying scrupulous attention to detail, then wait several more hours to learn if what you did worked, only to find that you have to start all over again. A couple of weeks wouldn't cut it. Before I knew whether this was a new animal species, I had to head back to National Geographic headquarters.

Months after we found that tiny lemur shivering at the bottom of the trap, I received the call that would change my life. My suspicion was confirmed. Eddie and I had discovered an entirely new species of primate. It was a scientist's dream come true. It's a moment you hope for but never think possible. I hung up the phone and sat motionless. This might very well have been the find of a lifetime. And then it hit me.

With only one sample and no photographs, how would we prove it?

It was Friday afternoon. On the fifth floor of the National Geographic building this meant happy hour. Aptly named the Exotic Liquors Club by its founder, Brian Armstrong, a well-seasoned producer and connoisseur of all things alcohol, the fifth floor was the place where explorers, producers, and execs came to sample liquor brought back from the latest expeditions. There were more than a hundred bottles to choose from, and every bottle told a story of adventure, exploration, and survival.

The flavored African moonshine made on a game reserve and delivered in test tubes was fiery and good. Usually, after a few sips I would be transported to the wild bush from which the drink originated. But the news I'd just received was weighing on my mind. Brian asked me what was new. I nonchalantly replied, "We just discovered the world's smallest lemur."

Brian suddenly got the look in his eye reporters get when they sniff a scoop. Before I knew it, he had written a proposal to go to Madagascar and film the discovery of this new species. This was just the solution to our no-proof dilemma, which otherwise would end with *the one that got away*. With a film crew and a National Geographic photographer on the case, this little lemur would become a star and, with luck, the face of renewed hope for all of the endangered creatures in that forest.

A few weeks later, I was heading back to Madagascar. My plan was straightforward: to confirm the greatest discovery of my career. All I had to do was find another mouse lemur.

Our Air France jet landed in the capital, greeted by the usual chickens and dogs on the tarmac. The familiar smells on deplaning triggered a nostalgia I had felt even on my first journey to this exotic island. I headed to the sign "Entry Visas," where a heavy woman with a cash box took my money, licked the back of four stamps picturing cattle, and placed them in my passport. I was soon back on the chaotic streets, jammed with old Renaults and Citroëns honking at rickety carts pulled by slow-moving, single-humped zebus.

Eddie would not be joining me on this expedition, but our Malagasy team, who had accompanied us on many expeditions, would be meeting us with equipment—most important, the traps. Eddie had trained this highly sought-after team to be proficient marksmen, and we were completely reliant on their skills and expertise in the forest. Without them, there could be no expedition.

But they were nowhere to be found.

Two days later, with our team still missing, I went down to the MICET office. There on the floor I saw feet sticking out from under some covers. I counted four pairs. The team was there. They were also asleep. Like a den mother, I called, "Salama! Rise and shine, boys!" They fidgeted under the covers without waking. Richard, the team's leader, finally got up and explained that they had just driven in from their village. It had taken them more than 14 hours because of bad roads and accidents. I sympathized, but there was no time to sleep. We had to rush to catch a flight.

It was only at the airport that I had a chance to check the gear. Part of the team's responsibility was to pack the equipment, most of which we kept stored in their village. Normally, when Eddie and I flew into the capital, we met up with the team at the airport and proceeded directly to the site, counting on the team to have all the equipment ready. I didn't for a second think any pieces would be missing, least of all the essential traps. But there were none.

"We have no mouse lemur traps! Zero!" I yelled. I was in shock. No, I was furious. The team hesitated; no one wanted to admit they'd forgotten the traps. It made no sense to go without them, but charter planes are very difficult to come by in Madagascar, and we had a pilot ready and waiting. I stood there looking at the dozen crates of gear, wondering how they could have forgotten those vital pieces of equipment. The pilot motioned us to board, and we had no choice but to cram into the plane. Trapped and trap-less, we were on our way.

From Tana in the center of the island, we took a short flight north to Sambava. Our pilot must have sensed my stress because he invited me to take the controls. That was a guaranteed way to lift my spirits. My free flying lesson amused Brian; my cameraman, Jeff; and my student, Angelo. But I noticed they all held on to barf bags. I wasn't the steadiest of pilots.

Down below I could see the jungle where we were headed; not much of it was left. Looking down from the clouds, it really struck me: If nothing was done in this region, our newly discovered lemur would be gone in less than two years. Fires burned up and down the hillsides. Although as long ago as 1881 Madagascar's Queen Ranavalona had made slash-and-burn agriculture illegal, the farmers continued to practice it. Every year about one percent of Madagascar's forests are destroyed for charcoal, logging, and rice paddies.

It was somewhere down in that patchy green abyss that I'd gotten my glimpse of the mouse lemur. Now I had to find it again. The thought of looking for the world's smallest primate at night in dense foliage was as daunting as searching for the pot of gold at the end of the rainbow. Only their shine at the end of our flashlights would reveal their whereabouts.

We landed at Sambava, quite smoothly I thought, given it was my first try, and immediately began brainstorming about how to improvise traps. It's a simple concept, really: You bait whatever you're using, and an animal should be able to get in but not get out. Angelo and I tinkered with ideas. Finally, we grabbed some plastic water bottles and cut the ends off with a pocketknife. I had no idea if these would work, but for lack of something better we made 20 of them.

A long drive and hike to the field site were still ahead of us. A little before sunrise, all equipment loaded onto a hired truck, we and our improvised traps were on our way to Anjanaharibe. This is the part of the journey when I long for a pillow to sit on. The roads are terrible. To make things worse, it was monsoon season, and a mud slide soon brought the vehicle to a dead stop. We all jumped out and pushed and pulled our way out of the mud. But that was only the beginning. All the roads were washed out. It seemed we had gone as far by truck as we were going to go.

We camped overnight on the side of the road and sent a message to the nearest village asking for 30 strong men to come and help us carry our gear to the campsite the next day. Despite the delay and less than ideal sleeping arrangements, it was comforting to hear lemurs in the forest; the voices of indris sounded like "Welcome back" to me.

Soon as the sun came up, the head porter arrived. Slowly, more and more guys started trickling in, some even bringing us pineapples for breakfast. But we still had to negotiate a price for their help, and they knew we were in a bind. These negotiations are never easy, but sitting on the side of the road with dozens of bags, crates, and a generator did not put us in the strongest position. After some haggling, posturing, and arm waving, we settled on a fee—eight dollars a day per man, which was more than they normally make in a week. The head porter shook his head and said, "Uh-uh," which in the U.S. means no, but in Madagascar means yes. Within minutes our bags and crates were off the ground and on their backs.

However, it seemed the stars were not yet aligning.

The problem now was that a huge, fast-moving river stood before us. I could see where there had been a bridge at one time, but only the frame remained. With more than 30 porters and a film crew standing behind me, I had to decide where the best place would be to cross. At last, waist deep and with bags lifted high above our heads, we managed to struggle to the opposite riverbank, fighting the current all the way.

Safely across, we were nearing our field camp, but the final leg was through thick jungle. Then it was all down a very slippery hill. Like a kid I would raise my arms and slide. We had only five minutes to set up camp before a downpour.

The entire team and all our equipment were crammed under one flimsy tarp, which barely held up under the storm. Camp life, I thought. Awesome.

Over the next few days, life settled into a routine of steady rain and empty traps. In this weather, it seemed we were good at attracting only one type of animal—leeches. The little bloodsuckers are common in Madagascar rain forests, and, unlike leeches in other parts of the world, are not aquatic. If you stand still for a few minutes, you're guaranteed to see leeches dropping from the trees. Onto your head if you're not careful.

I've read that leech bites do not hurt because the creatures release an anesthetic when they sink their teeth into you. But I firmly believe that the person who wrote that has never had a leech between his toes. They gorge themselves on your blood, seeking to consume more than three times their weight. In just one sitting, a leech is able to absorb enough blood to sustain itself for several months. Some misguided people have attempted to remove leeches by burning them with a cigarette; applying mosquito repellent, shampoo, or salt; or pulling at them. This, you should know, can result in the leech regurgitating blood into your wound and causing an infection much worse than the bite itself. Also, should a leech invade an orifice like your nose, you have a more serious problem, since it will expand as it fills with blood. I saw one drop from a guide's nose straight into his oatmeal. It could have been worse, though. If it had gotten stuck, he would have had to puncture the leech with a sharp object.

At this point in the expedition, I was ready to stab myself with a sharp object. My only hope was the National Geographic photographer who was supposed to be joining us soon and bringing professional traps. Our improvised traps were not doing the job. Without the real ones, I was genuinely afraid this expedition would be a complete failure. And I could not have it fail. Far too much was at stake.

With no mouse lemurs and not much else to do, I checked the gear and realized that something else was missing. I turned to Angelo and asked, "What's the smallest scale we have?" No answer, just a blank stare. That told me everything. The guides had also left behind the small scientific scale we'd need to weigh a mouse lemur—if we ever found one. With only large scales, I wouldn't be able to confirm that this new primate species was the world's smallest of the small. Usually calm and level headed, I now lost my cool. "There are just too many screw-ups on this trip! You guys can't just wait until we are in the field to tell me these things. You pack for every trip with great attention to detail, and yet here we've come out specifically for mouse lemurs, and you don't bring traps or scales!" The team looked at me in shock. Until now, they had only known Mireya the bubbly cheerleader. They had just met Mireya the fiery Cuban.

I stormed off angrily to my tent, already feeling guilty for yelling. Fact is, it was my fault. I should have double-checked the gear. I would apologize to the team for losing my temper, but the heat in the tropics was getting to me and first I had to cool off. I headed to the stream and sat underneath the waterfall, hoping to wash away these problems. But even a luxurious, tropical waterfall didn't help. I still felt terrible.

Not helping matters, the photographer was supposed to have arrived a day ago but hadn't yet. There was, of course, no way to communicate from here, and I was beginning to wonder if he was coming at all. The film crew had little else to film than streams of water. It reminded me of the line in the King Kong movie, "You know what it's like to try and make a film in the rainy season: months gone, money wasted, and nothing to show for it." I could relate.

Then, as if descending from the heavens, I heard, "Dr. Livingstone, I presume? Do you know where a guy can get a beer around here?" A soaking-wet Mark Thiessen, the National Geographic photographer I was waiting for, had finally arrived. With him was Conservation International president and my friend, Russ Mittermeier. Russ had supported my research since my first expedition to Madagascar. I was thrilled he'd come. If we were ever able to prove our new species, it was my plan to name it after him.

Russ had barely said hello when I noticed something moving in his eye. It was a leech. Removing it, I said, "Welcome to our camp. You wanted to see a leech?" Russ took it, rolled it into a little ball, and flicked it away. Not very conservation minded, I joked, but leeches aren't particularly endangered.

Now there was only one thing I wanted to know: How many traps had they brought? Tearing through their boxes, I spotted the shiny metal. Five traps. Better than nothing. I had counted on having a lot more than five but was relieved to have any at all. Now we just had to put out some bananas, set the traps up, and cross our fingers that a mouse lemur would go for one.

By candlelight, Russ and I talked about the importance of properly documenting this new species. A new species would attract the world's attention and was key to getting extra protection for the area. He said, "I think that with President Ravalomanana, who is really excited about conservation and seems to get it, there is real opportunity to turn the tide here and develop a whole new approach." With that, the rain finally stopped. I took it as a good omen. Perhaps more than traps, Russ had brought luck. We finished our Malagasy dinner of rice and beans and went looking for eye shine. Because mouse lemurs are so quiet, we rely on the reflection of their eyes in the flashlights to find them. Like house cats, they have tapetum lucium, a reflective layer over their eyes that causes them to appear to glow in the dark.

Under the forest canopy the only light that shone at first was from our headlamps and flashlights. Then, suddenly, glowing coals stared back at us. A mouse lemur! From about 18 feet up in the tree it looked right at us, holding perfectly still. Unfortunately, it was on the other side of a leech-infested swamp.

The coolest part was that this experience was an absolute first—the sighting of a new lemur species in the wild (by scientific observers, anyway). I was pretty confident that we had a good chance of catching the little guy in the tree. Since the rain had stopped, it seemed to me it might be hungry for some yummy banana. We set the trap right beneath its tree. Soon the adrenaline started wearing off, and we began to feel the leeches biting us. Yeah, the "painless" ones.

In the morning, Russ and I eagerly revisited the swamp, praying that our mouse lemur had found its way into the trap. The trap was closed! Russ's eyes shone with childlike excitement. Slowly, I peeked in. Fruit flies, damn it. The trap had caught nothing but fruit flies. But discouraging as it was to find another empty trap, we had to keep trying. I restocked the traps and crossed my fingers that the next morning our luck would change. Now I felt like the child, pouting.

We had only one more night to catch a mouse lemur. It was time we tried our own special brand of Malagasy magic.

The Malagasy team began singing a traditional folk song to call on the mouse lemurs. Loosely translated, the lyrics went, "Tomorrow we're going to find lots of mouse lemurs . . . there will be two in every trap." Around the campfire, we clapped and sang on into another rainy evening, and with heavy lids and heart I slipped into my tent and fell asleep.

During the night it cleared up, and my team, still feeling bad about all the forgotten equipment, headed out to look.

In my sleep, I thought I heard Angelo call, "Mireya, we saw a mouse lemur over there and are keeping a light on it. Hurry!" What a great dream. Then my tent started shaking. It was Angelo! I couldn't get out of my tent fast enough; Angelo had already taken off into the trees. Half asleep in the darkness, I yelled, "*Angelo*! Where are you?" I followed the team's faint voices just the other side of the forest. There, just a few feet above the ground on a branch, were those burning coals.

The guys and I began pulling back the trees surrounding the mouse lemur, essentially isolating the tree it sat on. This could be our last opportunity to capture this little lemur, and we were leaving nothing to chance.

We were going to try to catch it by hand.

I stood motionless as Laude, the tallest guy on the team, moved in. Even in the darkness I could see his hand shaking. Everyone held his breath. Slowly, we pulled the branch down toward Laude, and with one swift motion his large hand shot up and engulfed the lemur.

"He got it!" I fell to my knees and raised my arms to the heavens, saying, "Thank you, thank you, thank you." Laude and the other team members smiled from ear to ear. My anger completely forgotten, we high-fived and hugged. I then went over and gently took the lemur. He was beautiful. His huge eyes were incredibly wide and alert, and his tiny hand gripped my finger.

My little King Kong was at long last in my palm.

It was too late to begin taking blood and measurements; we would have to wait until morning. That night I would be sharing a tent with a mouse lemur. I hoped he didn't mind the mess.

The next part of the story will be news even to my producer. When I parted with the film crew that night, I placed the mouse lemur in a little mesh sack. Lying in my tent staring at the little guy, curiosity got the better of me. Who could resist that little face? I carefully took him out of the bag and held him close. But with a sudden jump the mouse lemur was loose in my tent, and for the next few hours I couldn't find him. What the hell was I going to tell the film crew?!

I looked in my sleeping bag, inside my backpack, and through every square inch of the tent, but he was nowhere to be seen. I worried that I might squash him if I didn't sit still. Morning came, and Brian stood at the opening of my tent asking if I was ready. "I'll be right out," I whispered. Then out of the corner of my eye I spotted my boots. I always keep them inside for fear of scorpions. They were the one place I hadn't searched. Nestled into the toe of my boot was the world's smallest primate. Thankfully, I hadn't tried to put them on before looking.

That morning we would turn our little beauty into the most photographed and documented mouse lemur in history (we weighed him using a scale we'd bought earlier in one of the markets in Sambava). And advance science in the process.

Finding the tiny, two-ounce creature was only the beginning. Our search was over, but my mission was not. Now that I had proof positive of this mouse lemur's existence, I had to take steps to make sure it continued to exist. That meant a journey from the jungle to the corridors of political power.

I managed to secure a meeting with the prime minister of Madagascar. I sat in the lobby of Madagascar's equivalent of the White House nervously looking at my watch. The butter-flies in my stomach were doing somersaults. Finally, the door to his office opened, and out came a gentle-looking man wearing a gray suit. When I walked into his office, I noticed wildlife pictures on the walls and *National Geographic* magazines and conservation books on the coffee table. Those were good signs.

I introduced myself and told him about our discovery. I sounded like a giddy girl. I showed him photographs of the new species and a map indicating where it was found. He was engaged, responsive, and nearly as excited as I was. I raised the possibility of creating a national park in the area, and to my great surprise, he answered, "We can do it." At first he said it in French, and I wondered if I'd understood him correctly. So he repeated it in English and added, "We'll get the process started." I was blown away. Obviously, the process is a lengthy one, so sensing the urgency of the situation, he said, "What do you need us to do tomorrow?" I couldn't believe my ears!

Governments don't usually see urgency. Even a span of months might be too late for this forest. If we acted quickly, the new primate would help save the home of thousands of endangered animals. Later, the government pledged to triple the nation's total protected area to 6 million hectares (14.8 million acres).

This tiny little animal became a huge ambassador for all wild things in Madagascar. And in a twist on the old story, a virtual Fay Wray had saved King Kong.

[*nine*]

Sharks, Squid Ink, and a Frying Pan

FEBRUARY 8, 2003: Full of adrenaline, I jumped in, hoping for the best while also thinking about the worst. But the sharks were on their best behavior. That is to say, they didn't eat me. In reality, humans are not the preferred prey item of the great white shark. I realize, too, that sharks get a bad rap from the media and movies, but as dozens of these huge creatures, no smaller than pickup trucks, with razor-sharp teeth as long as my pinky finger, circled around me, all rationale went out the window.

By the time I was offered a staff position at National Geographic as a wildlife correspondent, I had broken in several pairs of boots and become quite good with a machete. As much as I loved my primates, I was excited to get my feet wet working with other animals. As it turned out, my feet along with the rest of my body would get very wet. I had just finished a project in Congo and was sitting in my office at NG headquarters, when I was handed a film proposal that began with the lines, "Thirty years ago waters boiled and turned red with blood. One man lost his life, another barely escaped." I probably should have quit reading, but I went on. "Then it grew quiet. For three decades, the crystal waters of Guadalupe Island have been peaceful, and despite constant surveillance, rarely since then have Great White sharks patrolled the shores." It sounded like a bad sci-fi thriller, but I didn't know any better than to be intrigued. I suddenly noticed the title, "Killers: Up Close! With an Explorer in the Water." Good God, did they mean me? I was really hoping they didn't.

They meant me.

I would soon have to swim surrounded by man- (and, I have to assume, woman-) eating sharks. Yes, my next three National Geographic assignments were offshore.

After a quick detour to Seattle to check out some other sharks that were behaving oddly, the film crew and I would be heading to Guadalupe Island, Mexico, to dive with 1,800-pound great whites. I couldn't help but think of all the times I'd go to the beach as a little girl only to find that it had been closed due to sharks migrating along the coast. This is a common occurrence in South Florida, and growing up as part of the *Jaws* generation, I had the utmost respect for, if not outright fear of, what lurked in the deep waters.

We would be filming the sharks of Guadalupe because of the inordinately high aggression they'd recently been displaying, reportedly attacking local fishermen and because they were coming in closer to shore. I wouldn't tell my mom. The third assignment involved a large, tentacled sea creature with a razor-sharp beak, referred to as "devil of the deep," and thought to be a man-killer. I wouldn't tell my mom about that, either.

Despite the potential dangers hyped in the film proposal, I had no trouble agreeing to the projects. I'd always loved the ocean and had logged many hours underwater studying the colorful fish, mind-blowing anemones, and magnificent—not to mention increasingly rare—coral reefs on the ocean floor. As Her Royal Deepness Sylvia Earle, the famed oceanographer, has often reminded me, approximately 71 percent of the Earth's surface is covered by ocean, and we have a very limited understanding of it. Instead of Earth, "Ocean" would be a more appropriate name for our planet.

So off to Planet Ocean I went. Joining me on this underwater adventure would be extreme underwater cameraman Bob Cranston. Tall, lean, and sporting glasses, Bob looks more like an accountant than an underwater adventurer. But the man is fearless and, with thousands of dives under his belt, he's seen just about everything below the ocean surface. The one thing he wished he had not seen was the body of his idol, Al Schneppershoff. Bob's longtime friend was the guy eaten alive by a great white shark off Guadalupe Island, our destination.

In 1973, Al was hunting tuna and planning to become the next champion of the popular sport. But the hunter had become the hunted. He was killed exactly 30 years to the day we'd be diving in the very same waters. It was clear from talking to Bob that he was haunted by memories and frustrated by the decades-long disappearance of these "demons." He had never been free of the past. Now, for reasons unknown, the sharks were back here in full force. Bob wanted to find out why.

Before heading to Mexico to film the great whites, we would first dive into the frigid waters of Seattle, where four decades ago six-gill sharks had suddenly started hunting at night in shallow waters. Until then, they had remained unseen, in depths where humans could not venture. With small, fluorescent green eyes and black pupils, six-gills (most sharks have five gills) can grow to a length of 18 feet. Usually slow and sluggish, they are capable of bursts of high speed when chasing prey. These carnivorous predators feed mostly on cephalopods, crustaceans, fish, rays, and some marine mammals. They are unchanged from the Jurassic period, when their ancestors prowled the murky bottoms of the seas. Before 1966, the year they began emerging from the depths, no adult six-gill had ever in recorded history been seen by humans. What could be causing these feared predators to change their habits after millions of years? Bob and I hatched a scheme to find out whether their hunting preferences had adapted over the past four decades. Until now they had been thought unreceptive to the kind of bait that attracts more commonly seen sharks like great whites. Our plan was to chum the waters (with the same kind of bait) where the creatures were known to swim. It was kind of like giving broccoli to kids who would eat it only if they were starving. If they took the bait, we would have proof that they indeed had moved closer to shore in search of food. What forces were sending these giant animals to forage in the shallows? Was it this same impetus that explained the great white's recent behavior? The propensity of six-gills to emerge only at night, unlike great whites, had given humans little opportunity for contact. No one knew what the result of such an encounter might be.

We would be diving at night, when the six-gills undertake their vertical migration up to the shallower waters. The water was freezing despite my dry suit. Diving in a dry suit, which allows for better insulation, is completely different from diving in a light wet suit, as it affects buoyancy. I'm a warm-weather Florida girl who learned to dive wearing nothing more than a two-piece bathing suit and fins, so even in a warm dry suit I was very cold. My lips turned purple, but that wasn't the scary part: I had never before gone on a night dive.

For those of you who have never been diving, the depths of the ocean feel like another planet. In this case, I would descend into one where someone had turned off the lights. With giant underwater lamps, we made our way slowly down. In the black depths the six-gill shark was a successful recluse. Our visibility was extremely poor, and we could barely make out the sharks swimming only dozens of feet in front of us. Suddenly, I lost my bearings and didn't know if I was going up or down; the little light particles in the water glowing from our lamps made me dizzy. I became badly disoriented. Fortunately, Bob's assistant, an experienced safety diver, was nearby, and I was able to signal him that something was wrong. Slowly, he helped me make my way back to shore. Solving the mystery of the six-gill sharks would have to await another day. Disheartened that I'd had such a poor dive, I was happy to think that great whites made their living during the day and lived in warmer waters.

There is no question but that the sight of a great white shark sends most people into a panic. At first mention of this project, I, too, feared the jaws of these supreme predators. But as a scientist I know what I didn't know as a little girl. Great whites are shrouded in myth, unfairly portrayed as villains and man-eating monsters. *Jaws* did a terrible disservice to great whites; in actuality, the film was based not on the habits of great whites but on the aggressive and unpredictable behavior of bull sharks. A combination of popular movies and media stories about shark attacks created a universal fear of these toothy eating machines. What I didn't know as a little girl was that the dangers posed by sharks to humans are way overstated. *Globally*, sharks kill only about ten people each year. Very rarely do great whites attack humans. You're at least ten times more likely to die under the clumsy feet of ordinary cows, which fatally trample about 100 people a year in the U.S. alone.

These were the kind of arguments I used to convince myself I should be relieved to be filming sharks and not cows!

As I gathered my diving gear and prepared to head to Guadalupe Island, all my thoughts turned from sharks to packing bikinis. Let's face it, when I think of Mexico, I think of margaritas and Cabo. And if I'm going to be filmed being eaten by a shark, I might as well look good. What I didn't know was I'd spend the next month on the top bunk of a boat's very confined quarters with four other people,

My grandmother, Mima, along with thousands of other Cubans, was forced to "volunteer" cutting sugarcane in the early days of Castro's regime.

Compañeros del Ministerio del Interior y otras personas ayudan a una de las pasajeras de la MMM-Miami a bajar a la embarcación desde el espigón del puerto de Camarioca.

In 1965, at age 20, my mom made the news as she stepped onto a boat fleeing Cuba, the only home she had ever known.

Here I am with my three mothers and grandfather. Left to right: Aunt Ica, Pipo, Mami, and Mima. I am wearing a Snow White dress Mima made me for my birthday.

I proudly wore the nurse's outfit Mima made for kindergarten career day. But it was not to be.

This was my chicken, Maggie, a beloved member of the large menagerie that shared our Miami house. I bet she thought my orange socks were cool.

On this day I was a beach babe on the lookout for sharks, though usually I ran around with a net catching hermit crabs or anything that swam into it.

Game day was the payoff for hours of grueling cheerleading practice. Nothing beat standing on the field listening to thousands of screaming fans—or hearing the national anthem performed.

We Miami Dolphins cheerleaders were a wild bunch with big hair. Several of the girls remain among my closest friends. But we've straightened our hair. I am on the right, second from the top.

I got to play with a capuchin monkey on my first expedition, to Guyana's Amazon, in May 1996. From then on, I have never stopped dreaming of my next adventure.

A seemingly magical force drew me to the edge of Guyana's spectacular Kaieteur waterfall and made me want to spread my wings and fly.

Dr. Patricia Wright and I took the first ever measurements and genetic samples from endangered silky sifakas in Madagascar's Marojejy National Park. Later I posed with Pat, my mentor and friend, and two silky sifakas.

When I first read about the black Perrier's sifaka, an inhabitant of Madagascar's Analamera Special Reserve, it had scarcely been studied and there were no photos. The genetic samples we obtained confirmed it as a distinct lemur species.

No one said expeditions were easy, especially in Madagascar, where heavy rains often wash out roads. If I pretend to be taking this picture, maybe I won't have to push.

Who knew La Macarena would be such a hit among the Congo BaAka?

Standing over the severed hands of murdered Congo gorillas marked one of the worst days of my life. It's hard to believe tourists buy them to use as ashtrays.

You should've seen the faces of the human patients as we pushed a gurney carrying this leopard—en route to a "cat scan"—down the halls of the Namibia hospital.

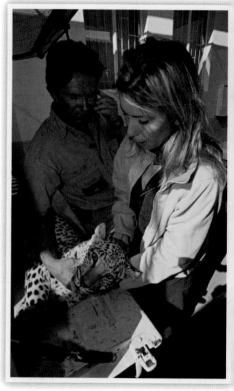

Capturing a giraffe here on the Namibia plain is incredibly intense. I was extremely relieved when the tranquilizer wore off and the giraffe began rising to its feet.

Great missing you, always! See you soon, I hope. Louis Sarno

To my surprise, I encountered an American, Pygmy music aficionado Louis Sarno, living in a remote BaAka village in the Congo. A kind soul with an adventurous spirit, he could be called the world's tallest Pygmy with a Jersey accent.

Even with hundreds of sweat bees hovering— not even my eyelids are immune—the gorilla in my sight keeps me smiling.

Leopards can be killing machines, but this one is like a large house cat.

My big, small discovery in 2001. The mouse lemur of northeastern Madagascar is the world's smallest primate. If he looks a little spacey, it's due to the tranquilizer, not my squeezing.

Education is key for conservation, and it's vitally important the locals be involved—especially the kids, who will inherit this land and these animals. Many children in Madagascar have never seen a lemur, even though lemurs are only found there.

On the side of Mount Roraima, a *tepui,* or tabletop mountain, in Guyana. I had never spent the night with a more gorgeous view. It was also the only time I lay suspended above the clouds with a small pin holding up my tent.

My grin atop Mount Roraima comes from having survived the climb and near starvation. We found a spectacular landscape up there—black, forbidding, primeval.

This worm, found on Mount Roraima and weighing a third of a pound, is the biggest I have ever seen. Can you imagine the fish you could catch with this thing?

I have yet to meet kids, such as these in an Amerindian village in Guyana, who don't love to pose for the camera.

Don't let the cage fool you on this expedition to study great white sharks in Baja California. The opening was wide enough for the shark to swim in but not for it to turn and swim out. See why I needed a frying pan?

One of the most epic journeys of my life— a 1,000-mile expedition across Tanzania for the 2009 reality show *Expedition Africa*— began on this ancient boat, which sailed us from Zanzibar to Tanzania.

Here I am at one of our Tanzania camps. It's the simple moments in the bush—savoring a cup of tea, watching wildlife, or basking in the African sun—that I miss most when I'm back in "civilization."

The two Maasai warriors who accompanied us for protection, Rafael and Lesordo, would stay up well into the night, keeping watch for lions and other predators.

Seems more often than not we found ourselves trudging through swamps, trying to avoid the crocodiles in the tall grasses.

This picture is classic. Just look at the faces on these guys as they argue. Kevin's jaw is clenched and his arms are crossed, Benedict is waving his hands in frustration, and Pasquale is staring at the ground contemplating murder. Also look at the Maasai sitting patiently, waiting for them to quit bickering.

My most cherished memory of the trek across Tanzania is captured here—time spent with Maasai tribesmen and Benedict Allen, modern-day Indiana Jones and kindred spirit.

This was my favorite part of the day. The African sun is starting to set, and after many hours of trekking, we would soon set up camp for the night.

I'm clinging to Rafael, dreading our goodbye. He gave me his warrior shield, which now hangs in my living room.

My favorite team picture. This was taken the moment we finally arrived at the very spot—in Ujiji in modern-day Tanzania—that Stanley shook hands with Livingstone. We had come a long way. Left to right: Benedict, me, Pasquale, and Kevin.

Watching gorillas can sometimes feel voyeuristic. Here I am observing the male silverback Kingo in the northern Congo jungle.

Kingo and his son, Ekende, share a moment.

Coming full circle: 1978 and 2010

So excited, nervous, thrilled, and terrified

I married my Tarzan, Roland. But this Tarzan wears suits. And he's German.

My little newborn monkey, Emma. It was love at first sight.

Just call me Dr. Mommy!

Roland is an amazing father. I can go off deep into the jungle knowing my girls are in the best hands.

My wild life . . . happily ever after

including a snorer, retching my guts out from seasickness. The only time I was not seasick during this expedition was when I was actually in the water. This was no umbrella-drink vacation.

I was met at the airport by the assistant producer, who was waving from behind the fence wearing a large Mexican sombrero and several local necklaces and holding a Corona in each hand. He had not been able to sign for the car because he was slightly inebriated, but they had let him drive off with it, anyway. I offered to drive us to the hotel, where we would meet up with the rest of the crew.

The next day our journey to the sharks began with a 12-hour boat ride to scout the remote cove where as many as 20 great whites had been spotted from the air. Guadalupe Island is a wild, harsh, forbidding place. Located 200 miles off Mexico's coast, it's a starkly scenic collection of cinder cones, ridges, and dramatic offshore rocks. The sea can be flat calm or brutally rough. This remote island is host to a large number of northern elephant seals, California sea lions, and Steller sea lions, all of which inhabit Guadalupe year round.

It was the second group, California sea lions, that raised the question of why these sharks were coming closer to shore. Hundreds of them frolic on the rocks and in the waters off Guadalupe Island, and they're usually the sharks' first choice of prey. So why were these sharks congregating in shallow water and not feeding on their usual diet of sea lions? Bob was no scientist, but he had an interesting theory. He believed that the sharks were after tuna, a somewhat bizarre hypothesis since tuna swim at about 40 miles per hour and are the fastest creatures in the sea. Even a determined great white would have a tough time catching one tuna, let alone enough to satisfy its enormous appetite.

While Bob surveyed the water conditions, I spoke to Terry Ingram, Al Schneppershoff's spearfishing buddy, who in exactly the same spot a year to the month after his friend was killed barely survived an attack by the same bad shark. Terry explained how Guadalupe Island used to be known for the biggest fish around, which is why the participants in his sport held their competitions here. Thirty years before, large schools of tuna were easily and frequently hunted by the Bottom Scratchers Dive Club, which both men belonged to. Yes, the Bottom Scratchers. The tuna disappeared, perhaps due to overfishing, at the same time the sharks vanished, and now that the tuna were back in numbers, the sharks were, too, lending credence to Bob's theory.

But it was this next piece of information that sent chills down my spine. It seemed that no one knew exactly how long these predator sharks lived, but some scientists had speculated it could be as long as 40 years. According to eyewitnesses, and Terry is one of them, the shark that attacked both him and Al was relatively small for its species, about 12 feet long, probably a young one. This meant that the rare man-eater might still be among the school of sharks we'd be diving with. The chilling part is that we would be filming on the exact day of the fatal attack, which also happened to be my birthday.

Bob and I began preparing our gear. He was diving with a re-breather instead of scuba (acronym for self-contained underwater breathing apparatus). A re-breather recycles exhaled breaths and allows a diver to spend up to 11 hours underwater. It has an added advantage in that it emits no exhaust of bubbles, thus not scaring away the tuna. Having more tuna swim nearby would attract more sharks. If the sharks became overly aggressive, and there's a good chance they would around the tuna, Bob would need to wait unobtrusively on the bottom until they left the area. Too rapid an ascent, especially with a re-breather, risks compression sickness.

Underwater visibility was close to 100 feet, and the sun was just peaking over the barren hills of Guadalupe Island. Bob declared the visibility good enough for a test dive. As far as we could tell, the "monster" shark was not around, but at least six good-size sharks circled our boat, and it was anyone's guess how many remained unseen. As most people know, it's not the shark you see that you need to worry about, it's the shark you don't see.

We had a short safety briefing during which Bob handed me a frying pan. At first I thought it was a joke. My next thought was that it was a weapon. Turns out, it was to bang on the cage we'd be descending in. The metal box offered a very false sense of security. To begin with, I would still have to swim for at least 20 minutes among the sharks before I could reach the cage, which was submerged far below the boat (we didn't have the mechanical apparatus to get in the cage and then have it lowered). They'd be the longest 20 minutes of my life. To make matters worse, one side of the cage was open so that the camera could get good shots of the sharks as they swam by. This meant that a shark could also swim right into the cage. More worrisome than a shark coming in was its inability to get out of the small cage, meaning I'd be in a cage with a stuck, pissed-off shark. Awesome.

Despite knowing how exaggerated the danger factor is, there was something very eerie, not to mention terrifying, about jumping into the water with aggressive great whites, in the exact place someone had been killed three decades before, on the very day I was born. Nevertheless, clutching my frying pan, I jumped in and, with my heart pounding out of my chest, began swimming like crazy for the cage.

But as I swam past the sharks, my fear turned to awe. I couldn't help but notice the beautiful fluid motion with which their mammoth bodies pierced the water. They were graceful like ballerinas, menacing-looking ones with big teeth.

Once inside the cage, we began testing our equipment. You see, my job was not just to stand in the cage. I had the important role of keeping a constant lookout for sharks that might sneak up behind or beneath Bob while he was filming outside the cage. My breathing air was supplied from the surface and fed through an apparatus nicknamed a "hookah" that would allow me to communicate underwater. That meant I could breathe normally through my nose and also speak, keeping in constant contact with both Bob and surface support.

Bob slowly swam off, spinning into the blue. Between us swirled hundreds of tuna. Soon I could make out several curious, 12- to 14-foot adolescent sharks gliding toward Bob. I apprised him of the whereabouts of each as they appeared and then disappeared amid the sea of tuna. Their proximity to the tuna seemed to further support Bob's hypothesis, though their taste for these lightning-fast fish was still a mystery.

One of the sharks started swimming straight toward my cage, and my eyes became locked on his. Looking into the eyes of a shark is nothing like looking into the eyes of the gorillas I am used to. When you look into a gorilla's eyes, you can see there is thought, insight, and emotion. Looking into the eyes of a shark, I saw nothing but steely black circles attached to an eating machine. I felt foolish but grabbed the frying pan. The shark swam right up to the cage opening and took a quick bite at the metal bars. He then just as quickly turned and disappeared into the blue abyss.

While I watched my shark swim off, a "monster" shark appeared like a ghost ship. One look and Bob signaled his belief it was the one that had been haunting him. This wasn't just another predatory fish; this shark was colossal. As it swam toward me, growing ever larger, my heart rate doubled and my respiration sped. I gripped the frying pan. Everyone topside was on edge. The crew strained to see over the side of the boat, but Bob was too far away for them to tell what was going on. As best I could, I continued to give them a play-by-play account. "Holy crap!" I yelled into my helmet. "Do you see this? It makes Bob look like Raggedy Andy in a wet suit." Just then something caught the enormous eating machine's eye, and it started zeroing in. "Ummm," I said in one of my more brilliant microphoned moments, "I think Cujo just noticed Bob." The giant shark was becoming too interested in him for anyone's comfort. No one knows why a shark turns aggressive toward humans, but it may be that fishing and chumming waters make them confuse us with their food. It was time for Bob to head back to the boat—fast. But there was a major problem: The enormous shark was now between Bob and the boat. I let the crew know to lower the cage.

The boat crew manned the winch, and the cage descended deeper into the water. Still filming, Bob started a steady kick to safety. As he grabbed on to the cage, the great white circled slowly. The crewmen gradually lifted the cage, keeping the shark closely in sight. Not a moment too soon, they yanked us into the boat. Huge, angry jaws shot skyward as the immense predator hurled nearly half its body out of the water.

Bob had finally faced the shark that had given him nightmares and perhaps obtained some closure. I, on the other hand, now had fodder for nightmares of my own. What brought the sharks back up to shallow waters was still uncertain, though Bob's idea about the renewed presence of tuna made as much sense as anything.

We breathed a giant sigh of relief to have survived our encounter, but we weren't done yet. Sharks are not the only underwater giants with a reputation for bloodthirstiness. There are far lesser-known man-killers lurking in the ocean's depth.

Next we would be going into deeper waters to film the giant Humboldt squid.

These extraterrestrial-looking sea creatures have powerful arms and tentacles, excellent underwater vision, and razor-sharp beaks that easily tear through the flesh of their prey. The elusive Humboldt, or jumbo, squid have a reputation so fearsome that they have earned the nicknames "devils of the deep" and "red devils." They are also known to eat each other, at least when one squid is caught on a fishing line. Such cannibalistic behavior has fueled the squid's reputation.

Finally back on dry land, the film crew and I headed to the eastern side of the Sea of Cortés. Bob and I met up with William Gilly in Guaymas, a port in Mexico's state of Sonora. To "Gilly," a biology professor at Stanford University, the mysterious squid, which can reach six feet in length, is a beautiful sea creature that provides important ecological clues. Gilly had studied the biology and behavior of the Humboldt squid for more than two decades, tagging them in the Gulf of California as part of a larger study of their movements in the Pacific Ocean. But very little had been learned about them, as these squid spend 95 percent of their lives at depths of 660 to 2,300 feet, well beyond those safely penetrated with scuba gear. They may be elusive, but they're not rare. Gilly estimated that ten million squid may be living in a 25-square-mile area outside Santa Rosalia, Mexico. At night the squid are known to rise from inaccessible depths to depths that are accessible but dangerous for divers. Bob and I would go in search of them. I couldn't wait to see one. Well, I could . . . but the prospect had my juices flowing.

For the first few days I spent time around the fishing villages on the Sea of Cortés. One of the benefits of my job is that I sometimes get to play with the local kids, so while Bob made arrangements for the boat, I watched another Bob get massacred. Armed with a Sponge Bob piñata, I made lots of little friends instantly. A little girl cracked open his head on her third strike. It was brutal, but the candy was a huge hit.

I hired a local fisherman with a beat-up pickup truck to take me around to the villages. I noticed the driver had a framed picture of Jesus Christ on his dashboard and said a little prayer every time he attempted to start the car. I needed to talk to him about the legendary sea monsters I would soon be pursuing, so I prayed with him. Although I'm sure my Cuban accent sounded foreign to him, we spoke Spanish easily together, and it helped me gain his trust.

The fisherman described how every night hundreds of Mexican fishermen nicknamed *pangueros* head out to the rough seas in *pangas,* small skiffs, to fish for the jumbo squid. It's no easy task. The catch is heavy, weighing in at more than 100 pounds, and every squid must be caught on a hand line. But the harvest is lucrative—the squid are sent to Japan, where they are a delicacy—and very important to the local economy. Livelihoods depend on the catch. Each boat, manned by two or three fishermen, typically brings back a metric ton (2,200 pounds) of squid every night. Fathers pass down their knowledge of how to catch them to their sons. The fisherman described how these giant creatures appear like ghosts up and down the Pacific coast and then just disappear. Fishermen sometimes fall overboard and are dragged down into the depths. Many are so scared of the squid they won't even eat them.

In every village I was warned by the local fishermen, "Whatever you do, don't fall in the water. They eat each other, and they will eat you." Who knew calamari could be so aggressive?

One of the fishermen offered to take me out on his boat to see if I could catch a squid, even though during the day it would be unlikely. Never one to turn down a challenge, I accepted. After so many tales about these alleged maneaters, I was morbidly curious to see them firsthand. The next morning before the sun was up I helped bail out a panga on the Sea of Cortés. Then we spent five long hours without so much as a squid trace. The waters were rough, and I was feeling seasick. All I wanted to do was get to dry land and lie down. We were about to head back when one of the men announced there was a squid on the line. Ironically, it was the one-eyed man who spotted it; he had lost his eye from a hook on a line cast from one of these small boats. My hopes of getting off this rocking death trap were diminishing. Feeling a pale shade of green, I grabbed on to the line and began pulling the wretched squid in. I pulled and pulled, my arms getting sorer and sorer. I was at it for 20 minutes. They say these jumbo squid weigh 100 pounds, but I was pretty sure the one on my line weighed closer to a ton. Leaning over the edge of the panga, hanging on to this heavy creature, I tried my damnedest not to fall over. More than a half hour later I had it on board. It was massive—at least five feet long and 70 pounds—slimy, and as alien-looking as anything you will see in this world. I was very happy to release it back into the sea.

After a day back on land, it was time to head out again. Gilly had spent the last several days with the fishermen, too, tagging more than 150 squid each day, falling only 4 short of his goal of 1,000. Listening to us talk about our plans to swim with the red devils, the boat captain Bob had hired didn't mince words. He looked at me and Bob and the crew and said, "Ustedes todos estan locos." I translated it for the crazy gringos. But Gilly insisted that the squid's ruthless reputation was unwarranted. "I've been snorkeling with them at night in just shorts and T-shirt," he said. "The squid would swim up to the surface, reach out their arms, and gently touch my extended hand. To meet them like this and shake hands was truly amazing." Gilly could get quite emotional talking about his beloved squid and had been known to shed a tear or two, a sight that made the film crew giggle.

The captain strongly disagreed with Gilly's emotional portrayal of the creatures and said he'd personally witnessed them pull several fishermen to their deaths. He described how they can propel themselves up to more than three times the speed of an Olympic swimmer; a human didn't stand a chance. He described how one squid would pull the man down and drown him, and then several more would join in the ambush and then eat the body. I was beginning to think I'd been better off with the great whites.

That night, several miles out in the ocean, the water was again rough. The plan was for Bob to jump in first and dive down to the dangerous depths. I would feed the electrical cord for the lights and wait until a jumbo squid ascended to shallower depths. Then I, too, would get into the water. We were using red lights, so as to not startle the squid with bright, white light. Underwater the squid themselves flash red on and off. Perhaps they would confuse us as one of their own. Why they flash, like most of their habits, is still a mystery to science. Some scientists speculate that it's a form of communication. Others argue that the flashing behavior might serve to confuse a lurking predator whale.

I was excited, but no one was as keyed up as Gilly. Despite having studied them for more than 20 years, he had never been deep-diving with these animals, and most of the behavior we would document he'd never seen. Bob's camera would become Gilly's eyes underwater. Bob jumped in and before long, I got the OK from him to dive in. In the dark waters only a few feet away from me swam both the weirdest and the most beautiful creatures I had ever seen. Their long bodies lit up and changed colors, like a spectacular underwater light show. I was transfixed by their movement, their long tentacles flowing gently through the water. Lethal and beautiful at the same time, they were hypnotic to watch.

At first it seemed the squid were wary of the lights. I was beginning to think that their aggressive reputation was undeserved and if anything they were shy at a distance. But curiosity soon got the better of them, and one of them went for the light, then the camera, then Bob's mask. Soon Bob was surrounded. I remembered his words topside, "You have to let them know you are big and bad, and they will have a fight on their hands if they don't back off." Another of the squid began spurting ink. With his camera Bob began pushing the attacker away, his free hand disengaging a tentacle from his mask. It quickly backed off. With bated breath I realized that as quickly as it began, the drama was over.

Heading back to shore, I couldn't wait to get out of my wet suit and back into my pink boots. The ocean is a mysterious and wondrous place, which I love and respect. We know more about other planets than we do about what lies beneath our amazing seas. I felt privileged to have spent time with these mystifying sea predators. But I had come to the realization that I am most comfortable on land, on my feet back in the jungles of our cute, closely related cousins. Gorillas I can read. Red devils and sharks . . . not so much.

ten

My Fear of Heights Conquered (Sort Of)

APRIL 1, 2003: Today marks the beginning of the last two weeks of this expedition. It is the most rugged and difficult journey I have ever done. After a grueling nine-hour trek, we set up camp and went fishing, as we are nearly out of food. My legs are covered in blistering red sores, most of them now becoming black scabs. Seems the antibiotic is finally working. But waking up on the ledge that sits high on the tepui's wall over a green abyss makes it all worth it. Sitting here above the clouds, never have I witnessed a more amazing sunrise.

A number of early explorers spoke of mysterious mountains that thrust skyward over South America's dense jungle. The mountaintops appeared like islands in the sky. Their descriptions inspired Sir Arthur Conan Doyle to write *The Lost World*, a novel set in an isolated place where dinosaurs and other prehistoric animals existed. The dinosaurs were fiction. But the mountains are real, and the present-day Guyana natives are superstitiously scared of them. It was in this remote, trackless, virtually unexplored jungle of southwestern Guyana that I would have one of my most memorable extreme expeditions.

And, yes, Guyana is where I almost died years before. History would repeat itself.

Our team's mission was both high risk and high return. At National Geographic headquarters, the producer Peter Getzels, an American with a British accent that seemed to fade in and out, sold me on the idea almost instantly. He pointed to the high probability of discovering new species, and that is always exciting. He said the place we were going was a place few people have been, and though we can locate it on a map, that doesn't mean we'd find it. Mysterious . . . I liked it. He also explained that several other expeditions had set out to survey the area and failed. We would be the first to explore and collect specimens. It sounded like a challenge, and I've never met a challenge I didn't like. But then he warned me that the expedition would include not only real science but also severe rock climbing. Hold the horses. "Severe rock climbing?" As in hanging from the side of a cliff wall thousands of feet up? No, thanks.

I explained that I had never been rock climbing, much less *severe* rock climbing, a laughably tough technical grade. I was born and raised in Miami, where the tallest mountains are landfills. Even if I wanted to, I wouldn't have time to beef up my climbing skills before the expedition was on its way. But Peter insisted that I take a lesson at a climbing school in Maryland and then decide if I was up for it or not. I agreed. What I didn't mention is that I am scared to death of heights.

The explorer gene in me must have beaten out my fear, because before I knew it, I was on my way back to Guyana. Truth is, I could never turn down an expedition, even one that involved high altitudes. On the departing flight from Washington, D.C., the entire coach section was filled with Guyanese wearing jackets and ties. I couldn't believe my luck when the flight attendant offered to bump me and the crew to first class. Then I learned why. The plane was full of mourners heading home for a funeral, with the deceased peacefully resting in coach. It made for an eerie if not foreboding start.

In Guyana I was joined by biologist Bruce Means and herpetologist Jesus Rivas, as well as by two of America's best climbers, Mark Synnott and Jared Ogden, both highly experienced with extreme peaks. Our survey of these cliffs would almost certainly bring to light species completely new to science. But nothing worth doing is ever easy. If our search for undiscovered creatures was to yield results, we would have to tackle the dangers of extreme climbing and rappelling, both in our ascent of the *tepui* and our descent into the darkness of a giant sinkhole.

There are more than a hundred of these remote, high, sheer, flat-topped table mountains called tepuis. They are found in Venezuela, Brazil, Suriname, and Guyana, but they are not well mapped or well traveled. Their biological value lies in that they are some of the earth's oldest geological formations. The sandstone rock of these formations was laid down as sediment about 1.6 billion years ago, making them more than three times older than the earliest macroscopic fossils. Over

millennia, the vast sandstone plateaus were fractured by movement of the Earth's crust and eroded by the day-by-day effect
of water. Even by geological time the formations are ancient,
and very little is known about the plants and animals that live
on their cliff sides and in their sinkholes. Virtually untouched,
this ecosystem is a link to Earth's prehistoric past. The tepuis
are places where time has stood still, and the result is an aston-
ishing landscape not seen anywhere else on Earth.

Our goal was to reach the summit of Mount Roraima,
famously known as "the lost world." It is Guyana's tallest tepui.
On the border of Guyana, Brazil, and Venezuela, this massive
mountain extends for nearly nine miles and is three miles in
width. Its wide, flat summit tops out at 9,094 feet. I was psyched.

Our diverse crew met up in Georgetown, Guyana, and after
a short meeting with the country's forest ministry, loaded piles
of climbing gear and scientific equipment onto a rattletrap
prop plane. Bruce, Jesus, Peter, and I would fly to a remote airstrip, hike from there to the mountain, and then the climbers,
as well as cameraman John Catto, would join us by helicopter later in the expedition. The only helicopter in all of Guyana, it would be borrowed from the military. This would allow
Mark and Jared to do an aerial reconnaissance of the climbing
route, complete with GPS readings. Armed with that expertise, we scientists would pursue our exploration and collection of the species of flora and fauna that inhabit the vertical
world of Mount Roraima's prow. Several scientists, traveling
by helicopter, had studied the tepui summits, but no one had
studied the plant and animal life of the cliff sides themselves.

We landed on a tiny grass landing strip in the shadow of the tepui, at the edge of the jungle. We unloaded and trekked to an Amerindian village named Pipillipai, with a population of 670, and were greeted by the Akawaio tribesmen. Because this entire area was unexplored, only the local Amerindians would be able to find us a route to the mountain. Here we recruited numerous guides, 30 porters, and 13 trail cutters, who'd lead the way with machetes, hacking away obstacles in the path. It was a hard recruit because they'd have to commit to leaving their wives and children for well over a month. They also knew that it was a dangerous mission, not least because of the deadly and feared fer-de-lance.

Personally, I am not a fan of such big teams on an expedition. I feel responsible for more lives, and it is a surefire way to see fewer animals, as the noise made by the group sends them fleeing. But expeditions had failed in the past because of lack of food. The dilemma is the more food you bring, the more men you need to carry it, and the more food you need for those men, and so on. In this never-ending spiral, I nevertheless found myself hiring porters for the porters and more porters for those.

For the next six weeks we lived in hammocks, moving from camp to camp. The going was hard and slow from the outset. The trek was nothing short of jungle mountaineering. Although the route is not that steep by climbing standards, it was up a 70-degree jungle slope. We alternately grasped plants and bushes to haul ourselves up and with machetes hacked them out of the way. As we struggled along, we found tiny frogs; spectacular bromeliads, odd tropical plants that live on other plants; brightly colored and therefore almost certainly poisonous snakes; and some fearsome-looking insects. Some of these species appeared to be unknown.

The strain of the trek was beginning to take its toll. With every step and biting insect and the constant rainfall, I was understanding why most tepuis had yet to feel the tread of explorers' feet. Excited as I was to go into this lost world of tangled, twisted, and suffocating disorder to find the real Jurassic Park, the jungle was proving much tougher and more inhospitable than any of us had anticipated. In four days we had covered barely 20 miles.

Then one day, as if the going wasn't hard enough, an old cheerleading injury reared its ugly head. I had once badly sprained my ankle and now, weakened, it blew up to the size of a baseball. I couldn't let this slow the expedition down. I would have to keep pushing through the pain until we camped that night. Fortunately, night comes quickly in the jungle, and before I knew it I was lying in my hammock. I could hear Bruce wading around in murky water with a headlamp looking for frogs.

Mornings here could be gorgeous when the weather was clear. A brilliant light spilled through the mist and treetops, giving a glimpse of heaven. I had a good night's rest, and my ankle was feeling better. But the jungle was relentless, and it wasn't just the difficulty of the terrain. Bruce woke up that morning with a painful ball under his toes. A creature had burrowed in his foot. He also had swollen lymph nodes, which generally means an infection.

In the rain forest there are several organisms that can take up residence under your skin. I once had a botfly, for example, living in my arm. The area was sore and bumpy, but it was only when the botfly stuck its breathing tube out that I realized what it was. Burrowing worms, entozoa, are other pesky critters. They burrow into human skin causing a boil-like infection, which eventually breaks, leaving the head of the worm protruding. You can't pull it out, or the worm breaks in the body. These entozoa often grow to be ten feet long. Natives draw out a few inches per day, reeling them on sticks as they emerge.

In what can only be described as jungle surgery, I dissected Bruce's foot with my pocketknife. Having no training in this—other than having worn a nurse uniform as a kid—I peeled the skin back and used my tweezers to poke around, evoking a few grunts and a little scream from Bruce. I found the culprit. Bruce's painful ball wasn't a botfly or a worm but rather a burrowing flea that dug into his flesh and became distended with eggs. One flea turns into hundreds, and they all feed on blood. I had to be very careful removing the mother flea, so as not to unleash the eggs.

With one problem solved, we could move on, but we were hardly in the clear.

The original plan was for us to establish a base camp in the jungle, after which the climbing team would bring in additional gear and provisions for the ascent. But what we thought was a day's walk to the prow had taken a week. We couldn't communicate our position to Mark and Jared because the satellite phone wasn't working. We had no way of knowing if we were on course. When a cackley call finally went through, all we could tell them was that we were about three miles northeast of the prow, near a waterfall.

With the muddy soil, protruding roots, and nothing but a single green rope—which was starting to fray—to prevent a 60-foot fall, the climb to Roraima's base was treacherous. My journal entry noted that the trip "marks the most rugged and arduous expedition I have ever done." We trekked no less than eight hours a day, and as there was no water source nearby, we could not bathe. I had enough ailments to last me a lifetime. They included terrible stomach cramps, which I could only guess were caused by parasites, and unexplained puffed-up lips, which looked like bananas when I smiled. I took comfort in the idea that they were as swollen as Angelina Jolie's, though, alas, not as sexy. Worst of all, I had red, blistering sores covering my legs, source also unknown. Even the thought of having to put wet boots on for another five weeks was more than I could bear. To top it all off, our food supply was dwindling, and if we didn't meet up with the climbers— and our additional food supply—soon, this expedition would fail like the others.

Everyone was also dehydrated. We carried only enough water for the day, assuming we'd find some kind of stream along the way. Though everything was saturated with water, it was not drinkable. Bruce pointed out that the bromeliads that blanketed the ground were full of water. I dumped one into my bottle and shone my headlamp on it; the water was thick, soupy, and swarming with thousands of microscopic worms.

We kept trekking. Pinned to a tree was a note left by the trail cutters, who were farther ahead, advising us to continue on and camp by a waterfall. It also said to arrive before night-fall. But we weren't sure how much longer we had to walk to reach it. We sped up as much as we could. Hours later the jungle finally opened to a place where water had been flowing for millions of years, carving a gash in the landscape. There in the clearing alongside a river was one of the most stunning water-falls I'd ever seen. We had finally reached the base of Mount Roraima, "the mother of all waters."

I jumped into the river fully clothed, swam across to the waterfall, and had my shower.

As the second week dawned, we still hadn't linked up with the climbers. The blisters on my legs looked disgusting; weep-ing and oozing, they seemed to get worse by the minute. Our food supply was now dire. For several days we survived on nothing more than a meal a day. Then that ran out. At night I would eat a granola bar from a stash I kept secretly in my backpack, but eventually those too were gone. If the helicop-ter didn't arrive soon with the extra food, we'd need to start walking back, which would mean hiking with nothing to eat. I wouldn't be surprised if the porters mutinied and headed back without us or our gear. I'd seen it happen before.

We spent the day searching for animals. Bruce and I dug up some worms he thought might be new to science. We found another worm he said was an alien species. Introduced by European colonists, they had invaded this primal area. We also found huge spiders; some of the world's biggest inhabit these jungles. Biggest of all were the tarantulas, which seemed to be a dime a dozen. Bruce and I killed some time playing with these hairy and fearsome-looking creatures. Though Bruce was afraid of spiders, he's a biologist, so I think this was his therapy to get over it. He let the tarantula climb on his head. The Amerindians laughed hysterically. Bruce just looked nervous.

The laughter didn't last long.

Eldon, one of our porters, was laid up in his hammock. I touched his forehead, and it felt very hot. We suspected he had cerebral malaria, common in this area. We all realized that the mosquito that had bitten Eldon could infect any one of us. But he needed to be carried out, and time was working against him. More than ever we needed that helicopter.

It was a problem for all of us, but the expedition had to stay on course.

We sent the trail cutters ahead to continue working on the route. Then suddenly a weather front moved in. An awful sound came off the tepui and with it a huge spray inundated the camp. A massive storm caused the waterfall to roar, and its spray alone became a torrent. Jesus and I began stringing up tarps, but the wind quickly ripped them apart. Standing there sopping wet in what had been my last set of dry clothes, I thought, "This would never happen in an office." But I hate cubicles.

Bruce was so absorbed in photographing the frogs in his tent that he barely noticed it was slowly starting to float away. He came out, drenched and shivering, with an aluminum blanket draped over his shoulders, and said, "Last thing you want to do is drown in a tent." The river was rising and the camp flooding. The torrential downpour went on for more than 16 hours. It was the worst storm I had ever experienced.

That night Eldon took a turn for the worse. We also officially ran out of food. If the helicopter didn't manage to get in, we'd have to start walking back, storm or no storm. Also out of food, the trail cutters were stranded on the other side of the river. It was running rampant and had risen too high to cross without technical gear. Jesus had rope and a harness. He rigged a line, and the trail cutters began to cross. One false movement, and they would have been over and under and gone.

One by one, the guys held on to the line. Every one of them went under the current but still managed to pull his body across. Once they had all made it, we spread blue tarps and lit fires, hoping the climbers would spot us from the air. Unbeknownst to us our smoke signals were fruitless. There were little pockets of steam that looked like smoke signals coming up from the forest everywhere.

By then the rain had stopped, but the expedition still hung in the balance. I went to the edge of the river and noticed that one of the Amerindians had carved MIREYA'S FALLS into a boulder. I smiled. Then, suddenly, I heard a chopper.

The helicopter flew overhead and missed us again and again. It finally spotted the camp just as our hope was running out. The climbers were completely unaware of the drama that had been unfolding below them. We ran out to clear off the tarps. The entrance was perilous, to say the least. Bringing a chopper in there is extremely dangerous, as forceful downdrafts make holding it steady nearly impossible. There was also not much clearance for the rotors. Unable to land, the helicopter hovered low, and the climbers jumped out. Gear and food supplies were thrown off, scattered in every direction on the jungle floor. My hair flying in the wind, I exclaimed, "You boys sure know how to make an entrance!"

With ropes, we got Eldon onto the chopper before it pulled out. Sucked down by the same forces that made it impossible to land, it appeared as if it might not have enough power to lift out. As it ascended, it was repeatedly pulled down by gusts of wind. We watched in terror, but the winds finally died down and the chopper pulled out, lifting into the sky.

The climbers had not brought in as much food as we had hoped.

We struggled across the river, holding on to ropes, and the going just got harder. As the climb became steeper, the jungle closed in around Roraima's base, creeping up its sides as if it was trying to strangle the rock. Clinging to a rope, the four or five line cutters in front of us had to cut every branch to clear the path. Finally, we stood below the cliff we'd be exploring over the next couple of weeks. Mark, the most expert climber, led off, with Jared setting the ropes. For those two the climb was tough but not desperate. For me, it was a totally different story. In the two-hour class I took in Maryland, I'd climbed no more than 50 feet above a padded floor. Now I was going to do what most world-class climbers wouldn't. And, as I mentioned, I'm afraid of heights.

There were other risks. To be bitten or stung by a venomous snake or insect up there could be fatal. Although ropes would prevent us from plummeting to the ground, getting bitten and falling away from the wall posed serious risks. You could easily break a bone or hit your head. If the bite was bad enough, the victim would have to be lowered, itself a long, laborious, and high-risk task. Snakebites can kill in hours.

Difficult as this climb was, we were doing it in the most benign way possible, so as not to mar the cliff face. No pitons hammered in, no bolts drilled. As we moved up the face, we tried to leave no sign we'd been there.

Because the climb was so slow and arduous and our time getting short, Bruce, Jesus, Peter, and I called for the chopper to pick us up in a clearing and take us to Weiassapu, a neighboring tepui, while the climbers continued setting the ropes at Roraima. Weiassapu had once been connected to Roraima, but time and erosion had separated the two. The animals on Weiassapu might have developed differently from their relatives only a few miles away.

The helicopter dropped us on the barren, windswept top. Bruce found more carnivorous plants than we'd ever seen anywhere. Because the soil is so poor, plants have found a way of surviving by trapping insects inside "bladders." Bruce also found a carnivorous bromeliad, a long tuberous plant with a slick, waxy surface on the inside, making it impossible for captured insects to climb out.

Meanwhile, Jesus and I took on a much more dangerous mission. We would rappel into an enormous vertical hole called a chasm (technically not a sinkhole but similar) that is hundreds of feet deep. What its bowels contained was completely unknown, and we hoped to find more new species. The longer I looked down on the hundreds of feet under me, the more I resisted, so I tried not to look down. If anything went wrong— if the anchors came out or the ropes frayed—we'd be dead.

Before the climb I called my mom on the satellite phone to let her know I was OK, thinking it could be the last time I talked to her.

Hooking my belt to the rope on the chasm's edge, I longed for those cushy mats and padding I had trained on. Most unnervingly, you must immediately put all your weight on the rope, and just trust that everything is tied up correctly. Thankfully, the rope passed the test. I yelled to Jesus that I was coming down, mainly to tell myself I was going through with this. I don't know why I kept looking down, but I did. Reaching bottom, I stood in a forest and ventured into some rocky caves, knowing I was probably the first to do that. Looking up, I saw a giant chimney of vegetation and moss. It was humbling and breathtaking. Once there I knew I would have regretted not doing this. With my headlamp, I found a huge spider and got tangled in its web. I put several spiders in canisters. Then I found a strange-looking toad and included that, too. I wondered if it had ever seen a human before.

Now we had to get out of the chasm. To get back up we had to jumar. Jumaring is the art of ascending a slope by rope, using a toothed, metal clamp. It is murder on your arms and legs. I began ascending and decided to take it slow. But, then, hanging hundreds of feet in the air, I looked up and noticed that my single, fixed rope was rubbing against the edge of the rock.

The rope had frayed. So had my chances for survival.

I was still quite far from the top, and my arms were giving out. I stopped to rest, feeling I could go on no longer. I was an insect trapped in a bromeliad. But I'd seen the fray in the rope, and a sudden burst of energy propelled me on. Somehow I made it back—in what had to be record time!

Bruce and I were absorbed by our discoveries. We took detailed notes on the specimens, drying and packing all the plants. Bruce was especially excited about the toads. They would test the theory of continental drift on animals, as each tepui is like an island, on which species have followed independent evolutionary paths. The camera's flash never paused in his tent. Then one of the guides brought us a *big* worm. It weighed a third of a pound and looked like a weird tube. I could only begin to imagine the size of the fish you could catch with it. Bruce made me lick it. He said it excreted a horrible-tasting substance that kept it protected from predators, and he was so right. But it seemed like a good idea at the time.

Back at Roraima, nearly 2,000 feet above, the ropes had been set. It was time to hook up with the climbers. The chopper delivered us back to a clearing, from which Jesus and I would climb to a camp established on the rock face.

Crude ladders, spindly ropes, and log stairways were the only ways to the barren cliffs above. We were back on a "trail," and climbing would again be very dicey. Most of it would be spiderlike. Only Jesus and I were going up. I was scared and excited but still noticed how grimy my nails were. No question, I needed a manicure.

Mark greeted us and hooked our daisy chains to the wall. All I could think is, "What a room with a view!" Then I saw where we'd be living for the next few days—a hanging "hotel." A three-foot-wide ledge, with a precipitous drop below. We would have to stay tethered to the wall. Accidents happen when you get comfortable, careless, or lazy and neglect to keep yourself hooked up at all times. Same goes for gear. Basically, anything you don't want to lose, including your backpack and camera, must be hooked to the rope. Jesus' very expensive camera fell, never to be seen again.

Mark and Jared had rigged up the "portaledges," hanging tents we'd sleep in that night. These accommodations were a flimsy sheet of nylon attached to the rock face by a single, six-inch steel pin. There was no privacy whatsoever. As I saw one of the guys unzip his pants and pee off the ledge, it occurred to me that at some point I would have to "go to the bathroom," too. What if I had to, you know, do more than pee? I decided to skip meals and drink minimally. I would pee only when everyone else was asleep.

As night began to fall, the reality of our low-impact style of climbing really hit me. Normally, on a huge wall like this, climbers would drill bolts into the rock from which to suspend the hanging tents. Those bolts can hold thousands of pounds each. But we would be entrusting our lives to "bat hooks," tiny metal hooks that simply hang over small flakes on the rock face. They'd be backed up by "friends," camming devices that Mark would slip into the little crevices. They expand and grip the rock. We hoped.

I lay in my hanging tent exhausted but unable to sleep. I kept staring at the tiny pin that was supposed to hold up both me and Jesus. My first thought was that we should have had less dinner. Then I noticed a spider the size of a dinner plate inside the tent. I was *not* going to sleep until that spider was out. I shined my light so as not to lose track of it. Then I called for Jesus. He asked if I had it cornered. "No. It has *me* cornered," I replied.

After very little sleep, I awoke at dawn and lifted the nylon sheet. The view was breathtaking. Above the clouds were the most incredible shades of yellow, orange, blue, and purple emanating from the sun. To this day, I have never experienced a more beautiful sight.

We still had to move up the ropes, and my fingers were seriously blistered. On the midline of the cliff, more than 8,000 feet up, was a hanging garden that might harbor species never seen before. Like everything on this trip it was risky. Just overlooking one basic step could cost you your life. At these heights you make only one mistake. You don't get the chance to make two.

Trying not to look down, I concentrated on the beauty that surrounded us, such as the colorful green bird that perched at eye level. His wings under the sun's rays were iridescent. Wedged into the rock wall, we found a scorpion with all her babies molted on top of her. The contrast was spectacular: the female, black as night, against her clinging, glowing white babies.

We continued on, and soon the summit of Mount Roraima, Guyana's Empire State Building, loomed in front of us with all its hidden treasures. It was unbelievable that we'd finally arrived. The place looked completely forbidding, with fantastic black rock formations. We all had chills, not from the cold, but because we knew the significance of where we were standing. We had the feeling we had discovered a missing place. I had never seen or even imagined anything like this: a landscape laid down long before the dinosaurs, even before there were fish in the seas. It was primeval.

In this veritable lost world, hot water had pushed its way up through this rock and crystallized, creating a garden of jewels in curved and haunting shapes. These diamondlike stones covered the floor and were striking against the black rock. Every few hundred yards, a massive waterfall poured over the rim, and geysers of water burst from holes in the sides of the cliff amid the surrounding electric green jungle. To our collection we added more plants and animals that had developed in complete isolation. A cute little pebble toad, resembling a small dinosaur, crawled on the palm of my hand.

As scientists we are trained to think in concrete terms. But when you go to a place like that, you *feel* the ghosts, the spirit of things that lived there eons ago. It's not something you see. It was nearly impossible to comprehend just how old this place was.

As we explored the top of this Jurassic Park, a storm moved in. We took cover in tents, but I worried for Mark and Jared, who had gone off on another climb, one none of the rest of us could have handled. They were too far to get back to beat the storm. Looking into the mist, it struck me that most climbers couldn't make that climb even when it was dry. Fortunately, they made it back.

The expedition was over. Although I was anxious to get home to my family, I was also sad to be leaving this extraordinary place. We heard the chopper overhead and quickly broke camp. I took one last moment to absorb my surroundings, trying to commit every detail of this lost world to memory. Once again, the view took my breath away.

Perhaps discoveries had been made and papers would be published. Regardless, as the clouds reclaimed the summit, time would just move on. Meanwhile, I had caught a glimpse of eternity.

eleven

Leopard on a Gurney

JULY 13, 2003: It is extraordinary how such an arresting coat blends so perfectly with the freckled light! Basking in the sun, he sat and watched us for a while, then, keeping us in his gaze, stood and began to approach. It was unclear to me whether he was stalking us or exhibiting predatory curiosity. The end of his long tail twitched as his nostrils tasted us. My survival instinct was now nudging me sternly. But then he turned arrogantly to the side, no longer interested, and sashayed through the bushes, turning as he did to give us disruptive bipeds a look of exasperated hostility.

The halls of National Geographic headquarters are filled with energy. At any moment, you might expect showgirls to burst from the cubicles and go right into a full-blown routine on creativity and adventure. These are no ordinary office workers. The corridor walls are lined with nameplates that read like a who's who of the explorers, filmmakers, and photographers who made National Geographic the most recognizable name in exploration and adventure. But sometimes those walls come alive. Bumping into one of the legendary Cousteaus, Leakeys, or Jouberts in the hallway reminds you that this isn't regional dinner theater, it's the Broadway of exploration. Then again, standing in front of the bathroom mirror retouching my lipstick alongside renowned oceanographer Sylvia Earle has also reminded me that my heroes are human, just like me.

Only days before a giraffe nearly kicked me in the ribs, I was looking out my office window over M Street in Washington, D.C., wondering just how it was I had gotten so lucky. On my office walls were masks from different parts of the world I had traveled to and a map reminding me of all the places I had yet to go. Second only to the African skies and stars, it was under this roof that I had come to feel most inspired and humbled.

It was also under this roof that I first met filmmaker Eric Cochran. More than a cameraman, Eric looked part bodybuilder, part surfer. Blond, fit, tan, and a native Californian, that description was no stretch. But he was also a well-seasoned shooter-producer, which meant that besides producing films, he was an accomplished cinematographer. He had spent years working in Africa and was back at headquarters to pitch a story I immediately wanted to be a part of. He was working on a project in Namibia involving wildebeests, giraffes, and leopards. It was a project so alluring that I was soon packing my bags and heading back to the African continent. Namibia would be the next stamp on my passport.

A country in southern Africa as big as Texas and Louisiana combined, Namibia has a population of about 1.8 million, making it one of the least densely populated countries on Earth. Dominated by the inhospitable Kalahari and Namib

Deserts, it is also one of the most arid. Cars are few and far between on its smooth, tabletop roads, one of the happier results of brutal German colonialism and apartheid-era South African control, the latter of which ended with independence in 1990. German influence may also explain Namibia's relatively superb infrastructure compared to other African countries. If there's one thing Germans can do, it's organize. I should know, I'm married to one, and I envy his side of the closet.

In Namibia we were to meet up with Ulf Tubbesing, a pioneer veterinarian who works with wild animals. When I first met Ulf, he was stepping off a helicopter toting a rifle on his shoulder and trailed by a bevy of German beauties. Who is this character? I thought. He was not your typical lab coat–wearing vet, but the babes were his students. You might say he was the James Bond of the veterinary world. He makes "house calls" from his Namibian clinic, tending to the needs of the continent's wildest animals, facing danger every time. When Ulf makes a house call, the patient isn't usually cooperative, and the location is almost never a house. He might be responding to a report of a baboon wreaking havoc in Windhoek, Namibia's capital, or tracking and tranquilizing a leopard that's raiding a farmer's crops. The animals often need medical attention, as well. We hadn't been in Namibia very long when he got a call requesting him to tend to a wild cheetah that had been attacked by a leopard. His work can make a real impact on seriously depleted animal populations like that of the cheetah—and every animal counts.

The wild animals Ulf treats are in trouble less because they've been attacked by other animals than because they've come into contact with humans. Namibia has very little habitable land, which poses a dilemma for both animals and people. What little there is is fenced in, so many of the nation's leopards and cheetahs are forced to live on farmland. Those predators see a free meal and go for it, killing livestock and creating an economic problem for landowners. In light of that, Ulf spread the word among farmers that he was prepared to remove animals that ignored their "No trespassing" signs. Whereas previously ranchers and farmers would shoot to kill, now many of them called Ulf to move the animals off their land.

Treating and working with wildlife or, more specifically, problem animals is incredibly challenging. Five minutes with Ulf, and you know he's doing it for love. But he told me that as a fifth-generation Namibian, he learned his marksmanship by watching wildlife through a scope. In Namibia love of wildlife usually coincides with hunting.

But Ulf was now a changed man, trying to save Namibia's heritage. Against the odds, he was fighting to give the wild animals a sanctuary where they could recover and roam free. He and some partners had recently established a 10,000-hectare (25,000-acre) preserve, whose goal is to restore the thriving ecosystem that once existed here but was hunted out. He was just beginning to relocate many of his patients to the area. He called it the Ongos Project. Because of several close shaves I had while there, I called it the End of Me.

There is no instruction manual on how to convert barren African land into a perfectly balanced wildlife preserve. But even without an exact blueprint, you know that the land must sustain predator and prey. A little leopard with some wildebeest sprinkled in would be a good start. How hard could it be?

So first on our agenda was to *get us some wildebeests*. The wildebeest is a mammal whose name comes from the South African (Afrikaans) word for "wild animal." It has a large, box-shaped head; sharp, curved horns; shaggy hair around the neck; and a pointed beard. Wildebeests are typically gray or dark brown with black stripes, tails, manes, and faces. Although heavily built in the front of their bodies, they support their weight on long, thin legs like their gazelle relatives. They are members of the antelope family, but they look more like oxen or bison than they do a springbok. Measured against the rest of the animal kingdom, they're not the most attractive. But don't tell them I said that.

Wildebeests have been the subject of many wildlife documentaries and are well known for their annual migrations to new pastures. It is an epic spectacle in which vast numbers of wildebeests cross rivers, such as the Mara, and die by the dozens as they attempt to reach the other side. Many are eaten by crocodiles, and others simply drown. That was the extent of my wildebeest knowledge. I didn't have the first clue how you might go about herding them, but I imagined myself riding horseback old-fashioned cowboy style.

No cowboy hats. No horses. No lassos. Modern-day wildebeest herding is done with helicopters.

But this wasn't your ordinary, run-of-the-mill helicopter. This helicopter looked like a death trap. Small and light, it could maneuver lower and faster than any other type of aircraft. My fear was that it didn't look strong enough to sustain heavy winds. Eric didn't seem upset that there were only two seats, none for him. I introduced myself to the pilot, certain he would offer me some reassurance. He didn't. On the contrary, he said he was nervous. What? You can't begin to imagine how nerve-racking it is when you're about to put your life in the hands of a pilot who tells you he's nervous. According to him, wildebeest herding is one of the most dangerous jobs in existence. Much to my horror, he confided that in trying to beat the odds, he herds only a few times a year. All I could think was that when the pilot tells you he's scared, there's probably a good reason for it.

Before I could change my mind, we were in the air. We flew high and then dangerously low above the Namibian desert. Then we began trailing wildebeests at a relatively comfortable distance. Once the helicopter's noise got them moving, we started diving at the ground, herding them into an enclosed area with a police siren. From the sky, the glossy backs of the wildebeests spread out, stampeding in every direction.

It felt like we were doing air gymnastics, or riding a roller coaster without tracks. It was intense and exhilarating. As we flew right over the trees, it struck me that one slight mistake could end in disaster. The pilot was so strongly focused on the animals that it was a wonder he didn't brush the treetops. Airborne, herding wildebeests, there is absolutely no room for error. In this profession, crash and burn is not a figure of speech. On the bright side, if we did take a nose dive, the helicopter's glass front would enable me to watch every harrowing second of my earthbound plummet.

The siren continued to blast across the desert, and the herd obediently thundered into the trailer that was being manned below. All wildebeests inside, my feet finally back on land, I was very proud not to have puked on the pilot. We drove four hours to Ulf's land, where we opened the back of the trailer, and one by one the large creatures ran past us without looking back. Ulf's dream of creating a safe haven for these animals was slowly being realized. The release was a beautiful sight.

No question, the wildebeest mission was a wild chase. Now that I had helped with one capture, it was time for another. Giraffes were next on the agenda. I was really excited about this for two reasons. The first was that giraffes are some of my favorite animals on Earth. With their sleek, long necks and spotted patterns like a leopard's, I also think they are some of the most beautiful. A giraffe is conspicuous like no other animal—long in the extreme, from its legs to its neck and head, from its tail hairs to its eyelashes. Standing between 16 and 18 feet, a giraffe could go eyeball to eyeball with a second-story window. They tower proudly over the dry savanna and thorny thickets. Nothing compares to seeing a giraffe in its natural habitat. But truth be told, the main reason I was happy about the giraffe capture was that you don't herd giraffes. No death-defying helicopters. What I didn't realize was that it would not be any less stressful, or dangerous.

It was painful to know that these giraffes could have been fated to die at the hands of hunters. Giraffes are hunted for their tails, hides, and meat. The tails are used as good luck charms, thread, and flyswatters. But it wasn't poachers who would kill these giraffes if we didn't get them out. The fatal bullets would be wholly legal, delivered by paying customers who had bought tickets to take aim at these incredible creatures. We had come to a game reserve that had more giraffes than it could possibly support. Hunting is actually a conservation measure to ensure healthy and genetically balanced herds. Regardless, if Ulf didn't shoot them with a tranquilizer gun and transfer them to his preserve, it would be a hunting gun that took aim at them.

In the midday sun, the giraffes waited anxiously for a turn to quench their thirst at the watering hole. We in turn were in the back of a pickup truck waiting anxiously to dart the giraffes. We trailed them nearly an hour waiting for the right moment for Ulf to shoot. Tension ran high.

A lone giraffe bull stood at the edge of the scrubby bush forest that opened onto a grassland. The grasses were yellowed and brittle. We approached to within 150 yards of the animal. It didn't seem bothered by our presence. Ulf adjusted the air rifle and tweaked the scope to get it into sharp focus. Sweat streamed down his face. Neither excited nor aggressive, the giraffe watched us calmly from its haughty perch, brown eyes bulging. We could see the fine, curving eyelashes framing its attentive eyes.

Ulf took a shot. He missed. The giraffe ran off and rejoined the herd, making it hard to get another clear shot. We kept after the giraffes as they ran, sun glowing on their backs. Giraffes have an unusual gait, in which the front and back legs on one side move forward together, then the two legs on the other side move forward. Because the animals are so large, the motion of their legs seemed almost in slow motion. With their center of gravity so high, they seemed to sweep along, hardly touching the earth. They were virtually floating. It was breathtaking to watch.

With a bang, my romanticized moment out on the African plains ended. Ulf had taken a shot and this time hit his target. This is the point when things can get hairy. The gunshot sent the animals running, and giraffes are extremely fast, capable of speeds between 30 and 50 miles an hour. Ready to jump into action, we had to wait until the sedative kicked in before going after the animal but not a moment longer. The drug was so strong that Ulf had to counteract it with a second drug. He had only minutes to inject the antidote before the giraffe would die.

A rhythmic dance ensued, animals and truck constantly starting and stopping. It was more mosh pit than samba. I was crammed into the back of the small truck with eight other people, trying to stay upright and slamming into every bump in the Namibian desert. Within minutes, the giraffe was showing signs of the drug. Its run was becoming sluggish, its head beginning to sway. We had to get to it immediately. We managed to get closer and Ulf, some of his assistants, and I jumped off the back of the truck carrying a coiled 100-foot rope. I was running at full speed. This was the most dangerous part of the capture for both us and the giraffe. Two of us extended the rope in front of its legs to slow it down and then trip it so the antidote could be administered.

Watching this soaring creature fall to the ground was not a pretty sight. It was like watching nature's version of the Eiffel Tower crumble. The giraffe looked nothing like the picture of grace it had embodied only minutes before. But there was no time to pause. Hearts pounding and completely out of breath from the chase, we had to quickly elevate the animal's head, or it would choke to death. It took all eight of us to lift the 6-foot neck, which alone weighed about 600 pounds. That's more than two linebackers.

Ulf prepared the drug, while I covered the giraffe's eyes and someone else inserted earplugs. Covering his eyes and reducing the noise would help calm him when he regained consciousness. Each person had a job to do, monitoring the animal's breathing, heart rate, temperature, and respiratory oxygen. After taking blood, Ulf injected the antidote, reversing the immobilizer drug and bringing the animal back to consciousness. It was difficult for me to take in the scene. There I was holding a rope attached to a giraffe wearing earplugs and a blindfold. That had to be about as surreal as it gets.

We caught our breath and let our adrenaline settle, allowing the giraffe to rest until ready to stand up on his own. That process was not pretty, either. A giraffe can't simply hop to its feet. It is entirely reliant on its head and neck to get up from a prone position. As I held the rope and watched, the giraffe began to throw his head and neck toward his back legs in an effort to rise onto his stomach. Frighteningly, it looked as though the 1,800-pound animal was having a seizure. But finally he made it into a sort of crouch. Another throw of his head and neck toward his tail gave him momentum to stand. Holding the makeshift leash around his neck, I looked up in awe at this amazing beast.

For the next hour I walked my giraffe. That's right. I walked him like I was cooling down a racehorse 18 feet tall. Our next task was to walk him into the trailer. This was not as easy as it may sound and should come with the disclaimer, "Lead the giraffe at your own risk." We began wrangling him and quickly realized this giraffe had a lot of attitude. Leaning his long body way back, he resisted mightily. We finally got him in, and I went to close the back gate. As if in retaliation, the giraffe kicked back, nearly hitting my rib cage. I jumped out of his way in the nick of time, relieved it was only a near miss. I wasn't impervious to the fact that a giraffe's kick can kill a lion.

One giraffe down, we still had one to go. It was a daunting thought, an intoxicating mix of excitement and danger. We needed a female if there was to be any chance of reproduction. By the end of the second capture I was exhausted, as were the giraffes we had set off running. The entire process of capturing and moving them to the new preserve had been even more intense than I'd anticipated, but the result would be worth it: the gradual rebirth of one of the planet's great natural environments. A giraffe couple stood in the back of the truck, and it was time to take them to their new stomping grounds.

Wildebeests and giraffes in place, Ulf's preserve was almost complete, but it lacked predators. In the natural world, every form of life is food for another. Most predators have special adaptations to catch and kill food. These may include good vision, a keen sense of smell, or strong legs for running. Leopards have all of those. They are capable of running just under 40 miles per hour and can easily jump 22 feet horizontally and 10 feet vertically. They have four-inch, razor-sharp teeth and claws as thick as rifle slugs. They have a terrible beauty. They're like an automatic weapon with the safety latch off.

Ulf had a couple of these potential killing machines at his farm (located not far from the preserve). They were orphan cubs brought to him by a local farmer. They were still too young to survive on their own, so Ulf had adopted them. He had always been crazy about leopards, and it was remarkable to watch them interact. He called them the "ultimate beasts" and described them as very moody. They were sometimes extremely cuddly and affectionate, but their behavior could change to vicious in a second. Though Ulf never forgot that these leopards were capable of inflicting serious injury, there was a bond there akin to father and sons. Unquestionably, these leopards saw Ulf as Dad.

One day we were cruising along with the leopards in the car and Ulf driving, when one of them decided to ride shotgun. From the backseat, it jumped onto my lap and reached to the left placing its large paw on the steering wheel. It was like having an extremely large house cat on my lap. In fact, other than being able to eat you, leopards really aren't very different from house cats.

Walking around the preserve, Ulf told me this was not the first time he had cared for leopards. It turns out that these cubs were members of a leopard family with a brain disorder that Ulf had been trying to help for years. It all started in 1999 when a farmer knocked on his door carrying a female leopard and said, "There's your leopard. Do with it what you want and then kill it." Cats are traditionally admired for their graceful movement, speed, and agility. This leopard cub could barely walk.

It seems safe to assume that most people would have put the cat down. But something about this particular cub made it impossible for Ulf to consider such a thing. She couldn't run or climb and fell over all the time just trying to walk. Ulf worked tirelessly doing all he could do to improve her quality of life. But nothing worked.

Ulf took his leopard to the local hospital in Windhoek to get an MRI. The tests showed she had severe damage to her nervous system caused by hydrocephalus. This condition, fluid on the brain, occurs in humans, too, and to date there has been no cure for it either in humans or animals. Having grown very attached to the leopard, Ulf was desolate. He continued giving her vitamins and then one day, on a whim, gave her a vitamin supplement used to treat humans with liver ailments. Within days, she recovered. Nothing short of a miracle.

I was fascinated by this medical story, but the rest would have to wait. Ulf received a call, and the next thing I knew we were headed to find a wild cheetah that had been attacked by a leopard. A wild vet's work is never done.

The cheetah was very badly injured. It couldn't walk or eat on its own. It was a sad sight to see one of the most amazing cats in the world writhing in pain. I would have much preferred to see it doing what it's famous for—running. The fastest of all animals, cheetahs can accelerate from 0 to 68 miles an hour in three seconds, reaching speeds up to 75 miles an hour. Unfortunately, they are still not fast enough to forestall the tremendous decline in population that has been threatening their survival. The world's biggest population of cheetahs—of only about 2,500 individuals—is in Namibia. More than ever, I realized what an impact Ulf's dedication could have on threatened populations, as in the case of cheetahs not a single animal can be spared. In any other circumstances, the injured animal Ulf and I found would quickly have died, but, remarkably, after a few weeks in his care, you wouldn't even know it had been attacked.

I was very curious to meet the hydrocephalic leopard Ulf had cured. She now lived atop rocks in a reserve near Fish River Canyon. Few wild leopards get the chance to make it back into the bush, but this was a haven for problem animals. Eric and I took a two-hour bush plane ride to pay it a visit. Natasha, Ulf's friend and owner of the farm-turned-wildlife-reserve, warmly greeted us and took us out to search for Ulf's rescue leopard. Natasha cautioned us that this was now a full-grown female, big and temperamental. I told her I had an aunt like that. After a long pursuit we saw her, barely, camouflaged well into the landscape. I stood still, trying not to make any sudden, jerky movements that might startle her. But she approached us, showing special interest in Eric. Not Eric himself, but the fuzzy, hairy microphone on the end of his camera. She was just a big cat, after all.

Eric and I flew back to Ulf's ranch. Ulf had decided to take his year-old hydrocephalic leopard cubs to the clinic in Windhoek, and I asked to go with him. You see, the medical angle of the story was fascinating to me, not only because of the leopards. It was also personal. One of my cousins, a hydrocephalic, had died several years earlier. Growing up, I saw the hardships he endured, including never being able to leave his bed. If Ulf had really stumbled upon a cure for leopards, would it be possible to extend that treatment to humans?

It's not every day that leopards are wheeled through the emergency doors of a hospital. Rolling a gurney with a leopard on top gets you a lot of stares, and you'd be amazed at how quickly the halls clear. The leopards had been anesthetized, but their large adrenaline supply required extra tranquilizers to ensure they did not run wild in the hospital.

We lifted the first one onto the scanner platform on his belly. His legs and paws spread, he was ready for his CAT scan. That is probably the only time I'll ever say CAT scan and mean it literally.

We awaited the results anxiously. With the vitamin supplement, the leopard's behavior had improved drastically, but how deep was the improvement? Had his brain physically changed, too? Minutes later, we had the results. No brain damage. Amazing. I couldn't help but think that this miracle cure of Ulf's might someday open new vistas for human medicine.

As I have learned so many times, some of the better things in life happen totally by accident.

Back at the preserve, the cubs were fully awake and so agile you'd never guess they had once been handicapped. They moved around the rocks much faster than I could. I also noticed that their cuddly qualities had gotten to me, and my guard was down. When I first met them, I was careful not to trigger their razor-sharp claws, but now I was taking naps with them. I won't lie—I had already been pawed several times and bear scars on my back to prove it. Sure they were young, tame leopards with brain disorders, but they could still hurt.

Then I had one last realization. Without Ulf, these leopards had been destined for a cage or a bullet. It was a beautiful and joyous moment for me to watch them run free. Even better—sheer heaven, in fact—was sitting in the Namibian desert, watching the sun disappear behind the hills, with one leopard rubbing against my leg and another leaning against my back.

[twelve]

The Vain Girl's Guide to Survival

JULY 2, 2006: I've had to add more and more holes to my belt from all the weight I have lost over the last few weeks. Food has been very difficult to come by. This wouldn't be a bad thing if I were an aspiring fashion model, but I still have endless miles to trek and several more weeks to endure. Physically, I am feeling quite weak. It also doesn't help that my body is doubling as a frozen yogurt machine. I'm fairly certain that small worms or parasites have attached themselves to my intestines.

Boys, feel free to head to chapter 13.

Where I travel seldom resembles what most of my contemporaries consider civilization. But the good life has very different meanings in different parts of the world. In some places you can be a rich man if you live in a hut with no electricity or running water and a dozen family members, as long as you have a cow. You can tell a lot about a culture in the eyes of its children. If the children are smiling and laughing, there is a good chance that their way of life, spartan as it may look to us, is a happy one.

When you go to places like that, you quickly learn to appreciate just how little we actually need.

In the "civilized" world most women carry small convenience stores on their shoulders. Known as purses, pocketbooks, handbags, shoulder bags, or "Birkins," they usually have neat little compartments for eye shadow, emergency snacks, rain gear, reading material, breath mints, contact lens solution, sunglasses, pens, dental floss, water bottles, lipstick, feminine products, mobile phones, Bluetooth headgear, spare batteries, hair brushes, and gum. Some women, those with improbably large bags, also carry over-the-counter medical supplies, sewing kits, hand wipes, Windex, bad hair day caps, garage door openers, Starbucks punch cards, and occasionally a teeny lap dog. Women who carry all of the above often actually run out of room. They are easily spotted in their native habitat (malls) with wallet and car keys in hand, as those items simply don't fit in their overstuffed bags.

Believe it or not, seemingly trivial items can be essential to several weeks in the wilderness. Dental floss, for example, is 20 times stronger than string and comes in a small package with its own cutter. If you don't use it on your teeth, one container of floss can build a full shelter and dozens of snares. The drug Percocet relieves pain and will treat diarrhea. It's also great for making that one person in the group who's freaking out shut up. And if you get cornered by a bear, squish the pills into little bits and drop them; the bear will consume them until it passes out—eight or ten pills should do the trick.

In my humble opinion, women's natural ability to be prepared proves conclusively that we are ideally suited for expedition work.

Most women hope they never find themselves stranded in the wilderness. If the situation arises, however, they are readier than they realize. So much of survival is just about common sense. And since they say necessity is the mother of invention, the everyday things many of us carry as a matter of course can actually save your life.

I didn't know any of this on my early expeditions.

When I packed to go to the Amazon for the first time, I carefully selected several matching outfits for each day and stuffed my bag with makeup, a jewelry bag, a hair dryer, an arsenal of hair products, pajamas, and enough sensible underwear for a small rain forest tribe. As I've mentioned, I also packed a little black dress and heels. You just never know, right? Nights before setting off, I lay awake thinking about coming across a Pygmy tribe that had never made contact with the outside world. What if the Pygmy king invited me to his hut for a ceremonial dinner? I would have to be prepared, right? In the morning I also packed my pearl necklace.

I eventually arrived at the dankest, muddiest, most remote place on Earth wearing what used to be called "traveling clothes," trailing an overstuffed rolling suitcase, and carrying the teddy-bear backpack. I'm not making this up—nobody could. I looked like a Catholic schoolgirl en route to summer debate camp—an expedition my mother would have approved of. In all, I think I actually used three things from that suitcase, and all of them were socks. But had there been an emergency, I would have been ready.

By the time I had a few other trips to remote places under my belt, I had become an expert packing minimalist, which, if you think about it, goes completely against any woman's natural instincts. What woman in her right mind would think she is prepared for a couple of weeks anywhere with only some tank tops, a couple of shirts and pairs of cargo pants, shorts, socks, a hat, extra pens, field notebooks, lip gloss, and underwear she could wash in a river filled with leeches? But seriously, as long as I have these few things, I am mostly good to go. OK, I still pack the little black dress. Some habits die harder than others.

But even cutting down my gear didn't stop my crew from calling my bag the monster. It always made me feel as if I had over packed. Not so.

The guys on the crews normally walk around unshaven, priding themselves on not having seen their reflection for several weeks. But when one of them got something in his eye and another felt a creepy-crawly in an unmentionable area of his body, they came to me. As much as they hated to admit it, they needed my mirror. They thought I had brought it to apply makeup. Makeup? Pshhh. Forget about it. Even if you wanted to wear it, you are usually in a place so hot that within the first hour you would perspire your foundation, blush, eyeliner, mascara, and lipstick right off your face and into your eyes. If you wear contact lenses, you know that is really bad. And even if it didn't melt off your face and into your eyes, you might soon find any number of bug species stuck to your mascara and lipstick. This is especially true of gooey lip gloss. Bugs in the rain forest, let me tell you, are some of the weirdest, creepiest-looking things on this earth, and I promise you don't want them pissed off and writhing in your lip gloss. Besides, when you are trying to habituate a group of lowland gorillas, it's probably best not to smell like Cover Girl. Take notes here, because this is the stuff they never teach you in anthropology school.

Also—and this will be on the quiz—such journeys typically take you to places where beauty is perceived on a different scale, so your usual allure is completely lost on the natives. While being thin is considered attractive by most Westerners, tribesmen are searching for a chunky, fertile-looking woman to bear their kids. Then, too, think about it: Who, exactly, are you trying to impress? I guarantee you that no silverback will allow you to get closer to his family because you smell like something expensive from Chanel. In nature, bar pickup tactics don't work, and you eventually find yourself realizing what a very odd species we are.

I assure you, the mirror I take with me is not intended to be used for applying makeup, though I admit to using it to check my hair. In many remote villages, the unexpected appearance of a painted lady might conjure up images of some feared she-demon. But there's no reason to sport crazy hair. I would never want to give my hosts the idea that I might actually be from their underworld. I suppose you think I'm kidding here. Dian Fossey famously used her unruly, thick, curly hair to scare the local bullies and primate poachers away from the gorillas she was studying.

Besides helping me keep my locks in check, a mirror is one of the most overlooked but valuable methods for attracting attention when you need help or are lost in the wilderness. When aimed correctly, the brilliant flash from the mirror cannot be ignored. It will reveal your position in the densest of vegetation or in the most rugged mountain landscape. I remember standing on a trail attempting to locate my team on a densely forested slope a mile away. After a frustrating hour of yelling, I used my compass to position myself, then the mirror and the sun as a signaling device—the flash immediately and accurately revealed my position. And so was born my admiration for the lowly signal mirror. Under ideal conditions, a signal mirror can be effective for more than 100 miles, but 10 miles is more reliable. You need to practice your signaling technique. A search plane will pass only once or twice over a given area before widening its search. A good signal can mean the difference between 36 hours lost in the woods and a week. Or more.

The crews also made fun of my tweezers. About the only real "grooming" you can do as a girlie-girl in the jungle, besides picking ants out of your hair, of course, is plucking your eyebrows. Once you've achieved the perfect high-arched brow back in civilization, there is no way any style-conscious girl will sacrifice it. Tweezers, therefore, are an essential packing item. Period. The last thing you want on your return trip is to be greeted by your loved ones sporting a Frida Kahlo unibrow. But it turns out that tweezers, in addition to keeping your eyebrows coiffed, are an essential jungle item. There have been numerous times when a tick has made its way into, how should I put it, private, hard-to-reach areas, and it has been my tweezers that have come to the rescue. Tweezers are also the ultimate tool to deflate a leech lodged in your nose, not to mention indispensable when long, skinny splinters have lodged themselves under the skin. Who you gonna call? Tweezers.

Jewelry? I actually have this leather and shark's tooth necklace that is my one piece for expeditions. It is my good luck token. Anything more would be overkill. Wearing shiny metal neckwear that could start a tribal civil war is not a good way to have a successful research trip. Nevertheless, jewelry, I have discovered, is universal. While mostly not made of precious stones or metals, necklaces, bracelets, and rings transcend cultures. In Africa, the noble Maasai warriors wear the most beautiful pieces. Still, it is best to leave your jewelry at home. In time, you learn to appreciate pretty things through the eyes of the native culture you're visiting. Much as with animal species, it is often the men who are most adorned. Such is the way with the Maasai.

Of course, no book about rugged wilderness expeditions around the world by a former professional cheerleader would be complete without mentioning hair care. Basically, there isn't any. That is, except for that rare day your team stumbles upon a waterfall, and the film crew thinks they are being completely novel by asking the one woman on the expedition to go bathe and wash her hair in it . . . while they roll film. And on that day you will find that not a single member of your expedition team has brought along shampoo. So you end up washing your hair with a bar of soap made of pumice used to get the grime off hands. And because the film crew wanted you to do the waterfall thing, tiny bits of pumice fall from your hair for the next three days, usually into your food. The locals might name you Tall Girl with Golden Hair Who Makes Rock in Her Head, but it is a small price to pay for dipping your toes into paradise and making the film crew happy—thrilled with themselves, actually, for coming up with such a brilliant idea.

One problem with being a cheerleader in the jungle is that after washing your hair you can't just sidle up to the only other girl around, a nursing lemur, and ask her where you might plug in your dryer. A motorized hot-air wind machine might scare off not just the animals you have traveled 8,000 miles to study, but your guides and porters, too. I have long hair I like very much. If you saw my salon bills, you'd understand just how much. When I go off into the wilderness, there's not much beyond basic hair care, and that is precisely how I justify my salon bills at home. When you travel with a film crew, however, they require electricity, which, happily for me, means lugging a generator through the bush. And my hair dryer has come in very handy when the crew's camera goes down from the moisture in the rain forest. Same holds for my hair.

As for clothing, style doesn't have to go out the window. If there were a window. On an expedition I am a scientist, and scientists are (usually) practical to a fault. So, when you go to work, you dress completely for function, which is exactly how I got myself in trouble in graduate school. But that doesn't mean your cargo pants have to be ill fitting, nor will your science be any less valuable if, God forbid, you match. Although it's true that on a good day in the jungle, your socks are dry.

On a really good day, you find a body of water that isn't contaminated or infested with crocodiles or piranha, one you can not only bathe in but even wash your clothes in without disturbing the hippos. And that is if, and only if, you don't also have to use it for drinking (nothing like having to drink your bath water). That's about it. As a Western woman, it really doesn't matter where you go—you are an oddity. Sure, just about any girl wants to be noticed, but it's a different thing entirely to stand out like some sort of apparition. Fashion sense doesn't need to be sacrificed. While being a girl in the wilderness has nothing to do with femininity or pretty things, it doesn't mean you have to look bad, as long as you use your wits and intuition and stay prepared.

Behold the tampon.

In addition to its intended use, removing the absorbent cotton from inside its casing and using it as kindling can save your life. It may seem like a small amount, but it's enough. On a particular African expedition, after walking something like 25 miles in a light rain, we made camp in a thicket. My socks were wet, as was everything else, for that matter. But the bigger problem was that all the kindling and underbrush were damp, and nobody could start a fire.

As hot as the days get on the African plains, the nights are chilly, and that night would have been miserable without a fire. Then there is the matter of prey. As the food chain goes, people are easy prey to many species in many remote parts of the world, and Africa is no exception. In the game of big cat versus human in a sleeping bag, more often than not neither the sleeping bag nor the human stands a chance. Without a fire to deter animals, we weren't going to sleep, and it would be a long, cold, and hungry night.

Being an old-school purse packer, I offered a solution. I produced one individually wrapped magic fire starter—er, tampon—from my backpack and handed it to one of the researchers trying to start the fire. Despite being married and living in the Westernized world, he looked at the package and then looked into my eyes the way a husband does when you ask him to buy you Pamprin. Abject fear. But once I removed the cotton wadding and showed him what it could be used for, he put it to work immediately. In no time at all we had our fire. That may have been the night we were really short on food, and the camp cook produced what he assured us was a delectable dessert of big, white, icky grubs. "Packed with protein and other good things," he insisted. Come morning, we were all completely green—sick as dogs. Nevertheless, we had our fire and dry socks for another day.

I mentioned dinner, so I should explain about food on an expedition. Since the only nutrition has to be carried on your back, you don't bring much, sustaining yourself many days on a ration of rice and whatever else comes your way. Literally. And believe me, although there are more things out there that can eat you than you can eat. Other days, the locals welcome you and share their prized delicacies. *Gag.* Chewing gum is a great way to distract you from hunger pangs and can be offered to the Pygmy king who has just handed you the coveted goat kidney, raw.

Most girls in captivity worry about their weight and try a number of different fad diets before discovering that diets simply don't work. Well, I have discovered one that does work: the Congo diet. You don't necessarily have to be in Congo; any developing African country will do. It consists of raw goat kidney, termites, grubs, and running out of food, which often happens on expeditions (at least, on mine it does). The parasite loads you acquire by drinking the water are optional (well, no, they're actually not), but they help a lot to keep you trim. I had a parasite load so large after one expedition that a doctor asked me if I had been licking toilets. I lost ten pounds that trip.

This diet, coupled with endless hours of hiking, running from elephants, trudging through swamps, and being so tired that you skip dinner altogether, is a surefire way of shedding unwanted pounds. Trust me.

Water is one thing you can never take for granted. I'm not talking about proper hydration to make your skin glow. I can't seem to run to the grocery store these days without taking a bottle of water with me (in a reusable container, of course). In the wilderness, water equals survival, plain and simple. And water is heavy. So if you can't carry it, you have to find it, which often isn't easy. I am always amazed that two-thirds of our planet is covered by water and so little of it is drinkable. When you are thirsty, really thirsty, your standards for drinkable water change. It might be brown, gritty, crunchy, or smell funny, but when you are in a situation where water equals survival, you purify it the best you can, drink it, and hope you'll live to see another day. Panty hose or dance tights, by the way, make a great water filter.

Speaking of dance tights, I have up to this point not discussed the amount of dancing I have done on expeditions. Seriously, I have danced with every tribe I have come into contact with. It's like they know I used to be a cheerleader. Sometimes the social gatherings are informal, but often the villagers will put on their best getups. That's where my little black dress comes in. Though I never made it into Girl Scouts, I learned to "be prepared." And going to a party underdressed is a big no-no in my book. I impressed the Maasai with my jumping ability (though I could not match theirs; not even Superman could). I wowed the snake dancers with my prowess, and I am a legend among the BaAka. As I mentioned in an earlier chapter, I wanted to teach them one of our dances in exchange for everything they'd taught me. I taught them La Macarena, and I fully realize it will ruin any future documentaries about their age-old rituals. Mea culpa.

But that is one of the interesting things about being on an expedition. I can't tell you how many times I have walked into the remote interior of a country only to be greeted by a tribal elder wearing a Hard Rock Hanoi T-shirt and a Cleveland Indians cap some missionary group gave him in 1985. It is like discovering that the Prime Directive on *Star Trek* has been violated. When Captain Kirk and his group landed on a foreign planet inhabited by early-development non-Federation humanoids, they were told, "Don't teach them how to make laser beams or flying machines or taffy." And don't, for that matter, teach them La Macarena. Oops. I suppose it is not too different from using a bikini photo of Kim Kardashian to get our gear past customs agents, but somehow, when you are far, far away from civilization, it just seems culturally intrusive. But cultures are strong and resilient to foreign influence. They are not living museums, and we shouldn't expect them to be. A Maasai wearing traditional dress with a cell phone on his hip is part of modern-day Africa. So what if the BaAka decide to summon forest spirits with a little Macarena?

No, it isn't easy being a girl scientist in the jungle. Nor is it easy to be a woman in a largely man's field. In fact, sometimes it isn't easy being female at all. But on those rare occasions in the wilderness when the stars align and the moonlight kisses the top of your head just so, every frustrating, awkward, and difficult moment is so, so worth it.

The Vain Girl's Survival Checklist
THESE ITEMS, IN YOUR BIRKIN OR YOUR BACKPACK, COULD SAVE YOUR LIFE.

ITEM	FIELD USE
Mirror	For signaling, tick checks, and minimal primping
Eye shadow	Need to get your oversize bag through customs?
Emergency snacks	VERY practical
Rain gear	VERY practical
Reading material	No *Us Weekly* in Brazzaville
Contact lens solution	Very practical
Sunglasses	Very practical

ITEM	FIELD USE
Pens	Very practical
Tweezers	For eyebrows, splinters, and tick removal
Dental floss	For emergency rain shelter and snares
Breath mints	Need to meet that hunky French pilot?
Lipstick	Great for writing SOS on windshields and rooftops
Feminine products	For starting fires, emergency wine cork
Mobile phones	Cell towers do exist in Africa; I've tweeted from Congo
Bluetooth	For hands-free Congo bush driving
Spare batteries	Because there's no corner RadioShack
Hairbrush	Hel-lo, Pygmy king!
Gum	For distracting well-meaning villagers bearing gifts of raw meat; see also hunky pilot
Over-the-counter medical supplies	Because Congo doesn't have Wal-Mart (yet)
Sewing kit	VERY practical
Hand wipes	VERY practical
Windex	For neutralizing flesh-eating fish bacteria
Bad-hair-day cap	ESSENTIAL
Garage door opener	You're kidding, right?
Starbucks punch cards	Not a shameless product placement—they're everywhere
Teeny lapdog	Big-cat diversion, appetizer

thirteen

A Near Disaster,
I Presume?

NOVEMBER 4, 2008: So hungry and thirsty I can barely walk. For weeks we have been living off little to no breakfast, raisins and peanuts for lunch and dinner if we are lucky. Water has been abysmal, almost nonexistent throughout. When we do find some, it is usually in dirty, muddy, water holes with cattle bathing and defecating in it. I have not bathed in days, and I am tired, itchy, and dehydrated. I have had diarrhea for almost a week now. We have just arrived in a village, and after several weeks without news of the outside world, we listened to every word coming through the transistor radio. Through the crackling I heard that Barack Obama has been elected, the first black President of the United States.

When I tell people I am an explorer, they look at me skeptically, as if there were no longer such a profession. It is true, we are a rare breed today and a rather anonymous one, especially compared to explorers of the 19th century, the rock stars of their day. They were the modern-day equivalents of celebrities like Michael Jackson and Jennifer Lopez, or athletes on the level of Michael Jordan and Babe Ruth. They were revered, and their adventures offered a window to unknown lands during an era when travel was difficult and most of the world remained uncharted. Their expeditions made headlines around the globe.

Unquestionably, Dr. David Livingstone was the biggest rock star of them all.

In Victorian England, Livingstone was a true hero, believed by many to be the greatest explorer ever. His journeys, lectures, and many best-selling books on the mysterious African continent were legendary. He wore many hats. As a gentle Scottish missionary, he dedicated his life to the abolition of slavery. As an explorer, he discovered numerous geographical features, such as Lake Ngami, Lake Malawi, Lake Bangweulu, and, lest we forget, Victoria Falls. He filled in details of Lake Tanganyika, Lake Mweru, and the course of many rivers, especially the upper Zambezi. Livingstone's explorations resulted in a revision of all contemporary maps and allowed large, previously blank regions to be filled in.

In 1865, at the age of 52, Dr. Livingstone set out on his most famous journey. Obsessed with finding the source of the Nile, he led an expedition into the center of the Dark Continent. He had already survived numerous deadly diseases and a lion attack that crushed his left arm, rendering it forever useless. He was seemingly indomitable. The Nile expedition was his latest great voyage.

Then Dr. Livingstone disappeared.

Rumors swirled that he was being held captive or, worse, that he was dead. Months rolled by, and then years without the outside world knowing what had become of him. Just imagine if, say, Brad Pitt suddenly disappeared without a trace. The public's fascination with Livingstone's whereabouts reached a fever pitch. Enter American journalist Henry Morton Stanley. Stanley's boss, James Gordon Bennett, Sr., the American tycoon who owned the *New York Herald,* dispatched Stanley to find both Livingstone and the biggest story of the decade. Stanley was no explorer, nor had he ever been to Africa, but he wanted the scoop. After almost nine months and the death of most of his team members, Stanley found Livingstone on November 10, 1871, in Ujiji, a small village on the shore of Lake Tanganyika in Tanzania. A thin, frail Livingstone stepped out of his mud-and-wattle house to meet him as Stanley bowed, took off his hat, and spoke the now famous words, "Dr. Livingstone, I presume." Deep in the jungles of Africa those words have come to represent the most celebrated encounter in exploration history.

Zanzibar Island in the Indian Ocean off Tanzania's coast was where pioneering European explorers began their journeys into Africa and where both Livingstone and Stanley began theirs. It would also be where I started my next expedition: to retrace the footsteps of Henry Morton Stanley's famous search for Dr. David Livingstone in the unknown heart of Africa.

There was nothing ordinary about this mission. It was part of a Mark Burnett reality series but was neither a competition nor a game. Although Burnett is best known for his hit series *Survivor* and *Apprentice,* there would be no million-dollar prize and no one would get "voted off." Burnett wanted to test whether some of today's top explorers could survive the same terrain, dehydration, hippo attacks, and jungle fever that challenged Stanley. We would be stripped of satellite navigation, phones, tents, sleeping bags, water filters, even matches. Using only a compass and basic maps, we would attempt to relive the spirit of one of the most remarkable adventures in recorded history. This expedition was an authentic, visceral journey of survival. Only this time there would be cameras.

Cryptic discussions with Mark Burnett's producers preceded the trip. I was not given so much as a clue as to who else was going. My only information was that "four elite explorers—each experts in their own field" had been selected. I was one of them; I wondered if I would be the only woman. The only thing I knew as I headed for the airport was that, in the company of three strangers, I would face the spectacular yet highly dangerous landscapes of Tanzania—its unforgiving terrain, ferocious wildlife, and deadly tropical diseases. I would get a glimpse into a world few have explored. And I would have to do it with no modern technology. Mind boggling.

The moment I stepped off the plane in Stone Town, I was enraptured by the beaches and sultry sea breezes of Zanzibar. The architecture mixed Arab and Indian influences and had a genuine Old World feel. Most impressive of all were the doorways—massive, carved, and elaborately decorated.

When a house was built in Zanzibar, the door went up first and showed the status of the owner. The richer and more prominent the owner, the larger and more elaborate his front door. I was intrigued that many of the doors were studded with sharp brass spikes to prevent their being battered in by war elephants—purely decorative, as the elephants must have been long extinct before the Arabs built houses there.

Aside from the trip in to my hotel, I did no sightseeing. I was told upon arriving that I would have to spend the first three days within the confines of my hotel. The producers wanted to keep me and the other explorers in seclusion so we wouldn't meet before the expedition began. A "minder" in the hotel lobby made sure I didn't leave. To further ensure that we wouldn't run into each other, we were all placed in different hotels, each with our own watchdog.

Excitement and fear about what lay ahead prevented me from getting more than three hours of sleep a night. In preparation for the journey, I had read all of Stanley's and Livingstone's journals, which revealed their worst fears and experiences. Livingstone's journal entries on confrontations and massacres were vivid and horrible. Stanley described Africa as "the eternal feverish region." Although Africa has clearly changed since their time, the challenges of diseases like malaria and typhoid and the powerful and deadly animals and insurmountable terrain have not. Their fears were now my fears. But like Livingstone, I have the love of exploration deeply embedded in my soul.

It was finally time to meet the others. My eyes welled up when I arrived at the British Consulate, the location from which the world's most admired and accomplished explorers once set off. Nineteenth-century maps decorated the walls. Humbled to be there, I could feel the ghosts of Burton, Speke, Stanley, and Dr. Livingstone, all of whom I felt a kinship with through their books and journals.

I was anxious about meeting the rest of the team, sure they'd be more accomplished. Later I learned we all felt that way. I was so wonderstruck at my surroundings I didn't even notice the tall, handsome, blue-eyed Brit standing in the room. He shook my hand and in a lovely accent said, "I am Benedict Allen."

Benedict is a modern-day Indiana Jones, complete with leather hat. He was there as our survival expert, having come back from the dead half a dozen times. He even had to eat his dog on his first expedition. That's one professional survivalist. I hoped our survival wouldn't come to eating travel companions—each other. Benedict and I chatted about our experiences, trying to size each other up.

Next to walk into the room was U.S. war correspondent Kevin Sites, a clean-cut journalist if I ever saw one. Kevin wasn't an explorer, but he was very accomplished at covering war zones. Like Stanley, he had never been on this kind of an expedition.

Kevin was quickly followed by Pasquale Scaturro. A gruff American mountaineer of Italian descent with a thick mustache, Pasquale is a life force. He has led expeditions for more than 30 years and was especially proud of having taken the first blind man up Everest. I have no idea how many times he mentioned "the blind guy" on our expedition, but it was a lot.

He began citing his résumé and navigational know-how and quickly moved to assume the leadership role.

The four of us really did look like a group from central casting.

From the start, it was apparent that there'd be head-butting, especially between Benedict and Pasquale. But that wasn't unexpected, as cast conflict is a hallmark of almost any Burnett production. That's why he picked four type A personalities. Sure enough, a power struggle ensued. The role of expedition leader was up for grabs, and we all wanted it. I may have been the only woman on this testosterone-filled team, but I have more than enough determination, estrogen, and cojones to level the field. Conflict and drama were inevitable, and I was ready for it.

Accompanying our trek would be a film crew who'd follow our every step and listen to our every word 24-7. It would be *Big Brother* meets *Survivor*. The rules were tough and would be strictly enforced. The crew would not be allowed to say a word to us, help us, or interfere in any way; even "hello" was forbidden. We wouldn't know their names. We had to completely ignore their presence, even if our lives were at risk. If one of us became deathly ill or a lion attacked, their only duty was to film it. We had been chosen because of our extensive experience and were expected to handle whatever came up, however deadly, as we would on our own expeditions. Only the two field producers could have any contact with us, to ask questions, and that was only once we'd stopped; they could not help or direct us in any way.

My teammates and I sat around a table at the consulate, four complete strangers with only 24 hours to gather supplies and plan a month-long expedition. Studying Stanley's old maps, we knew it wouldn't be easy. We broke into two groups. Kevin and Pasquale would seek out a dhow, an old-style boat with a massive sail that we'd use to cross the 25 miles of Indian Ocean to Tanzania. It is the same type of vessel both Livingstone and Stanley employed, and it is still used by the Zanzibar locals to reach the mainland. Meanwhile, Benedict and I headed off to the old market in Stone Town to buy provisions.

There was no magic formula. We were basically guessing as to what and how much to buy and how long we'd need to subsist on it. We had no idea how or when we'd be able to resupply.

Benedict isn't just a survivalist, he's a minimalist. He would have been happy with nothing more than a banana and a bag of peanuts. Pasquale, on the other hand, is Italian and likes cooking and comfort. He wanted us to come back with pasta, tomato sauce, and spices. I found myself mediating between these two different approaches, urging compromise between too much and too little. Consider this a foreshadowing.

If I had to choose a favorite, already it was Benedict, who had a wonderful sense of humor and, despite his toughness (I mean, the man had crocodile-teeth scars on his chest), was gentle and charming.

Still, I could sense conspiracy building. We had yet to agree on a lot of important things, and both Pasquale and Benedict seemed to be trying to co-opt me as an ally. They were appealing in completely different ways, I thought, but I predicted their egos and stubbornness would one day lead to an explosion. During our short meeting, they even compared the lengths of their knives. Boys. You never see women pull out their lipstick tubes to compare the relative length of their creamy accessory color. You know what I'm saying.

The "reality" aspect was daunting. We had to do in 30 days what took Stanley almost nine months to complete. For that reason, we would skip over sections of Tanzania that were now populated, traversing only the harshest of terrains.

Benedict and I made one last hectic trip to the market to revisit a kindly man who had earlier offered to find us a large tea kettle and some oil lanterns. We were really excited to head off that very day and begin the long-awaited expedition. Back at the British Consulate, Kevin and Pasquale were laying out the green canvas bags and supplies that would get us through the journey. We weighed the bags, hoping to keep them under 50 pounds, as we were uncertain how much our porters would agree to carry.

That led to the next argument. There was a major discrepancy between the number of porters each of us thought necessary. Accustomed to traveling light and alone, Benedict wanted only ten. Kevin, having no experience with expeditions, naively agreed. Pasquale and I saw eye to eye on that one, feeling that 20 was a more realistic number. In the end we shoved our gear into 22 bags, hired carts and men to pull them, and set off for the port and the waiting dhow. Hiring the boat cost a mere 150 shillings, the equivalent of $150.

The port scene was crazy, with hundreds of people in the water around the dhows yelling to each other in Swahili. It had the energy and hustle of New York. As we loaded our gear on the boat, it hit me hard that these men would be my closest companions for the next four weeks, yet I had known them for less than 24 hours. Benedict and I had already forged a tight bond. "Kindred spirits," he called us. We all helped raise the sail. The winds were favorable. We waved to the crowd as the dhow glided through the waters. It's healthy to be a little nervous on a journey like this, because it forces you to keep your guard up. I was sure Livingstone must have felt the same combination of excitement and trepidation when he left this same shore in an identical vessel, headed on the same arduous journey. Zanzibar was now behind us, Africa's horizon ahead.

At first it was smooth sailing, but as we grew closer to the Tanzanian coastal town of Bagamoyo, the waters became rough and choppy. The wind blew so hard the boat began filling with water. We tried to get the dhow's 500-pound mast down while being knocked around by the storm. We struggled, trying not to slice off our fingers with the rope. I started getting seasick. None of us was an experienced sailor, and it quickly got scary. Before our eyes, the mast of the dhow in front of us ripped off and blew into the ocean.

We soon were close to shore, as far as the dhow could take us, and one by one we jumped into the waist-deep water carrying our gear on our heads, making multiple trips to retrieve it all. We set up camp on the shore. In the morning, our head porter, an experienced Tanzanian named Julius, came to meet us. Key to the success of the expedition, Julius would be there to translate and to help oversee the men, safeguarding against mutiny or dishonesty. He was joined by two Maasai warriors who would help guard our safety. Members of a beautiful and proud seminomadic people, Maasai males are expected to kill a lion or a leopard with a spear at a young age, which both our warriors had done by 14.

We went into town and, in consultation with Julius, selected our porters. Quickly, we returned with them to camp, loaded the gear on our backs and theirs, and began our trek. We argued about how much water to bring and, in our haste to leave, brought none.

We'd be taking the old Arab slave route through the mangrove swamps. It was the route Stanley had taken, but in the mangroves you can't see more than a few feet in front of and behind you. On Day 1, only a few miles into the expedition, we'd already lost a team member. Kevin was nowhere to be found and, as the least experienced, was the last guy you wanted lost out there. But one of the Maasai was with him, so we knew he would be OK. Cleverly, he had brought along a little whistle, so we soon found our missing explorer.

Sticking together the rest of the day, we arrived at an area where we could camp, happy that it was surrounded by water, though we quickly discovered it was brackish. Water would be our greatest concern throughout, as it had been Stanley's. We'd neglected to secure the most important element to our survival. Kevin headed back to the last village with some porters and his whistle and, sometime after sundown, returned to camp lugging containers of the precious liquid. We would never make that mistake again.

The next morning, only a few feet from camp, I found a spitting cobra. They don't actually spit but can spray their venom with precision and, usually aiming straight for the eyes, can cause permanent blindness. There are 29 species of venomous snakes in Tanzania, known as "snake country." As Pasquale pointed out, the only tools in our snake kit were a hatchet and a sharp knife.

That afternoon we began crossing the swamps. Crocs were bountiful, and now was the nesting season, when they are most aggressive. I could barely lift my feet out of the thick mud. So much for my pink boots, now brown along with the rest of me and everything else. Trekking through mud up to our knees carrying far too heavy backpacks was nearly impossible. More than once I sank waist deep and had to be lifted out. We were all struggling. Finally, we came to the edge of a river too deep to cross by foot. That was a relief, as it, too, was infested with crocs. Few of the porters could swim. At a village we hired dugout canoes that were so unstable we knew there was a real risk of drowning our nervous porters. As we paddled, I became aware of the dozens of crocs nesting in the banks. You could almost smell the danger. One of the porters in our canoe started to panic and stood up; the canoe began to wobble, and water poured in. Benedict tried to calm him, knowing we could capsize in seconds. And seconds is all it would take for the crocodiles to have us in their jaws. Somehow we got through that and arrived at the other side.

Once there, more arguing ensued. It was never ending. We argued about where to camp, when to camp, which route to take, how much water to carry, and a host of other concerns both serious and trivial. Pasquale never listened, only yelled. He made it very clear to us that an expedition was not a democracy. I was sure that if the crocs didn't get us, the bickering and backstabbing would. On those first few days of our journey, Pasquale treated me like a little girl. I'm not very good at taking orders, and my patience was wearing thinner and thinner. It infuriated me that all he could see was my gender, not my credentials as an explorer.

Benedict incessantly questioned Pasquale's navigational calls, and they bickered like schoolchildren. But we were now well into the swamp, and there was no turning back. Pasquale was a loose cannon, and loose cannons roll around on the tops of ships. When seas start to get rough, loose cannons either hurt people or go off unexpectedly. We could afford neither. It was early in the expedition, and we were already lost, even though Pasquale wouldn't admit it. Then Kevin began whining that he wanted to go back to the river, afraid we were running out of water again. I argued that we couldn't take the river on a leash and we had to keep pressing on. It was a battle of wills . . . and won'ts, as in, "I won't let these egotists ruin this expedition."

In two days we had covered only 9 miles. We had more than 900 to go.

Burnett's film crew (of more than 100 people, we later learned) traveled parallel to us in vehicles, unseen, and stayed in satellite camps. Every once in a while, behind a bush we'd spot one of them. We began referring to them as "the others," from the TV show *Lost*. They could not reach most of the remote places we were traversing but were there to provide logistical support for the handful of producers, cameramen, and sound techs who did follow our every move. This team worked in shifts because of the arduous nature of the journey and the 100-pound cameras they had to carry. They were with us all the time, even when we slept. (On occasion, when we were really desperate, we tried to think of ways to steal their water and food.) They were flies on the wall, documenting every step of our misadventure. They were what you might call "extreme cameramen," who were adept at high-risk expeditions and had been part of Mark Burnett's other series, *Eco-Challenge* and *Survivor*.

The first couple of days we were very much aware of the cameras; they were so big, it would have been difficult not to be. But soon we were forced to focus all our energies on sheer survival, and there was no way to do that and worry about image or how we'd look on TV. As a result, the effect was raw and often far from pretty—certainly not our best sides. But we were always real.

We finally arrived at the base of the Uluguru Mountains. Stanley had gone around the mountains, but we took a more challenging route directly over them. It didn't take long to realize we had too many porters and too much gear and would have to get brutal in cutting back. We even cut back on our toothbrushes and towels. When it's on your back, every ounce counts.

The peak of the Uluguru Mountains is 6,400 feet high. Once you start climbing, you are pretty much committed. If anyone tripped or lost their footing, it could be fatal. It was more than 100°F, and we were huffing and puffing trying to keep a steady pace. Pasquale wanted to move faster. The rest of us tried to convince him to slow down. When Benedict suggested I lead the way instead, Pasquale lost it. He couldn't bear the thought of not being in the front. I would taunt him by walking a few steps ahead. It drove him nuts, but even so the gruff taskmaster and I were beginning to bond. We spent the rest of the expedition walking side by side or with me a step behind him when the trail was narrow, because he couldn't stand for me to get ahead of him.

In fact, being a woman on this expedition had its clear advantages. The guys seemed able to open up to me in a way they couldn't with each other; I got to see another side of them. Perhaps they felt less threatened. Kevin told me about all the tragedies and deaths he had witnessed on the front lines. Those images still gave him nightmares. Benedict and I would talk about everything under the stars, sometimes well into the night. Pasquale and I would have long talks about love and life. I could even tease him a little bit. Most telling, I was the only one he ever let walk in front of him, however grudgingly. Even the Maasai warriors, who were not allowed to show fright or pain, confessed to me their one and only fear: women.

The climb was steep, and there was no slowing Pasquale down. Once again, he reminded us of the blind guy who kept up on Everest. Suddenly, we heard a thud. A porter had gone down. We took his pulse and poured some water on his fore-head. He was boiling hot and hyperventilating. After we got him stabilized, we had two porters take him down the mountain and back to a village. We had to move on. The expedition couldn't wait.

You plan and plan and plan, then Africa happens.

We continued the climb and stopped to camp at 4,276 feet before darkness hit. It was a serene, calm setting with incredible views. But that night a windstorm came through like I've never witnessed. We tried to secure our shelter and gear. The wind was so loud and strong no one slept that night. The next morning we had to complete our climb, more than 2,000 feet, on much steeper terrain. As tired as we were, it was hell.

We literally walked through the clouds and into the oldest forest in Africa, 25 million years old. Soaring trees nearly reached the sky. Benedict and I wanted to stop and take notes, but Pasquale insisted we keep pushing, joking that we should just pick a flower, put it in our pocket, and talk about it at camp. It is always a tough balance on an expedition, staying on course and still absorbing everything you can.

There's a climbing saying, "Going up a mountain is optional, going down a mountain is mandatory." It was now time to descend, and we knew it would be dangerous. The fact is that there are more deaths going down Everest than going up. Ours was a slippery slope and our feet were tired, so staying upright was difficult. It took us more than eight hours to reach a place we could camp.

Everything was damp and humid. Benedict, obviously well trained, broke out a tampon and started a fire. But the warmth didn't last. A thunderous rainstorm set in, and everything we owned was soaked by morning. We were trying to stay ahead of the rainy season, and that was a sure way to kill an expedition. Stanley called the Uluguru the "misty mountains," and he was so right. That mist percolated into everything. There was no way to start a fire in the morning. Even the old tampon trick failed us. The team's mood was as damp as our clothing. Regardless, we had to push on, even though we'd had hardly anything to eat and were all feeling lethargic. Making matters worse, for days I had been suffering from diarrhea. I was beginning to feel like a frozen yogurt machine.

Kevin was shocked when he saw the sheer cliffs we had yet to traverse. He tried to convince us not to attempt it, insisting it was unfair to the porters. They might not have been happy, but we felt he was projecting his own fears onto them. Pasquale, Benedict, and I felt frustrated. As explorers we knew there'd be risks, and this was one of them. It's the nature of the beast. An expedition can't just come to a halt every time things get dicey. Outnumbered, Kevin had no choice but to go on.

The climb was hairy, but we lost neither Kevin nor a porter. We did, however, happily stumble on a tiny village. Kevin went off to sulk under a tree, perhaps feeling he had overreacted. The rest of us feasted on pineapples and bananas. It was paradise. Then Benedict spotted a goat. The next thing I knew, the goat was ours and had been named Lucky. It was lucky for us, not so lucky for the goat. As the Maasai skinned it, they offered me a piece of the kidney. They said it would boost my energy instantly, so I ate it raw. I wouldn't say it was delicious, but it wasn't the worst thing I've had. At least it wasn't dog.

Full of goat kidney–induced energy, Benedict and I—along with our other two companions—camped and danced with the villagers into the night to the sound of their drums. They pulled in a few nine-foot pythons to join. Dancing in my once pink boots, I had a magical night.

Pasquale was always the first one up in the mornings, and he brought Benedict and me cups of coffee. (I have no idea if aloof Kevin drank coffee in the morning, but he never got any from Pasquale.) It was one of the nice things about Pasquale. From my tent, I looked forward to seeing his feet approach, especially after the long night of dancing. Refreshed, we broke camp and threw on our packs, heading to the Makata Plains—lion country. It felt like a scalding frying pan in dry season. I know I just said we were running from the rainy season, but that's Africa.

We walked on parched, cracked ground with no water in sight. You can survive two or three weeks without food, but you can't go more than a day or two without water. Getting through this part must have been a true test of Stanley's will, and it would be for us, too. Like Stanley, I was dehydrated and suffering from dysentery. For several days I was forced to stop every few steps and duck behind a sparse tree, hoping against hope that a snake didn't bite me on the ass. Or the cameras didn't catch me. The upside was that the dysentery gave me a few rare moments of privacy.

We were still 880 miles from Ujiji.

Scattered bones now covered the ground, giving it the feel of a huge graveyard. There wasn't a lot of life, just heat and thorn bushes. The Maasai said that a buffalo carcass we found had been eaten by lions. Soon we were walking through the tall grasses where lions like to hide, knowing that we too could be the hunted. We could see only a few feet in front of us. It felt very much like we were walking into a trap. One of the grasses snagged my hand, and blood spurted everywhere. Kevin wanted to stitch it up, but I insisted we keep moving. The last thing I wanted to do was just sit there, bleeding, with lions around. Kevin insisted I at least splint it, but I wanted to have both arms mobile. He called me stubborn, which I would never dispute, but he had a tendency to overreact.

After several hours of trekking in temperatures of more than 100 degrees, we entered a forest and searched for a place to camp. Survival was our first priority. There were elephant highways everywhere and no suitable place to set up. When elephants stampede through the forest, they leave a tunnel—an elephant highway. There were also hippos everywhere. Hippos are one of the most dangerous animals out there, responsible for more human deaths than any other animal in Africa. They are extremely territorial and will not allow you to get between them and their water source. Hyenas and jackals were also a concern. Not shy like lions, they are capable of taking a fully grown man and dragging him off.

Ordinarily, we would have built bomas and lit fires. Bomas are barriers of thorns you set up to act like a barbed-wire fence, deterring lions. But as tired as we were, we just built the fires. With nothing but tarps on the ground and wool blankets, we were completely exposed. It was a risk, and we knew we'd be vulnerable but were too exhausted to care. The Maasai stood guard all night. No animal attacked, but the Maasai reported seeing eyes around the camp.

The next morning we awoke to the sight of towering giraffes and a watering hole filled with hippos. We lifted our heavy packs onto our increasingly frail bodies and continued the trek. Pasquale continued to insist on calling all the shots; Benedict grudgingly obeyed, and Kevin moped. When we happened upon a troop of baboons, I couldn't help notice the similarities between the monkeys' hierarchy and my teammates: an alpha male, a subordinate, and a juvenile.

We found an abandoned camp and decided it was a good spot to rest for the night. While we were setting up, a group of Maasai men from a nearby village came toward us, suspicious of our presence. But after we explained, they were welcoming, even staying into the night to party. When the Maasai dance, they chant and jump, their bodies effortlessly soaring skyward. This is how they find a mate, the highest jumper getting the girl. Under a full moon we jumped into the night, and in the morning they made us breakfast. I was hoping for eggs. Instead, they brought one of their beloved cows to bleed. Joy. They tapped into its blood without actually killing it.

To the Maasai, blood is the breakfast of champions.

From a shared gourd we all drank the cow blood, most of which was coagulated. There was actually more chewing than drinking. This is definitely an acquired taste, and I had little desire to acquire it. But we were guests of the Maasai and could not reject their hospitality. These warriors rely on cows for everything. To them the cows represent prestige, wealth, and survival. Their blood is literally the lifeblood of the community, and the warriors were willing to share it with us. It was an honor.

With bellies full of blood and parasites we trekked on. It was 116 degrees, and we were desperate to get to the next camp, where the map indicated a river. But when we found it, the water was still and milky brown. We ground some charcoal and filtered the water before boiling it, hoping to kill off the parasites. But water was water, and it looked inviting in the scorching heat. No sooner had we jumped in than a herd of cows numbering in the hundreds came running through, bringing any thoughts of a nice cool soak to an abrupt end.

Our next goal was the Segarra Mountains. On Day 12 of the expedition we were still trying to stay ahead of the rainy season. Pasquale was getting increasingly irritated with Benedict's frequent stops to point out trees. It was a constant battle, and soon the rain was again upon us.

The porters had no rain gear, and the packs were not waterproof, so we unpacked one of our tarps and piled some dry wood, the gear, and ourselves underneath. When it starts raining that hard, trekking has to stop. And once the rainy season really begins, it never lets up. There is nothing worse or more dangerous than being constantly wet and cold on an expedition, as you can quickly succumb to hypothermia.

Of course, the film crew was there, but they weren't helping. Only watching and documenting our suffering.

We had only an hour of light left. Running out of food, we were now relying on the small villages we stumbled on, but often they had nothing to offer but a few tomatoes. Living on just peanuts and one small meal a day, we'd all lost a lot of weight and were feeling weak.

It rained all night, and temperatures dropped below 40 degrees. The shivering cold, blisters, and bug bites were all getting to us, as was Pasquale. He argued with us about everything. The Segarra Mountains are where Stanley was shot at by his team members. I wondered how close Pasquale was to being murdered.

From the lower coastal plains we walked and walked in the rain, finally arriving at the summit of the Segarras. We camped underneath an amazing baobab tree hundreds of years old. Baobabs are the only trees that can withstand the ravages of elephant tusks. We were back in snake country, too, and there were snake holes everywhere. But it wasn't the snakes or even Pasquale that got us that night. It was Benedict. My charming friend produced a pod a local had given him. Inside were larvae, still moving, which Benedict proposed we eat. The locals considered it a delicacy. We cooked them up, and I ate one or two of the squishy things; for some reason, Kevin ate dozens. It was a foolish move, and he paid the price, violently throwing up all night. He was so sick he couldn't have blown his little whistle if his life depended on it.

The next morning we tried to hurry and make up for lost time, but we got only a few feet from camp when another porter went down. Aching and burning up with a fever, it was clear he had malaria. Malaria had killed many of Stanley's porters, and we weren't about to let that happen on this expedition. We gave him what treatment we could, said tearful goodbyes, and sent him home. Expeditions make you or break you, and this one was clearly beginning to tear us apart.

Temperatures and tempers were now hitting the boiling point. It was Day 19, and we had at last reached the Bahi Swamp, 600 miles from Ujiji. But at this time of year, it was a desert, unimaginably dry and desolate. Think Death Valley, only less inviting. We had to trek more than 15 miles that day with no water source or shade. Now short-handed, we entered a village and hired two donkeys. Stanley had employed dozens. Much stronger than humans, these beasts could carry enough water to last us two days. In the 120-degree heat, they were our best chance of surviving.

When the donkeys arrived, we tried to saddle them with the water containers. Hilarity ensued. Benedict and I couldn't get them to cooperate. The expression "stubborn as a jackass" came quickly to mind, though not for the first time on the expedition, given our teammate Pasquale.

With the water containers finally aboard, we tried to move forward, but the donkeys dawdled. Impatient, Pasquale charged ahead with Kevin on his heels. Benedict and I trudged along with the donkeys, which were snorting and wheezing and protesting every step. The team was now clearly divided, both geographically and in spirit. Pasquale was far ahead and had not looked back once. Never on an expedition had I abandoned a team member.

As the hours went by, we could no longer see Pasquale, Kevin, or the porters. The Maasai had stayed with us, and in all honesty, if we had come upon danger, there was no question of whom I'd prefer to be with. Not to mention the water. Nevertheless, if we went the wrong way, we were screwed. We hadn't a clue where we were going, and Pasquale had all the maps. Ominously, animal bones were scattered across the salt plains. We were becoming more pissed off by the moment.

When we finally caught up, I exploded. Kevin and Pasquale apologized for abandoning us, though they didn't sound very sorry. We continued on to a village of a few huts belonging to people known as the Wagogo. During Stanley's time, the Wagogo tribesmen were aggressive and attacked during the night with spears. They were making spearheads as we approached but seemed in no way hostile. On the contrary, they gave me a bow and arrow.

With another long trek ahead of us, we camped and got an early start in the morning. When we tried to replenish our water supply, bees were hovering over the source. They're drawn to ammonia, which is found in urine. It was used as a toilet. The local people had as hard a time finding fresh water in this parched country as we did, often walking miles in search of it to no avail. Water was such a problem the guys and I often had to bathe simultaneously out of the same bucket.

When Benedict and I stopped to examine a tree, Pasquale flipped out. It was becoming more and more his expedition. He acted as though he was dealing with novices he could boss around. It only made me more determined. What is the use of being an explorer if you don't explore? There's more to it than simply getting to a destination. If Benedict and I wanted to look at a tree, we damn well would. I was beginning to understand why Pasquale had loved leading the blind guy up Everest: He didn't stop to look at a thing.

Again, the donkeys were slowing us down as we climbed a steep escarpment. And again Pasquale and Kevin left us well behind. We decided to release the donkeys and carry the water up the hill ourselves. As we removed the containers, we noticed that one of them had broken, and some of the precious water had leaked out. A little longer and we would have lost most of it.

When we reached the top of the cliff, I made a beeline for Pasquale and told him what I thought of his behavior. Initially, he blew me off, but perhaps to intimidate us, he then began yelling. As stubborn and temperamental as Italians can be, they can't hold a candle to an irate Cuban. At the top of our lungs, Pasquale and I screamed and cursed at each other. Then he started wagging his finger in my face, elevating my anger to a whole new level. Benedict joined in. It was the mother of all fights, and this is saying a lot on an expedition where we argued and fought about *everything*. By now completely exhausted, hungry, and worn down, we even argued about whether or not we were on a mountain. The expedition was coming apart at the seams. It was like a cockfight, with the battling back and forth. In the end, we all just walked away, still stewing.

After a night's rest and a little food, we started off the next day in better spirits. Benedict jokingly carried me across the river. He and I had become soul mates, spurring rumors later that we were romantically involved. But in reality we were close friends who respected one another and kept each other sane. When my turn came to carry him across the next river, I dropped him midpoint, giving everyone a good laugh. Everyone except the sound guys, that is; we ruined their expensive microphones.

On our path I spotted a green mamba snake. It was a baby, and babies are more dangerous than adults since their venom is more powerful and concentrated. The bite of a green mamba can kill you in 30 minutes, and there is no antivenom. It was a reminder that Africa is full of animals that can hurt you.

But usually, it's the ones you don't see that get you.

Benedict woke up feeling ill and drenched in sweat. We had just broken camp and headed down the road when he began vomiting. At least, we were lucky to be near Tabora, a sprawling town on the savanna. With large houses and lush gardens, fruit orchards, and well-tended fields, it was like approaching nirvana. During Stanley's time, Tabora was occupied by wealthy Arabs and was a center of the slave trade. Dr. Livingstone kept a house there.

In a horrible ironic twist, Benedict succumbed to malaria near Livingstone's very house, only steps from the grave of John William Shaw. Shaw, who himself died of malaria, was Stanley's best friend and trusted companion. Benedict was mine. It doesn't take long for the harshest realities of Africa to set in.

We ran to get assistance at Tabora, and within minutes an ambulance was there. I helped Benedict to the ambulance. Soon he was slipping in and out of consciousness, nearly incoherent and slightly delusional. The medic tried to place an IV in his arm, but Benedict's veins kept collapsing from dehydration. Once that was successful, I had to hold his hands to stop him from tearing out the line. He was shaking uncontrollably and trying to get up, nearly causing us to topple out of the back of the parked ambulance. The medic asked Benedict if he knew where he was. Sumatra, he answered.

I stepped out of the ambulance and couldn't hold back my tears, both distraught at his misery and worried about myself. How could I possibly continue on the expedition without him? We'd gone through such intense experiences and relied on each other to survive. We knew more about each other than most friends learn in a lifetime. I feared the prospect of leaving Benedict behind and having to walk to Ujiji essentially alone. As companions, neither Pasquale, who I came to love despite everything, nor Kevin, who'd become distant, disengaged, and curt, could replace him. We carried Benedict out of the ambulance and made a bed for him under the Livingstone house veranda. Still restless, he eventually fell asleep. I prayed that the treatment had been in time and his health and strength would quickly return. Pasquale wanted to leave him, but I was adamant that that wasn't an option. The truth is, I wasn't so sure.

We were still 480 miles from Ujiji.

Though still very weak, Benedict did in fact wake up feeling better the next morning and insisted on coming with us. I was extremely relieved, to say the least. We left the Livingstone house and headed to Ugalla Game Reserve. There I spotted a dik-dik and some guinea fowl, and for the first time in days thought of food. Then by the river we saw 5 crocodiles, upstaged only by the presence of more than 50 hippopotamuses. I had never seen so many hippos in one spot—it was a spectacular sight. The hippos emitted low, deep grunts, and their jaws gaped 140 degrees. Awed, I watched as they peered at us and wiggled their ears before disappearing under the murky waters.

We crossed the river at a sandy bend and followed a hippo trail on the right bank. We argued about where to camp, Benedict and I pointing out clear evidence of hippo grazing and elephant dung and tracks all around us. There were three hippo trails going straight through the spot Pasquale had picked, as well as evidence of recent hippo activity. But Pasquale ignored us and starting setting up the tarps. Only when I spotted a nest filled with thousands of bees directly overhead did he agree to move our camp a few yards away. He was using Benedict's weakness to assert himself even more strongly. I wasn't going to let him take over.

Then Pasquale announced that we were to ask him every time we wanted to drink water. My blood began to boil. None of us was an infant needing to ask him permission for anything, least of all water. I leaped up and confronted him. Again we were screaming and cursing, but this time I didn't walk away. "Fuck you, Pasquale!" There, I had finally said what we had all wanted to for weeks. There was a long uncomfortable silence. In the end, Pasquale relented, and out of that fight we forged a truce that would get us through the worst to come.

We still had to collect water from a croc-infested river. It was nesting season, too. I walked down to the edge of the river with buckets and realized our water situation was not going to improve. The muddy waters were disgusting, full of tadpoles and hippo shit. I would definitely have to skip tea that night.

I'm not sure which one of us had read that hippos didn't like fire, but back at camp, we collected firewood and lit four gigantic fires to keep them away. There were enough flames to guide a plane in. Along with the Maasai, we all took shifts during the night sitting up and vigilantly watching. The fires must have worked because not a single hippo came into camp. Though I heard lions in the not too far distance.

We needed to find a source of food, as we were almost out. In the morning I helped Benedict find wood and got a lesson in building guinea fowl traps. It was not unlike basket weaving. After setting the traps, Benedict went to rest, and I went fishing, foolishly standing at the edge of the river where crocs were known to take villagers. I saw several of them on the opposite bank going in and out of the water. Suddenly, I felt a pull on my fishing line. I had a catfish. As I reeled it in, I could see hippos approaching out of the corner of my eye. I ran up the hill with the fish floundering on the hook.

I snuck off with some buckets of water to a secluded spot in the forest so I could bathe and dye my hair. Yes, that's what I said. I had more roots exposed than the 25-million-year-old forest and was in desperate need of coloring—even using muddy river water. It was not something I wanted to do in front of the guys or the cameras. So I excused myself and disappeared for longer than usual. Standing naked with caked dye on my head, I was terrified a hippo might appear and I'd have to run out of the forest. I would never have been able to live that down.

Later, I practiced shooting the bow and arrow I got from the Wagogo and amazed myself. Not only that I was such a good shot, but that I was stupid enough to use one of our big water containers as a target. I spent the next several hours trying to hide the evidence by plugging the holes where water was now leaking out.

Before going to sleep, we had our usual supper of rice, beans, and mud-water coffee. Later, in the middle of the night, we woke up to a scream. Ramadan, one of the porters, had been stung by a scorpion. After taking care of his wound, we all returned to our tarps and checked the bedding.

We had lost a couple of days allowing Benedict some recovery time, so we started our trek at 4 a.m. to try to regain them. We hiked through hippo and elephant territory for several hours in pitch darkness with nothing more than lanterns for light.

We stopped at the first village to get water. I was extremely dehydrated, not having been able to bring myself to drink much of the muddy hippo water from the last couple of camps. Unbeknownst to us, we were about to enter the final and most difficult part of the journey. We had to let all of the porters go now, 29 days in and 80 miles from Ujiji, because the journey on the next river, the Malagarasi, heading into Lake Tanganyika, would be too dangerous for nonswimmers. Only Julius and the Maasai stayed with us.

We were very anxious to get to Ujiji, just as Stanley had been at this point. We again boarded dugout canoes and began paddling. Pasquale pointed out, correctly, that the worst day on the river was better than the best day on the mountains. The glassy water was peaceful and serene, masking the dangers beneath. Crocodiles crossed our path repeatedly, but the end was within our grasp. Soon white caps from Lake Tanganyika were in sight, making it look more like an ocean than a lake. With 20-mile winds, the waves repeatedly came close to toppling us.

Next, we hired two small sailboats at the edge of the lake and began what seemed like a roller coaster ride. I was bailing out our boat, when Pasquale and I noticed that Kevin and Benedict's sail wouldn't go up. We were way ahead of them and, with the wind at our backs, there was no turning around in these boats. The sails were nothing more than rice sacks tied together with fishing line. Benedict and Kevin were in trouble.

Hours later, we arrived on the shore and waited anxiously for any sign of their boat. They were nowhere in sight. It was possible that they would be stuck out there overnight, without gear or lanterns. Then I caught a glimpse of Benedict waving his hat from the boat. As the sun set, they finally arrived. Kevin had essentially withdrawn from the expedition weeks before and had, reported Benedict, literally turned his back on him in the boat and never uttered a word, leaving Benedict to wrestle with the faulty sail.

Benedict, Pasquale, and I spent the night on the shore listening to the sound of the waves crashing. Kevin went off on his own. He, more than anyone, was ready to finish, and, though close, we weren't quite there yet. To be clear: Kevin was no wimp. He had covered every major war zone, including Iraq. But an expedition, particularly one as long and arduous and contentious as this one, has a level of hardship and stress like nothing else, not even a war zone. It can easily break you.

It was on nights like that one that I really felt bonded to Benedict and even to Pasquale, in spite of all the bitter and nasty moments between us. Pasquale was arrogant and egotistical, and I doubted Benedict would ever go on an expedition with him again. But there was another side to him, the much softer, gentler side that brought me coffee every morning. And it helped that Benedict and I had each other to vent to when he especially pissed us off. My Cuban mothers fight a lot and then kiss and make up; it was kind of the same with Pasquale and me, except he didn't do it in Spanish.

Back in canoes, we paddled up a tributary that ran through a swamp; it was slow going. A blood red torrent of unknown origin came out of the swamp and reminded me of descriptions in Stanley's journals. When we couldn't go any farther, we stepped out into the swamp.

There were snakes and crocs everywhere. We were treading through mud up to our waists when suddenly my bad cheerleading ankle gave out on me. I tore a toenail off as I landed face first in the mud. This was no spa treatment. In the process I lost my shoe and would have to walk through the swamp barefoot, getting slashed by razor-sharp grasses while being sucked into the mud. Tanzania had already kicked my ass, but it was nothing compared to these last few miles.

Morale was nonexistent, and if we didn't get to high ground quickly, this expedition was going to come to a screeching halt. It was the first time I thought we actually might not make it. But suddenly, almost miraculously, we were on dry land, on the outskirts of Ujiji. We had been through so much to get there, almost a thousand miles, and just a half mile remained.

It was only when we arrived in Ujiji that we could look back and take in the full scope of the expedition. Our journey had begun more than four weeks before, 20 miles off the coast of eastern Africa. We four modern-day explorers had sailed toward the unknown, into the deep interior of Tanzania. We had traveled through the most stunning, epic, and unforgiving African terrain, fraught with danger. We had argued incessantly and sometimes laughed till it hurt. Now, as we approached a mango tree–lined avenue, it looked like the Garden of Eden, little changed from Livingstone's and Stanley's day. We were about to stand in the very spot where Stanley met the great explorer and uttered his immortal words, "Dr. Livingstone, I presume."

The immense hardships and dangers of the trip and the pain of missing my children seemed small prices to pay for the pride and joy I felt at that moment. As we turned the corner, we were surrounded by thousands of people who had come to celebrate our journey. The locals danced and clapped, overwhelming us.

For the first time in the entire expedition, we walked side by side.

Despite our differences, we had persevered, had survived one of history's most treacherous expeditions, and would now forever share memories and a bond that few others could ever know. Benedict, Pasquale, the Maasai, and I forged a friendship that will last a lifetime. I still talk to them—or in the case of the Maasai, email them—regularly. (Unfortunately, Kevin to this day has kept his distance.) My two most prized possessions came from this journey. Rafael, one of the Maasai, gave me his warrior shield, which now hangs proudly in my living room, and months later, Pasquale gave me the very compass that got us through it, engraved.

My hero, David Livingstone, died in Zambia on May 1, 1873, from malaria and internal bleeding caused by dysentery. He was found kneeling in prayer at his bedside. Britain wanted his body for a proper ceremony, so his loyal attendants Chuma and Susi carried it on a dangerous, 11-month journey to coastal Bagamoyo (where we started our expedition) and handed it over to the British authorities for transport and burial in Westminster Abbey. Before the body departed, however, a tribesman who knew Livingstone's deep love of Africa cut out his heart and buried it under a tree near the place he had died. It was what Livingstone would have wanted.

After this expedition, it is, I thought, what I would want, as well.

fourteen

Machismo, Gorilla Porn, and My Worm

JULY 1, 2009: By the road, a man pushed a wheelbarrow holding two plastic bags with pictures of the Eiffel Tower. He was well dressed, and under different circumstances he could have passed as a real estate agent or a banker. But what he carried in those French bags would reveal his profession. As he opened them to show passersby, I could see the anorexic carcasses of smoked antelopes. Then the tail of a smoked monkey leaped out as if crying for help. I couldn't help but think of all the damage we humans have done at the expense of these beautiful, harmless creatures. He then grabbed his bags and entered the restaurant across the street. He came out empty-handed, presumably having sold his goods. It was the very place we had dined the previous night.

Just 20 years ago, another lost world was discovered in the vast African Congo, revealed from high overhead on a satellite image. This secret swamp, an oasis concealed by hundreds of miles of dense jungle, was christened Mbeli Bai. The great revelation was that previously undiscovered, rare western low-land gorillas regularly visited Mbeli. The entire primatology world immediately sat up and took notice, and the stage was set for an earth-shattering performance.

Sure enough, in 2003 a female gorilla named Leah did something remarkable.

Leah was photographed wading across Mbeli Bai, danger-ously out of a gorilla's comfort zone, as gorillas don't normally go in the water. She then broke off a tree branch and used it to test the depth of the water. Her ingenious tool enabled her to safely navigate the deep swamp. This was a scientific revela-tion, for in more than a half century of study, no wild gorilla had ever been seen using a tool.

It was a giant leap for gorillas, one that immediately ele-vated Leah's species, in intelligence terms, to the level of their tool-using chimp, orangutan, and human cousins. So who was Leah, this super-brained female? What was her story? Was she just a one-off, the Einstein of the gorilla world?

Answers came just a year later with a second extraordinary photograph at Mbeli Bai. Sitting at the water's edge, another female gorilla, called Efi, was struggling to reach plants in the swamp. She solved her problem by leaning on a tree trunk, which balanced her weight, giving her just the extra stretch she needed to pick the deep-rooted herbs. Then Efi improvised again and used the tree trunk as a bridge so as not to get her feet muddy.

It seems that gorillas are master tool users, so why hadn't we seen this behavior before? Was it just coincidence that both gorillas spotted using tools were females? Both sightings occurred at the same location—what's so special about Mbeli Bai?

Back to the Congo I went to look for answers.

At Mbeli Bai I met the German researcher Thomas Breuer, who had witnessed and captured the remarkable photographs of the first-ever known gorilla tool use. Thomas had now studied the gorillas of Mbeli Bai for more than ten years and can recognize every individual gorilla in the region. He is a world expert on silverback behavior. Together, Thomas and I observed the gorillas from a 60-foot observation tower.

I had a theory that was about to seriously rock the boat. Until now, few had dared to question that the giant, muscular silverbacks control gorilla society. When a silverback charges, the ground quakes. Who could argue with that? But it seemed to me there was more to gorilla hierarchy than brawn. I thought it was the females—like Leah—that secretly ran the show with their brainpower. Perhaps coy female apes had been overlooked by researchers, while they quietly reigned from a safe place behind their silverbacks. If I was right, there was a jungle full of female ape rulers.

That thought reminded me of growing up with three mothers.

The Congo's swamps are the only places in the world where hundreds of gorillas regularly converge. Much more than just a feeding place, Mbeli Bai is also the metropolis of gorilla society, where gorillas build lasting relationships over the years, "friendships" that reduce aggression levels. The "bai," or swampy clearing, is key to understanding gorillas' unique interactions.

But when the light fades on Mbeli Bai, the gorillas retreat into the jungle to sleep. The swamp offers only a snapshot of their lives. They spend 80 percent of their time ranging through the thick, dark jungle, where their secrets are safe. There is, however, one place where western lowland gorillas are fully habituated to humans and it's possible to observe them up close: a bai called Mondika a few hundred miles west of Mbeli.

My time at Mbeli was over, but that was only the first leg. After a short stint at home, I was headed to Mondika.

A 17-hour flight took me back to the Congo with a National Geographic crew. The airport at Brazzaville was its usual chaos, with everyone pushing and shoving, cutting in line, rushing to get to customs only to wait there for hours.

The luggage carousel must have been there for decor, as I had never actually seen it circling. I was relieved when I saw my monster bag being hauled in from the runway. As usual, trying to leave the baggage claim area was a nightmare. The concept of waiting in turn is just not part of the culture. After being shoved to the left and right, we finally made it to customs. The customs officer eyed every page of my passport as I smiled nervously, awaiting the new African stamp that would allow my reentry to this remarkable continent. But we weren't leaving anytime soon. Together the crew and I had more than 15 bags, and the guard wanted to inspect every single one of them. All the while a dozen porters fought over who would carry our bags out.

Once we were out of customs, our Wildlife Conservation Society (WCS) contact, Rene, and our driver, Patrique, failed to spot us, despite our looking, I thought, incredibly obvious.

Cab drivers surrounded us, all screaming that they were the cab next in turn, the one to overcharge us for the ride to our hotel. After we loaded several cabs, the WCS staff showed up.

We proceeded to unload our bags and shift them to the WCS pickup truck, with the cabbies yelling that we owed them money. A short ride later we were at the Hotel des Ambassadeurs, hyped to be one of the best hotels in Brazzaville. Once there I was reminded that a four-star hotel in an African town is the equivalent of a half-star hotel in Middle America.

We set down our gear and headed off for a quick dinner at the Hippocampe. The great thing about the Hippocampe is that you can feast on Chinese cuisine *and* get Internet access. After some nem, noodles, and Twitter, I popped my daily dose of antimalarial and, back in our half-star resort, slumbered into vivid dreams under my holey mosquito net. I know . . .

In the morning, Patrique picked us up more than an hour late, which is on time in Africa, and drove us to the WCS office. We were greeted by the director of WCS Congo, Paul Telfer, a tall, handsome, 40-something man with salt and pepper hair and a friendly manner. It took me a little while to notice that he had only three fingers on his right hand, and I wondered how he had lost the other two.

Paul let us know that our filming permits were not quite ready and that the Congolese government was making more demands. In lieu of actual fees, it wanted a photocopier, laptop, and projector. He was scrambling around Brazzaville trying to find them and assured us not to worry. Later that afternoon, the government agency also insisted, curiously, that we provide

350 sheets of tin. Paul had whittled them down from 400. We agreed to all of their requests, just thankful we didn't have to bring the sheets of tin from the States.

Paul introduced us to Dr. Ken Cameron, a field veterinarian carrying out a project on viruses, with a strong focus on Ebola. A classic example of the kind of emerging virus people fear—it kills both wildlife and humans with horrible efficiency. In people, Ebola causes fever, headache, joint and muscle ache, sore throat, and weakness followed by diarrhea, vomiting, and stomach pain. In addition, many suffer internal and external bleeding. The virus has primarily affected remote villagers who most likely contracted the disease from infected bush meat. In rural Africa, hunting has brought Ebola out of the jungle and into the marketplace. Outbreaks in Congo and Gabon in 2002 and 2003 alone killed as many as 5,500 gorillas and an uncounted number of chimpanzees. It also flared among people in the region, killing dozens.

Ken and his team were working on developing a vaccine and trying to find ways of administering it to gorillas perhaps via fruit. But that was complicated, as dosage would be difficult to control, and other animals might eat the fruit. He assured us he would contact us if he found any gorilla carcasses. Hazmat suits would be the required attire.

Later that night we met again with Paul and Ken, this time for dinner. Sitting by the Congo River overlooking Kinshasa, the capital of the Democratic Republic of Congo (formerly known as Zaire), Paul told us stories of living in Sierra Leone during the civil war of the 1990s. He recounted sitting in his car watching guards as one by one they pointed their guns at vehicles lined up at a checkpoint in front of him and pulled the trigger, killing the occupants. He said a guard was poised to shoot both him and his wife, Trish, when another young guard recognized the rat sticker on his car that identified his project. The guard recognized Paul as the man who had saved his mother's life and yelled, "Don't shoot! He saved my mom!" They spared Paul and his wife. I wondered if it was during that war that he lost his fingers.

Four years later, Paul and Trish returned to the war-stricken country and stayed for several more years. He showed us a picture of a chimpanzee that had been anesthetized and pointed to two gloved hands. He said, "Those are my hands. I was helping chimpanzees suffering from Ebola, when one of the chimps turned on me and bit off my fingers." Just then our appetizers arrived. Finger food.

Paul warned us that Kingo, the male silverback, and other members of the group that we'd be following for the next several weeks at Mondika get "dangerously close," especially the two juveniles. If I were to get between Kingo and his kids, I'd be in for it. "Gorillas," Ken added, "like to bite your head, the worst place to be bitten. Or they aim for the balls." It would make a wonderful visual. But I felt safer knowing that. Another reason women make good field researchers.

Back at the hotel, I shuffled into my cocoon of holey mosquito netting, where I transformed into a grumbling grub.

I emerged predawn, still pretty grublike. The crew and I took an early Air Congo flight to Ouésso in the north. One large waterproof equipment case went missing in transit, but everything else, including my monster bag, arrived. Seconds after we stepped off the plane onto the runway, the skies opened and soaked us and our luggage. A duck wrapped in cardboard was unloaded from cargo; it must have been grateful for the rain shower, probably its last.

We were met by Rolan, our Congolese guide from WCS. I found myself now the translator, as he had spent 12 years in Cuba and spoke fluent Spanish. We loaded our bags onto the backs of two pickup trucks and headed to the port by the Sangha River, where two pirogues awaited us. Pirogues are normally propelled by oars, but these were motorized and furnished with camping chairs. It would have felt like a relaxing cruise had it not been for the beating sun.

We passed the Cameroon border and within an hour and a half arrived at the edge of a village, where naked kids played in the river. The children ran out of the water and threw on some tattered clothes, eagerly posing for our cameras. A truck soon pulled up, and we set off on a four-and-a-half-hour bumpy journey to Mondika Base Camp. On the way we passed a few villages and logging trucks loaded with mahogany trees. We eventually arrived, and an Ambien and an antimalarial later, I was out.

In the morning we loaded the truck once again and drove nearly an hour to the beginning of the trail, where our porters met us. We set off by foot to Mondika and reached a swamp a short time later. Because of the rains, I had imagined a much wider and deeper crossing so was relieved to find the water only thigh high. It was a 20-minute swamp walk, though, and

I felt bad for the 16 porters carrying our heavy gear, especially the one who had gotten stuck with the generator.

Nearly four hours later, we arrived at the Mondika camp to an awkward and lukewarm welcome from Patrice, the site's Congolese manager. It appeared we had awakened him, and, still groggy, he was not the least happy to find cameras and a crew asking for food and tents. My cameraman, Andy Mitchell, quickly went native, walking around the camp barefoot in his boxers and bathing in the stream by the kitchen area. James Manfull, my producer, spent the afternoon in the outhouse. We made a great first impression.

An Italian researcher named Roberta quickly filled us in on the two gorilla groups we'd be following. She described the two playful juveniles in Kingo's group and two of the females: Mekome, who liked to stay near Kingo at all times and had a son with him named Ekendi, which means "love" in BaAka; and Ugly, who had furrowed eyebrows and didn't like people, often taking swats at them and biting three. One of the trackers still bears the scar on his knee. I asked for a good physical description, as I'm keen on keeping my knees.

The second group was not nearly as habituated, still charging two to five times a day. That group had one very aggressive female that recruited the others to join in. Roberta warned us that the females would come very close and try to grab us by the legs. She cautioned that if the gorillas managed to grab us, they would undoubtedly bite.

She then enumerated all the other things that would bite us at camp—namely, tsetse flies, filaria-carrying mosquitoes, and, not least, the leeches and black water snakes in the river. I glanced back to see Andy prancing in his skivvies in the leech- and snake-infested water.

The next morning I woke up at 5 a.m. after having been awake late into the night. Seemed the BaAka workers were a happy bunch and fond of loud music on their crappy transistor radio. But what had really kept me up was the sound of gun- shots ricocheting in the dark. This prompted me to search for my knife and keep it next to my sleeping bag. What I would do with it, I had no idea. The next morning everyone said they'd heard the gunshot, too, but had no explanation.

I walked into the dense forest with the film crew, Patrice, and the trackers. We found Kingo, the gorgeous, 400-pound silver- back, nearly 45 minutes into our hike. His juveniles approached me, as I was told they would, and sat a mere three to four feet away. This was absolutely awesome. They began running in cir- cles and chasing each other, and I was careful not to get between them and their father. But we soon got a chest beat and a charge. Not from Kingo, but from the kids, who tried their best to dis- play like their enormous father. They looked disappointed when their efforts elicited only giggles from us, so I shot them a scared look. That seemed to please them.

It was hot and muggy, and the insects were enough to drive you mad—sweat bees and ants, in particular. That day we spent nearly five hours with the gorillas. Gorillas are big eaters; they munch, belch, and fart all day long. Mostly, we watched them feed on leaves and fruit. Kingo would make contact with the females by approaching them and making deep, short, grunting sounds, before dozing off while the little ones slept only a few feet away. Gorillas spend about 30 percent of the day eating, 30 percent foraging and playing, and 40 percent resting and sleeping. That is really all they do all day. Gorillas, I thought, know how to live.

We left the gorillas sleeping in the swamps and went back to camp, where, following their example, I ate and went to sleep.

The following day I was exhausted. I had spent most of the night scratching bug bites, unable to resist the urge. After removing a tick (good ol' tweezers) from my inner right thigh, I saw that I had an unusual swelling on my leg. Rather than worry about it, I quickly jumped into my clothes and went for breakfast. The dining hall, or "hell," was filled with filarial flies. I took breakfast to go, opting to eat in my tent even though it felt like an oven. The sun was beating down on it something fierce, but it was the only place to steer clear of the bugs for a while.

We set out to track the gorillas, and by the time we found them my skin was so oily, I might as well have rubbed myself all over with my spam and mayonnaise sandwich. It was brutally hot and humid. Kingo was resting against a tree eating mangos that were falling out of it and crashing dangerously to the ground around him and us. If I was going to die on that trip, I hoped it wasn't a mango that did it. How embarrassing would that be?

Kusu, one of the juveniles, wandered over to my backpack lying by the trail, and while I fussed with my camera, he peeked inside. One of the trackers yanked it away. Distracted by that for a moment, we didn't see another gorilla group arriving. Kingo and the male began vocalizing, and in an instant we were in the middle of a face-off. Kingo's females tried to lead him away, but he headed right for the intruders. This was a sign of a supremely confident silverback. Kingo puffed up to almost twice his size and began chest beating. Just like that, the intruding gorillas were gone. Busting with pride, Kingo walked down the trail, his huge, muscular body strutting through his wild kingdom. He then turned and slowly walked toward me, stopping less than five feet away. Just close enough to get my blood pumping.

Rain interrupted the moment, and Kingo headed back to the group. In the pouring rain, we rushed back to camp and arrived an hour later, me looking like a mop. There was a small stream running through my tent. The sponge mattress I slept on was soaked to the core. It continued to rain for hours, and my only consolation was that dinner did not contain sausage weenies, sardines, or spam.

Back in my tent I noticed that the red bump on my leg was looking dicey. It was swollen and oozing, itchy, and sore. It was a filarial bite. Mosquitoes transmit larvae, which in adult form live in human blood and lymphatic tissues, causing inflammation and obstruction. The latter can lead to elephantiasis, a disease characterized by the thickening of the skin and underlying tissues, especially in the legs and male genitals. The name refers to the resemblance of the victim's skin to the thick, baggy skin on the limbs and trunks of elephants. In some cases, the disease can cause certain body parts, such as the scrotum, to swell to the size of a softball or basketball.

Elephantiasis (commonly referred to as elephantitis) caused by lymphatic filariasis is one of the most common causes of disability in the world. I stared at my legs, intently looking for any additional signs of swelling.

It was then I noticed that I hadn't gotten the tick completely out of my inner right thigh. I fished out more tick parts with my tweezers and the aid of a headlamp. When I was finished with the tick, I went outside to brush my teeth and got smacked in the face by a bat. Then it was time to go to sleep on my wet mattress. I hoped that as the last straw elephants didn't come stampeding through my tent. Mostly, I hoped I didn't start to swell into one.

On our way to the gorillas the next day, we heard chimps and saw elephant dung near camp. At the gorilla site, it seemed that Dad had been left to babysit, as the females didn't show up until the afternoon. One of the little ones, which had not yet been weaned, spent most of the day crying for his mom. We heard another silverback in the distance, and Kingo hooted several times. His posture and demeanor changed, becoming tense and upright before he led his females off to a neighboring feeding site. Ugly and her baby sat about ten feet from us, and I was mesmerized watching the baby feeding on fruit. This was the first time anyone had seen a baby sharing food with his mom. As I sat there surrounded by gorillas, I felt my Dian Fossey *Gorillas in the Mist* moment had at last been fulfilled . . . wild hair and all.

Genetically, gorillas are 98 percent related to humans. In such close physical proximity, it is easy to see just how similar we are to our hairy cousins. A gorilla's hands and feet resemble those of humans more than the hands and feet of the other apes do. The most striking similarity is their eyes. I've looked into the eyes of leopards and sharks. They are steely and cold. Gorilla eyes look human, capable of showing fear, mischief, trust, and love. It feels as if you are looking into the eyes of your friend, or your brother, not a stranger. Their eyes are the windows to *their* souls, and I am certain they can see into ours, too.

When I got back to camp, I gave an English lesson to one of the young trackers, while he prepared a dinner of rice and beans with a choice of the inescapable weenies or sardines. I did some laundry and took a much needed jungle shower using two buckets of hot water. It was a small luxury, but, more than that, hot showers help in the removal of passenger ticks. When I am in the jungle, I almost constantly feel something crawling on me that may or may not be there but is, nonetheless, maddening.

Five minutes after my shower I was again soaked in sweat. Once more I lay in my tent on the damp mattress with thoughts of being crushed by a stampeding elephant. At night, the sounds in the forest are so loud that I am convinced an elephant is approaching. Rain began to crash down on the tent, not helping to ease my fears. I know there is only a small chance of being crushed by an elephant, but there *is* a chance.

The next day began pretty uneventfully. I know most people would deem any day with wild gorillas eventful, but after ten days, watching them munch and sleep and munch and sleep leaves you longing for a good gorilla wrestling match.

The juveniles, on the other hand, were never bored or boring. They jumped on each other, ran around in circles, and annoyed the females, giving us hours of entertainment.

Then things got exciting.

Kingo began his "mating whinny," a call silverback gorillas make when they are ready to mate. And mate he did. His first tryst, with an independent, high-ranking adult female named Mama, lasted no more than 30 seconds. This was scientifically significant because it had been four years since Mama Kingo had mated, following the birth of their son, Kusu (the mating interval following the birth of a lowland gorilla baby was previously unknown). When he finished his business, he unromantically stepped on her as he dismounted. A few minutes later, he mounted another female and did the deed. That one didn't last very long, either, but still I was impressed.

But Kingo wasn't finished.

Emilie, a beautiful young female, started shaking a branch. This is the female's way of letting a male know she's in the mood. Kingo approached her, and things got steamy. Emilie wrapped her arms around his neck while lying on her back. They were mating face to face! This behavior was not typical of gorillas, and in this group it was apparently reserved for Kingo and Emilie exclusively. Observers have witnessed hundreds of mating events amongst this family of gorillas and never seen this—every other time the female has faced away from her silverback. Kingo and Emilie liked to look each other in the eyes. The entire lovemaking session lasted a record 40 seconds, but it was exciting. It was full-on gorilla porn.

We left camp at dawn the next day and found the gorillas in the trees. Kingo made several of his mating vocalizations, but none of the girls was interested. What the females wanted was to go to the swamp to feed on herbs and fruit. Kingo, like me, didn't want to go and changed course. At the swamp gorillas are more likely to encounter other groups, and he probably preferred to avoid other males.

One of the females suddenly let out a chilling scream.

Kingo made a run for her. Andy and I began running after him in the direction of the swamp. When we got to the female, we were cut up from branches and out of breath, but it appeared that nothing was wrong. The entire group ended up going to sleep once all the females arrived; they never sleep away from the silverback.

Researchers have long believed that when it comes to gorillas, it's all about the male. The silverback's weight of more than 400 pounds is more than double the weight of females. Evolution has sculpted silverbacks like Kingo into the very figure of masculinity, nature's prize sumo-wrestler. Brawn is everything to a silverback; their dominance depends on it. Kingo is solely responsible for the group's protection against leopards, human hunters, and, most commonly, marauding gorilla males that will kill his offspring and steal his females. Even in the daily domestic routine, Kingo is in charge. He decides where the family goes and what it eats, and he *always* gets first pick of the food. He also settles any disputes.

Likewise, the prevailing thought has been that female gorillas are, without question, the weaker sex, forced to play by the rules. At least, that is what researchers had been reporting for decades. However, most of those researchers were male.

So, I wondered, had this female screamed deceptively to get Kingo to the swamp? She couldn't physically force him there. But she could outsmart him. This could help support my theory that physical inferiority encourages mental superiority. Had she just manipulated the silverback? Clever.

The next morning, upon the insistence of the females, Kingo went into the swamp. We were forced to follow. If I haven't said it before, I hate the swamp. Everything bad lives there. It's easy to fall in, and you can't reach out to nearby branches because the thorns are almost as long as your index finger.

The bugs are worse in there, too. I had a nest of ants fall on me as we were leaving that day. They bit me like mad and were caught in my hair, my pack, under my clothes. I couldn't wait to get out of there. After a two-hour walk back to camp and a hot water bucket later, I finally felt ant free. Sort of.

The next morning at 5:30 a.m. I woke up to thunder and a downpour. A few minutes of heavy winds and rain created several rivers big enough to be named, which naturally ran through our camp. I realized how dangerous it was to stay in my tent given the likelihood of a tree falling (a common cause of death in these parts), but my cozy sleeping bag beat out the worries.

When I crawled out of it at last, I was extremely itchy from our recent visit to the swamps, and then I noticed that a worm was living in my foot. That's what I said. A worm was living in my foot. The area kept getting redder and more swollen and itchy as the hours went by. Roberta confirmed that it was indeed a worm, either from the swamps or elephant dung, that had taken up residence. In an attempt to serve eviction papers to my worm, I soaked my foot in scalding water mixed with salt, then applied an antibiotic cream.

That night, the BaAka drummed away on buckets, tins, and canisters, while dancers wearing grass and leaf skirts emerged. As usual, I danced the night away. The worm danced, too, as I wasn't about to let a worm get in the way of tradition. I woke up in an unusually good mood, considering it was 5 a.m. and I still had the worm, the filarial bites, and the infected tick bite.

Andy and I set out to film the less habituated group of gorillas referred to as Bukka's group. The forest was so thick, sunlight barely shone through. The trackers led us to gorilla nests, some built in trees so as to avoid ground moisture, others on the forest floor. I took the liberty of lying in one, seeing how it was unoccupied. Spongy and bouncy like a mattress, I was envious of how much more comfortable it was than my own soggy mat at camp. Having learned from experience I got out carefully, as gorillas defecate around their nests before leaving. Clearly, they only use them once.

The trek in search of these gorillas felt tense, and I was much more vigilant than with Kingo's group, as they could ambush us at any moment. But when we finally found them, hours later, they were in the midst of a fruit feeding frenzy, and, though it appeared they wanted to charge us, they seemed unwilling to take a break from their sugary snacks. I spent the rest of the afternoon dodging fast-falling mangoes. I also managed to run into a five-and-a-half-foot termite mound. Impressive.

Back at camp, I again soaked my worm-infested foot in hot water. As I lay in my tent, I could hear an elephant trumpeting. Once again I was apprehensive about falling asleep and having my recurring, elephant-stampeding nightmare. But I knew I had to rest before heading out early the next day. I finally dozed off, unsure of whether I was hearing my heart pounding or an elephant's footsteps approaching.

The next day, Andy, the trackers, and I spent five hours searching for Bukka's group, but we didn't find them. More than once we thought we were hot on their trail, only to come face to face with an angry silverback, which would charge from behind a thicket and then run off. None of those were Bukka. Because we had to walk hunched over to get through the vines, my back was killing me. Bukka, it turns out, means "back breaking." No kidding. The BaAka trackers would cut vines out of the way, but since they're five feet tall at the most, we giants still had to crouch. I couldn't help but think that this would be far easier if we had taller trackers.

The evening was hot, muggy, and buggy, and I still had a worm in my foot. In my bed a spider awaited me, so apologizing in advance, I killed it. I'm territorial like that. I was already covered in enough bites and bruises. At two in the morning I was awakened by one of the trackers assigned the duty of "elephant watch guard." He was walking around my tent impersonating an owl.

The next morning it took us only two hours to find Bukka's group—we were more persistent than we'd been before. They seemed really agitated by our presence. One of the females with an infant charged us twice, one time nearly jumping over a wall of thickets to get at us. She tried recruiting Bukka to charge us, but he was too stressed from what he perceived as our threatening advances. We held back and gave them some distance. After the gorillas had scampered off, I noticed that Bukka had left a pile of diarrhea where he had been standing. Our close advances had stressed him more than I'd thought. Like Bukka, my producer had nearly pooped his pants when we were charged.

Back with Kingo's group, we spent the most arduous day yet chasing after them through the thickets. Kingo slept a total of only four minutes, which probably explained his grumpy mood and frequent charges. He had a much more intimidating charge than Bukka, and he shot me a look I would not soon forget. But it wouldn't be his worst.

Finally, after 11 grueling hours of observing them, Kingo and the group took off at an incredibly fast pace in the direction of the swamp, but it was too late for us to follow them. I wasn't exactly disappointed.

A half hour into our walk back, we turned a bend and stopped dead in our tracks. An elephant, a male bull with two enormous tusks, was in the center of our path. The trackers quickly motioned us to go back. Andy and I fumbled for the camera. In front of it, pulse elevated, I described what was happening for TV viewers and walked forward so he could get better shots.

The trackers, one in particular, were hysterically urging us to run in the other direction, but Andy and I insisted on getting closer. When we saw the bull bat his ears, a common threat display, we knew it was time to start running. We took off at full speed, the elephant rapidly gaining on us. We ducked onto another path and hid behind a tree, knowing the elephant was capable of detecting our scent. My adrenaline soared. Fortunately, the elephant passed us and kept going. Eventually, we came out of hiding and continued back to camp drenched in sweat. We later learned that the hysterical tracker had lost his mother when he was three years old. She was killed by an elephant as she protected him.

After my jungle shower, I tended to all my wounds, bites, and the worm. Repeated hot soaks and antibiotic treatments finally banished it. I gave Roberta some medication for a terrible staph infection on her leg. I then gave Andy some Cipro for the diarrhea he'd been experiencing all week. James came by and showed me the awful rash he had all over his back and butt. A bottle of Bactine and some antibiotic ointment later, I had performed my duties as Congo nurse. I was beginning to see this place less as a camp and more as a petri dish.

I was reading John Irving's *Hotel New Hampshire* in my tent with the usual fear of an elephant foot being the last thing I see on Earth. It was an odd book and particularly upsetting when the mother and son die in a plane crash, the worst possible book to read only days before I'd be boarding a commercial flight in the Congo. Congolese airlines are not exactly known for their maintenance or high standards.

I had spent considerable time wondering how I'd say goodbye on my last day with the gorillas. After peering into their lives for a month, it seemed so anticlimactic, not to mention rude, to just stop showing up. I would never do that to neighbors. But I soon learned that you don't say goodbye to gorillas . . . they say goodbye to you.

I imagined that the gorillas would think their maintenance people—we were always trimming vines—had just stopped appearing. They might be perplexed by our absence, or relieved to be able to argue and mate in the privacy of their own forest again. But I should've known everything is on their terms. On the last day, during the last camera take, Kingo said goodbye *his* way.

As I crouched only a few feet from him, Kingo crouched in front of the camera, feeding on vegetation, seemingly undisturbed. I looked at him and then turned to Andy's lens and said, "Clearly, the silverback is the dominant member of the group." I was about to add, "But females still exert power," when I felt tension brewing behind me. I turned back to see an angry-looking, canine-baring, 400-pound silverback coming straight at me. I guess he disagreed.

Textbook instruction to just sit and look submissive when a gorilla charges went quickly out the window. I jumped out of his way, narrowly escaping. As I scrambled away, I heard him at my heels. I thought this might be a brief and painful goodbye. But then he stopped. He grabbed a tree and broke it in half, as if to show what might have happened to me had I abided by the textbook.

I knew I would never forget the look on Kingo's face, or the speed with which he moved toward me. In that sense, it could not have been a more perfect goodbye. It was on his terms. Calmly and indignantly, Kingo disappeared into the thickets, and that was the last contact I would have with the gorillas.

But it would not be the last time I came close to death on this expedition. For it was on our way back to Brazzaville that our plane went down in the jungle.

We'd retraced our way back from Mondika to Ouésso by truck and pirogue down the Sangha River and spent the night in a hotel. Not one with hot water, alas. The next morning our flight was very late taking off, but finally it did, ascending quickly to 10,000 feet. I soon realized it was descending, however, and before long skimming the jungle treetops.

Almost immediately I heard my mother's voice warning me of the dangers of this work and saying, "I told you so." More than ever, I hated to think she was right.

As the panicked passengers went into crash mode, my mind flashed to my daughters, my husband, the rest of my family, pets, all the places I'd been, and whether they would call me "a real-life Lara Croft" or "the female Indiana Jones" in press stories about the crash, which no one would even know about for days. I saw a split image of my little girls' faces, and I couldn't bear the thought I would never see their beautiful smiles again. I was also reminded that as an explorer, no insurance company would cover me, and I hated to think of my children growing up not only motherless but penniless as well.

The plane came in hard, the wings snapping the tops off trees and shattering the landing gear, as the pilots dragged the fuselage to rest in the dusty outskirts of a village way too small to be on maps. Andy and I looked at each other as if to confirm we were alive. There was no commotion, only shock and confusion. It was eerily silent as passengers looked around wondering what to do next. Everyone gathered their belongings, and I checked my legs. They were still attached and so were my pink boots.

We clambered out of the plane, our gear on our backs. Without a single person or building in sight, I wondered how long before we could be rescued. I felt like I was in my very own episode of *Lost*. Andy, a strong mountain of a man, and I hugged and cried and shared a Xanax. We were not allowed to retrieve baggage from the cargo hold, but that was a detail. Eventually, trucks arrived to collect the passengers and crew, and we climbed into the back of one and headed down a dirt road to the village. Our truck stopped at what looked like an unfinished hotel, but no such luck. I soon learned it was a brothel. Normally, I'd be upset at the thought of a bed that had seen everything but actual sleeping, but not this time. I was on the ground, and I was alive. In the morning I awakened with my head on a perfumed hooker pillow, and we're not talking Chanel No. 5.

Wreathed in gear, Andy and I caught lifts on motorbikes to something resembling an airstrip. My bike's owner gave me a funny look as I jumped off; clearly, he was wondering what I had been doing in the brothel. I spotted a villager in a conservation agent's shirt, pushing a barrel full of endangered crocs. The scene was surreal. But I didn't stop to think much about it; my focus was just on getting home.

Men loitering at the airstrip told us that finding a flight out that day would be impossible, but returning to the brothel on the back of a rice-cooker was not an option I wanted to consider. Just then a tall, uniformed pilot oozing that unmistakable pilot bravado appeared, and my hope was renewed. I asked Andy to hang back and took off my shirt, revealing a tank top that left little to the imagination. For this move I would later be hailed as a hero.

Still smelling of not Chanel No. 5, I sauntered over to him. The tank top caught his attention and without removing his cigarette from his lips he said, "Bonjour." I thought, Crap, he speaks French, and I barely do. In a combination of franglais and tank top, I proceeded to explain that I had just spent the past few weeks hacking my way through the jungle with a machete, nearly getting my head ripped off by a gorilla, surviving a plane crash, and spending the night in a brothel. (I didn't at this point know about the worm in my eyeball, but mentioning that would have ruined the effect.) Batting my eyelashes, I asked if he had a spare seat to Brazzaville. Not wanting to suggest there was male competition, I would bring Andy's seat up later.

Frenchie quickly pointed out that the plane in front of us was the minister of defense's private plane, and that it would be as difficult for me to get on it as to get on Air Force One. I continued to flirt long enough to convince him to ask the minister's staff. Eventually, he convinced one of the crew to let me onto the unpaved airstrip to meet the minister himself, who politely listened to my desperate story and motioned to his security to let us on. But I would still have to negotiate our way past the ground crew. Payment would be involved. I was out of Kim Kardashian photos, so I took all the cash we had and handed it over. We ran on board before they could change their minds and breathed a giant sigh of relief as the plane took off.

I looked out the window and smiled as we flew over Brothelville and headed to Brazzaville. I looked forward to being inside four solid walls and a net cocoon.

fifteen

Expedition: Life

SEPTEMBER 27, 2010: Can hardly believe I am leaving again for the Congo tomorrow. Seems like I just got back yesterday. I've got a million and one things to do to prepare for this expedition, but I hate to steal even a moment away from the girls. This afternoon, while I packed frantically, throwing my clothes into a suitcase, Emma and Ava unpacked it and sat inside. They looked at me with mischievous little faces, fully aware that their mommy was leaving again. I stopped to change Ava's diaper and wipe Emma's runny nose. This is the last chance I will have to do either for months. I am cherishing these little moments.

On July 3, 2009, having just survived a plane crash in Congo, my head rested on a pillow wafting *not* Chanel No. 5. At 3:23 a.m. I stared at the moldy ceiling, listening to the sounds of the enthusiastic customers with their hookers, wondering just how it was that I, an NFL cheerleader turned Ph.D. explorer, could be so happy. The answer was simple: I was alive. I had two little girls waiting for me at home whom more than anything I wanted to see grow up. Only hours before, my worst nightmare of never holding my daughters again had almost been realized, when a rickety plane descended into the heart of darkness and crash-landed.

Before I went on my first expedition, I envisioned myself surrounded by gorillas and wearing stylish safari outfits and a ponytail, with just the right dirt smudges highlighting my cheekbones. I was sure the natives would see me as a goddess.

I was single and had no children. I didn't think about the "what ifs" in the life of an explorer. I didn't want to die, but the possibility seemed so remote I never thought about it. I thrived on adventure, danger, and the unknown. Single-handedly, I would save critically endangered animals all over the world, perhaps even stop global warming. Why not? With my machete in hand, I would slice through the forest, wrestle pythons, and dodge elephants. I was, in my mind, invincible.

But having a baby took me from superwoman to mere mortal, from the very second I was handed the little bundle of flesh, whose tiny hand clung to my finger and big blue eyes stared into mine. This wrinkly little creature was totally and completely depending on me for love, nurturing, and survival. For the first time in my life, I was afraid to die.

My life on the road, where there were no roads, had not been conducive to relationships or children. More often than not, I dated researchers I met in the field. It was where I spent most of my time. Besides, the jungle can be wildly romantic, and I loved the idea of marrying my very own Tarzan. We would wear matching safari outfits and raise our kids among chimps in a tree house with a floating garden. It was the perfect dream. Fact is, I was engaged to a couple of Tarzans, and then I married one but not for long; he turned out to be less like Tarzan and more like Cheeta.

A relationship between two people who both seek adventure and yearn for the wilds, and seldom are able to journey together, rarely, if ever, works. My dream was just that—a dream. I wouldn't meet my Tarzan in the remote rain forest. In fact, the love of my life wouldn't be Tarzan–like at all.

The man I would marry literally made me see things in a whole new way. He gave me binoculars.

I was at a bird fair in a small village in England. This is not exactly where you'd expect to meet your future husband, unless, of course, you're a birder. You see, birders, or "twitchers," are a funny bunch. Twitchers are committed bird-watchers who think nothing of traveling long distances to see a new species to add to their "life list," their "year list," or some other twitcher list. They practically have their own language. Don't get me wrong, I love them. Some of my best friends are twitchers. I wish I was able to recognize a bird by a feather barely exposed behind foliage. Nevertheless, it can't be denied that twitchers are a strange breed.

The bird fair took place only a few weeks before I was leaving for my next expedition, and I was in need of a good pair of binoculars. In my opinion, Leica makes the best. So I went to the Leica booth and introduced myself to Roland, the managing director. Little did he know he was meeting his life bird.

Right off the bat, I was struck by the brightness of his blue eyes. He was tall and handsome with a strong chin and even stronger German accent. We talked for a while about which binoculars would best suit my needs. He offered Leica as a sponsor for my expedition, meaning I'd get the binoculars for free. This was great because Leicas are not cheap. Then he invited me to dinner. Throughout the weekend I kept running into him. It was no accident. I track gorillas and jaguars for a living—I'm a professional stalker. He later admitted that he was trying to bump into me too.

I went off to Madagascar with my new binoculars and sent him a postcard thanking him. After I returned to the States we emailed one another incessantly. Thousands of dollars in phone calls and text messages later, we were in love.

I went back to England.

I was sick as a dog when I got there. He took care of me. While he went to a regular office job, I stayed behind in his loft and wrote grant proposals and scientific papers. Throughout the day, I would stumble on love notes he'd left for me. My colleagues and I would talk about science and adventure, and then Roland would come home and we'd talk about the nonevents of our day. He brought me flowers. I made him dinner. It was the most normal relationship I had ever been in. It felt strange.

I began to wonder if this routine would get boring. I was used to living out of a suitcase and venturing into the unknown for months at a time. Where was the adventure in weekends in Notting Hill and Chelsea? Could Roland handle the swamps? Would he want to? I was flooded with doubt.

Then I asked myself the most important question of all: Does it matter?

I really loved this man. I even loved being domestic. We didn't both have to want an adventurous life for this to work. The security of being with someone who loved me unconditionally and wanted to take the most important journey—life—with me outweighed my fears. He was supportive of my dreams, even if they were not his. That's what mattered.

In my newly evolved domestic bliss, one small detail went unnoticed. I'd missed my period.

By the time I noticed, Roland was in Germany for business meetings. I went to the store and bought half a dozen pregnancy tests. They were all positive, so I bought some more. Maybe I was harboring a large parasitic worm from my last expedition, producing false positive results. I peed on the last stick and hoped for a large worm. It, too, was positive. *Fuck.* How could this have happened? Well that's *exactly* how this happened, but I digress.

I knew exactly how and when.

I sat on the bed and stared at the pee stick. Then I grabbed the phone and called Roland on his mobile. He was in an important meeting but picked up the phone.

I said, "You need to come home."

"I can't, I'm in a meeting. In Germany."

"I'm pregnant."

"I'll be right there."

I cried my eyes out. I had only been with this man for a few weeks. I barely knew him. Sure, just five minutes ago I considered him my best friend and soul mate, but it was different now. I began listing his flaws. First on the list: He snored.

Not loudly, but still. Next on the list: He was organized. His closet looked like the after picture of my before picture. Who wants such an organized man? Was he going to expect me to label all of *my* shoeboxes? And he was *German*. There, I said it. He was German. I was Cuban. It could never work.

But the flaw that probably scared me the most: Roland had a big nose. Our kid would be a genetic freak.

In mere hours, my organized, big-nosed German was home. He drew me into his arms and smiled. He kissed my forehead and pulled me in closer. Then he said, "I am so happy. This is great news."

That was the last straw.

Great news? What was so great about it? We were strangers. I didn't want to live in England, my career would be over now that I wouldn't be able to explore remote corners of the world, *and* I was going to get fat. This was the furthest from great news I could possibly imagine.

But Roland remained calm and in his confident and tender way said, "It will all be OK." Something about the way he said it made me believe him. I told my subconscious to stop trying to fuck up a good thing.

Roland selflessly offered to quit his job and move to the States so I could be closer to my family when the baby came. Back in Miami, I took a teaching job and prepared a nursery. We happily looked at cribs and baby clothes.

With a heavy heart, I packed my field gear and clothing away in trunks. I resigned myself to the fact that I was embarking on a new life: I was going to be a mother.

The months went quickly, and before I knew it, I had gained almost 60 pounds. I couldn't see my ankles and longed to get this huge, ten-pound nose out of me.

As fate would have it, that year I was nominated for two Emmy Awards for my documentaries "Into the Lost World" in South America, and "Girl Power," my film about sex in the animal kingdom, featuring lesbian monkeys. But I couldn't attend the awards ceremony because I was too far into my pregnancy to fly to New York. Plus, I really didn't want to be seen on the red carpet looking like Kirstie Alley. In the end, I didn't win, but I would still get an "Emmy." We were naming our little one Emma.

When the moment came, I wasn't sure I was in labor; I just knew I was in terrible pain. It was either contractions or the Mexican food I'd eaten. It had to be the nachos—wasn't water supposed to gush out of me? Nope, I was in labor. Already, all the books I had read were wrong. Roland grabbed the overnight bag he'd meticulously organized, and off to the hospital we went.

Wearing one of those humiliating and unflattering hospital gowns that expose your ass, I practiced my breathing. Roland had relaxing music playing in the background and scented candles throughout the room. Everything was under control.

Then the real pain started, and all thoughts of natural childbirth went out the window.

Yes, I was a hard-core explorer who withstood severe stings, bites, and even stitching up my own wounds without an anesthetic, but that wasn't by choice. Now I was not in a mud hut but in a building with drugs in every cabinet, on every floor, and in everyone's pocket. And I can say that a snake-bite is nowhere near as painful as the pressure of a head the size of a melon pushing against an opening the size of a grape.

"Nuuuuuurse! I need drugs! A lot of them!"

"It may be too late for that. Let me take a look."

"Too late?! But there's no baby yet. I promise I won't let her come out. Just get me drugs."

As the nurse lifted the covers off my freezing toes, her eyes grew wide and she summoned the doctor. Why the startled look? Was the nose already out?

"Is everything OK?" I asked.

"Yes. Everything's fine. You're crowning. The baby is coming right now."

I tried to stay calm but began sobbing. I was more frightened in that moment than at any other in my entire life.

The nurse asked, "How are you feeling?"

"Terrified."

"Well, if you're scared now, just wait until she's 16 and asks you for the car keys."

I laughed but then worried about that. I made up my mind then and there that I wouldn't let her drive until she was 30.

The doctor came in, and with my two mothers (my aunt and my mom) watching and Roland holding my hand, I pushed. The pain was unbearable. Throughout the contractions, I thought, how do women survive this? And why would anyone knowingly do it more than once? I pushed again, this time tearing into Roland's hand.

"I can see a lot of hair!" said the doctor. "Push again!"

A lot of hair? Could she see the nose yet? I pushed.

Three contractions later, our baby girl took her first breath.

Eagerly waiting to meet my daughter, I watched as they cleaned her off and weighed her. Within a few minutes, she was in my arms. She had a full head of dark hair, enormous blue eyes, and—much to my surprise and relief—a wonderful little button nose. She was the most perfect, beautiful, wrinkled little monkey I had ever seen.

As a primatologist, I had watched monkeys and apes take care of their babies. I saw the way the infants clung to their moms and suckled their breasts. I witnessed how protective the mothers became when outsiders approached and how they would fight to the death to protect their babies. In some species, the mothers mourn the loss of their young, often carrying a dead baby around for days. I saw the monkey mothers groom and care for their own little bundles and had no doubt they loved their babies the way we human primate mothers do. As I stared into the eyes of the innocent soul I had just brought into the world, it occurred to me: All I knew about motherhood and babies, I had learned from monkeys.

What kind of a freaking mother learns from monkeys?

Motherhood was tough, tougher than I could have imagined, especially those first few weeks. The baby did nothing but sleep, cry, eat, and poop. My sore breasts were her pacifier. I was more exhausted than ever, but I was also happier than ever. I was adapting to being a new mother, and I hadn't even dropped her once.

I knew the meaning of true, unrelenting love for the first

time and, like a gorilla mother, that I would fight for her to the death. As I nursed her, bathed her, comforted her, and obsessively watched her breathe throughout the night, it hit me: Those monkey moms had taught me well.

Watching Roland hold and play with our little angel made me love him and our new life even more. Barefoot, with our infant in tow, we got married to the sound of crashing waves on a beach in Key West. It was intimate and perfect. I loved being a mother and a wife more than anything else. But there was something missing, and I knew it.

I missed the jungle.

Emma was nine months old when I started planning a trip to Madagascar. Though Roland agreed to come along to help, we were apprehensive about taking our baby into the rain forest, and into a malaria-prevalent area. But I felt there was no choice: I really needed to return to the wild, and I didn't want to give up breast-feeding. I also wanted to share with my daughter the precious animals I had worked so hard to protect.

As soon as we arrived in Madagascar, we realized we'd been rash in coming. Several of my guides had malaria, and there was a typhoid outbreak.

In the rain forest, I was careful to keep Emma's arms and legs covered at dawn and dusk, when mosquitoes are most active; at night she slept under a net. I worried about her constantly. But then the moment I had dreamed of actually happened. My daughter saw her first wild lemur.

Emma, now ten months old, was mesmerized by the large black and white creature jumping in the trees. Captivated, she looked at the lemur with the same wonder and amazement I felt the first time I laid eyes on one. It was nothing short of magical.

Walking down a path, we stumbled across a long, brown python coiled near a tree. My daughter nearly leaped out of my arms in excitement when I pointed it out. In fact, it was the reptiles and amphibians she seemed to get most excited about, especially the big red tomato frogs. A budding herpe-tologist, I thought.

I put my Emma on the ground and carefully lifted the snake, something I had done hundreds of times. At once, my daugh-ter began screaming to be picked up. The snake wrapped itself tightly around my right arm, while my daughter tugged on my left. I scooped her up and held them both. The locals almost immediately began to point and scream. I assured them it was OK and tossed them our camera for a family picture. But they continued to point and yell, and when I looked at Emma, I realized why.

My daughter had put the tip of the snake's tail in her mouth. She was using it as a teething ring.

Even monkey moms teach their young not to do that.

A year later, in 2007, I was back in Washington, D.C., accepting the National Geographic Society's prestigious award and title of Emerging Explorer. Shortly before I walked on stage to accept the award, I discovered I literally *was* an "emerging" explorer. I was pregnant again.

Roland and I were ecstatic, and I felt much more confident with this pregnancy. But everything changed during our first visit to the obstetrician.

During a routine examination, the doctor looked concerned. She asked, "Have you been bleeding?"

I was stunned. Taking Roland's hand, I said, "No."

"I see a lot of blood. I need to do an ultrasound."

My eyes welled up. I was frozen with fear. I placed my hand on my stomach to protect the little being I had yet to meet and already loved. I couldn't believe what was happening.

The doctor squirted cold lubricant on my stomach and began the search. There on the screen was my baby. OK, it looked like a small kidney bean, but still.

As the doctor began to speak, I braced myself for the news. She said, "There is a hematoma separating the baby from the placenta. It's bigger than the baby itself." Then she added, "Expect to see blood in a few days. I'm sorry."

"Is there anything I can do?"

"I can put you on bed rest for the next two months, but the chances of keeping the baby are still not good."

Bed rest for an explorer is like a death sentence. I was only allowed to get up to go to the bathroom, and even so she suggested a bedpan. The days went by slowly, with me terrified every minute that the doctor would be proved right.

But after several weeks, I was still pregnant.

I swore to myself I wouldn't gain 60 pounds this time around, and I didn't. I gained 65. But I was so happy the baby was OK, I didn't really care. I had recovered quite quickly the first time; there was no reason I wouldn't be able to this time.

Suddenly in the delivery room, the tables turned, and it was *my* life on the line.

I began losing too much blood, and the doctor was insisting on performing a C-section. I told the on-call doctor I wanted to keep trying. I had already done it once; I could certainly do it again. Plus, I had a bikini line to protect.

I kept trying, but the bleeding only got worse.

The doctor turned to me and said, "You have already lost far too much blood. If we don't do a C-section right now, you will die."

"Will? Or could?"

Shaking his head, Roland said, "Honey, it's all going to be OK. You tried."

Again, I knew I could believe him. And with that I was rushed into surgery.

When the nurse came over and handed me my baby girl, I couldn't believe how beautiful she was. I noticed that her little head was perfect, as was her little nose. Not having to squeeze through the birth canal has clear advantages.

In honor of our meeting at the bird fair, we named her Ava from the Latin *avis* for "bird."

At only minutes old, her eyes were already alert and wide. She looked at me as if not for the first time. She was an old soul.

Having lost so much blood, I needed a transfusion, and I experienced an adverse reaction to the anesthesia, making my recovery slow and painful. I wasn't able to lift Ava, and walking was excruciating. But I wouldn't hesitate to do it all over again to get this precious little miracle. Giving birth is not unlike going on an expedition. Somehow you forget all the pain and suffering once it's done and immediately begin to plan the next one.

When Ava was born, I decided to use the time I had at home taking care of two babies as productively as possible. It was time to finish my Ph.D. I had the data; all I needed to do was write it up and defend it.

As any doctoral graduate can attest, writing up a Ph.D. thesis is hard and stressful under the best of circumstances. With a toddler and an infant, it often seemed impossible. The minute I sat down at the computer, they wanted their mommy. I was either up changing one or the other's diaper or feeding them. I was still breast-feeding, so as I typed with my free hand, Ava nursed. In fact, I wrote while they napped, I wrote while they played, I wrote every spare moment that came my way.

Within a few months, I was at long last a doctor. I know—not the real kind.

When I set out to get my Ph.D., I wanted more than just a diploma. I wanted the opportunity to explore wild places and immerse myself in different cultures. Now that I was a mother, I felt it was my duty to stay home and be with my kids. I felt guilty that my desire to delve into remote and unknown regions and continue protecting animals on the brink of extinction still tore at my soul.

Then I got a phone call from my agent.

Mark Burnett was interested in interviewing me for the series *Expedition Africa,* to join an expedition that would retrace the footsteps of Stanley's famous search for Dr. Livingstone in the heart of Africa. Committing to that project meant I would have to stop breast-feeding months before I'd planned to. It meant I'd miss Ava's first steps. I would miss her first birthday. I would miss Emma's dance recital. Worst of all, it meant I would have to be away for six weeks, without any form of communication whatsoever.

I wanted to go more than anything, yet I almost didn't accept.

You see, for me the toughest part about being away on expeditions now isn't the mosquitoes, or the snakes, or living in wet clothes, or even the starving. The toughest part is being away from my family, especially my two young daughters, and not knowing if I will ever see them again.

Leave it to my mom, the woman who wouldn't let me join the Girl Scouts and who cried and pleaded with me not to leave on my first expedition, to say that I had to go.

"But Mami, I feel so guilty about leaving the girls."

"Your daughters want a mother who is happy and whole. You are a mother. You are an explorer. For your girls, you need to be both."

She was right. Again.

Being an explorer isn't my job. It's who I am. Exploration is deeply embedded in my soul, coursing through my veins. I am convinced that explorers are not made, they are born. Being a mother is my greatest joy, but giving up being an explorer would be a serious blow to my spirit.

Roland understood what an opportunity this would be for me, but as he read Stanley's journals describing the dangers, he became increasingly anxious about my going. To ease his fears and gain his support, I agreed to better prepare myself by enrolling in a boot camp and taking shooting lessons, even though I had no intention of carrying a gun.

There were still many friends and relatives who questioned my decision. They thought it was selfish of me to travel and leave my young daughters behind. But I knew I wasn't being selfish. Quite the contrary. Every step of that journey and every journey since I have taken for them.

I want to set the example my mother set for me: a strong female role model, who faces challenges, takes risks, and conquers fears. I want my children to know that as women, they can do whatever they dream, as long as they believe in themselves. More than anything, it is my responsibility to instill in my daughters the knowledge that they can have a family and everything else, too.

There is also the fact that so much wildlife is being threatened with extinction, and I feel a vital obligation to help stop it. We humans have more than doubled our numbers in half a century and are expanding into wildlife habitats for food and shelter, literally squeezing the animals to the margins. Today one bird in eight and a quarter of all mammals—including nearly half my beloved primates—face extinction. There are so few individuals left in the top 25 primate species, you could fit them all into one football stadium.

When I am out there, I think of the strong possibility that my children, their children, and future generations will no longer find the animals I have come to love. There is a wonderful Native American proverb: "We do not inherit the Earth from our ancestors; we borrow it from our children." We have created an environmental mess for our children, and I must continue to do my part to clean it up. Plus, the truth is, I still can't believe you can make a career of stalking monkeys in the wild.

At lectures women often ask me how I manage a family and a career. The answer is simple. I couldn't do it without my husband and my mother. While I am away chasing elephants and wrestling alligators, Roland and Mom are home looking after our toddlers. Roland gets them up and dressed, makes breakfast, packs their lunches and takes them to school, shuttles them to ballet class and swimming lessons, and colors with them by the hour. He even gives up his favorite ESPN for Nickelodeon. And all while working full time. He's an extraordinary father and husband. Mom helps in innumerable ways. I am so aware of how lucky I am.

Still, as every working mother can attest, my kids don't like it when Mommy leaves. I try to do things to help them cope. We make a countdown calendar with a picture of me in the jungle at the top and a picture of us all together at home at the bottom. I make them little scrapbooks to look at in my absence. I bring them souvenirs made by the locals. Sometimes if I have a satellite phone connection, I talk to them from the jungle. Often they try to negotiate special gifts, such as when Emma requested I bring home a gorilla. She was three at the time. When I arrived home, she was genuinely surprised and disappointed that I hadn't brought the requested primate. But she still loves the chair and necklace the BaAka made for her.

Leaving my husband for weeks—without being able to talk or write to each other—puts a certain amount of strain on our relationship. Yet he, still German, packs my suitcases.

Inevitably, we argue when I ruin his perfect packing job by throwing in last-minute things, but he still hides little love notes in my backpack for me to find throughout my journey.

And Mami still insists on ironing my field clothes.

There are days I feel like I'm failing a bit as both a mother and a scientist. At times when I'm home, I'm dreaming of the wilds, and on expeditions I have days when I can't bear how much I long for my girls. I hate missing even one night of tucking them into bed. It's not simple. But the vast majority of my days are glorious, and I am in the moment, happy to have all that I love most in life.

My daughters have inherited the frilly dresses Mima lovingly made for me. And like my mother, I have enrolled both my little girls in ballet classes. I sometimes meet up with my former cheerleader friends and their kids for play dates. Like their mother, my girls come home, go out in the yard, and spend hours chasing lizards.

Part Susie Homemaker (very small part), part Indiana Jones, I'm not sure I will ever find the perfect balance. I'm not even sure such a thing exists. I think what I have found is the strength to pursue my dreams with the love and support of my family. I have accepted who I am. I do what I love and am passionate about. Once you do that, you just find the way to make it work.

Life itself is an expedition full of beauty and unexpected challenges. I started life a sheltered little Cuban girl; became an NFL cheerleader; and suddenly decided to venture into the Amazon with no camping experience, an aversion to mountain climbing, a lousy sense of direction, and an affinity for pedicures and air conditioning. I am now a Fulbright scholar with a Ph.D., a serious explorer, a TV host, a mother, a wife, and a daughter. Everyone's life is a journey, and there are endless routes you can take. The outcome depends on your determination and perseverance to keep going for it until you succeed.

I was never the best dancer on the cheerleading squad, and I wasn't the prettiest. I am not the smartest scientist, and for an explorer I have a terrible sense of direction. But I work hard, I never quit, and everything I do, I do with heart.

So to answer the question I am most frequently asked, "How does an NFL cheerleader end up an explorer?"

I wanted to. It was my journey.